HEALTY MEAL PREP COOKBOOK

600 Super-Easy, Time-Saving & Weight Loss Recipes
For Smart Meal Preppers With Ready-To-Go Dishes

Emma Barnes

CONTENTS

SEAFOOD 87

LUNCH & DINNER 95

DESSERTS 110

INTRODUCTION

Have you ever had the feeling that your life has become dominated by activities revolving around your job and your food? A typical week consists of waking up, rushing to work, commuting, working, hasty lunch break, commuting home, cooking dinner, running errands? Then you may have noticed there's not much time left for anything else. Not to mention the money flowing out of your wallet to satisfy your food whims.

Can't resist buying from a burger stand or dropping into a bakery for a croissant? The world doesn't end if you do so once in a while. However, if added up, you may quickly realize you are spending too much money on stuff you could easily do without.

We may argue that's just the way life is or not, but one thing is for sure - it doesn't take much to make it way better. Planning meals in an organized way for the week (or more) may sound like a big investment, but in reality, it saves us a lot of time and money.

How much happier would your family, partner, or friends then be? How much would you develop yourself, having more time to follow a passion or hobby? How much money would there be left in your pocket if you stopped spending it randomly whenever you have a whim? A lot.

Whether we like it or not, our world is accelerating, and new forms of cooking and storing food are springing up. This book is a culinary response to that acceleration and current needs.

WHAT TO EXPECT FROM THIS COOKBOOK

The pages of this cookbook will be guiding you through the process of meal prepping, how to follow healthy cooking, and how to get the most out of it. You will learn how to organize yourself, get everything ready, and what the actual cooking process looks like.

I will explain how to get on this journey without feeling overwhelmed or unmotivated. You will also learn everything about healthy cooking, as well as the pros and cons.

Finally, I will present you with plenty of exciting and inspiring healthy recipes that will cover all your daily meals and needs, taking you to the extraordinary lifestyle you always dreamed of. You will also learn plenty of tips that will help you cook your meal prep meals most efficiently and save lots of time. Let the fun begin!

WELCOME TO MEAL PREP

A solution in the era of a constant rush

Meal Prep or Meal Preparation is about cooking dishes in advance for a few days or a week in order to save time and streamline your healthy eating habits. The idea is to cook a big portion of one type of food, divide it into parts, pack it into containers, and store it in the fridge or freezer.

Meal Prep is very helpful for everyone: busy people find it easier to cook dinner once a week because they simply have a tight schedule during the week-days; sports-oriented people cook in advance in order to control intakes of fat, protein, carbs; dieting individuals monitor their calories intake; people on a low budget prefer Meal Prep because it is one of the most economical ways of eating. The list is endless because Meal Prepping is a versatile tool to schedule your eating habits as well as make your nutrition more wholesome. When you prepare your meals in advance, you will forget about eating cheap fast food during the day, because you will have your homemade healthy lunch box.

WHAT ARE THE BENEFITS FOR YOU?

From planning meals to planning life

A great positive side effect of meal prepping is that you learn how to better organize your life.

The first step is to plan your shopping carefully. If you have never used shopping lists before, it's perhaps time to start. That will help you adjust meals and portions accordingly. You will prepare and eat just enough without having leftovers or overeating. If you prepare meals for the whole family, you will save yourself the trouble of preparing different meals several times a day and then cleaning it all up. The alternative is eating out, but that's expensive and, most of the time, very unhealthy.

Planning your meals develops you as a person because once taken care of, that skill may go beyond cooking and will surely help you better organize your life.

The Long Desired Weight Loss is Finally Easy to Achieve

When you have your daily schedule prepared, you are less likely to snack outside the schedule. Having a general plan for anything in life strongly builds a sense of discipline.

Therefore, a combination of healthy foods and meal prepping will ensure an excellent lifestyle where weight loss is not a goal in itself, but merely a means to an end. You will not have to obsessively focus on counting, yet you will see results soon enough. No more calories count, weight loss, or how I refer to it as staying fit, will be easier than ever. Losing weight will occur automatically.

Eat Clean! No Room for Junk Food Anymore

By organizing your meals, you decrease the risk of snacking on unhealthy, processed food and fast food, tempting you from every corner. Getting food from vending machines will also become a thing of the past. This is because you are less likely to throw out something you spent time and money on.

You will quickly realize that meal prep helps you feel great and be healthier. When you organize your eating habits you feel more energetic, disciplined and not only that you have a sense of control over your life, but this type of food prepping is also the key to long-term happiness.

Think of the food as your fuel and of yourself as a top-class luxurious car. Would you fuel it with low-quality gas that could damage the engine? Probably not. Meal prepping allows you to skip low-quality fuel and treat your engine better.

Nutritional Education

If you want to become an excellent meal planner, basic knowledge about food will come in very handy. A proper content of proteins, fats, and carbs in an adequate ratio will help you remain satiated for a longer period. As a result, hunger pangs will diminish and you will stop snacking on foods your body doesn't really need. You will not only develop a genuine interest in healthy eating habits but you will be challenged to learn how to pack and store food properly. Simple as it sounds, a bit of know-how is necessary.

Last but not least, labeling pre-made meals keeps your food organized and gives you control over the freshness. Meal prepping does not mean eating stale food.

MY TIPS FOR A GREAT START

PLAN AHEAD. PICK A DAY AND STICK TO IT.

Sunday is considered the best day to prepare food for the whole week.

Draw up a list of meals and days on a piece of paper. That never fails. Better yet, learn to plan two or even three weeks and you find the perfect balance and meal-prepping days for you.

GO FOR DIVERSITY

That means not repeating the same dish seven times a week. It would be too boring and unhealthy at the same time. Prepare two to three alternatives so you can avoid nutritional burn-out. It may be something as simple as changing the source of proteins or a different type of vegetables.

MAKE A LIST BEFORE SHOPPING

This will train you to stick to the plan, not toss impulse items into your cart. You will save money and time and keep yourself from buying junk food, however crispy it may be. If something is not in your fridge, you will not eat it.

KEEP IT SIMPLE

Although trying more difficult recipes is most welcome, I recommend that you stick to simple recipes at the beginning. Over time, as you become more adept, you may increase the complexity or try your own recipes.

COOK MORE ITEMS AT ONCE, WHENEVER POSSIBLE.

A good example of that would be roasting a couple of things in the oven or on the stove. It's not only time-saving, but your electricity bill will look way better.

INVEST IN GOOD-QUALITY CONTAINERS AND MASON JARS.

These will help you store things longer without the risk of wasting food, plus they look fancy. Eating from such containers even makes things taste better.

I would also recommend buying larger pots and frying pans.

BUY PRE-CUT VEGETABLES

Even though they may be a bit more expensive, they make your life easier and will save you additional time and effort.

DRINK LOTS OF WATER

We often confuse hunger pangs with dehydration. Water fills your stomach and you don't feel hunger, which is why every diet makes you drink plenty of water.

STORING

Most recipes call for airtight containers and mason jars to store the food in. The glass ones are the best since they preserve the freshness of the food the longest. In sauces and dressings, please keep them separate from the salads, meals or proteins, and only apply the dressing right before consuming them. Some foods do not freeze properly (salads for example) and should not be put in the freezer.

For reheating prepped meals, I recommend doing it for about 5-10 minutes in preheated at 350 F oven. You can also use the microwave, though place paper towels that are slightly wet over the containers so the food stays fresh and does not dry out. Do not overheat; you will destroy the flavors and micronutrients.

FOOD STORAGE CHART

FOOD	FRIDGE	FREEZER
Salads	3 to 5 days	Don't freeze
Cooked Fish & Seafood	3 to 5 days	2 to 3 months
Cooked Meat Dishes	3 to 5 days	2 to 3 months
Cooked Poultry Dishes	3 to 5 days	2 to 3 months
Cooked Vegetable Dishes	3 to 5 days	2 to 3 months
Soups & Stews	3 to 5 days	2 to 3 months

ABOUT THE RECIPES

Preparing food at home is one of the best and most important things that you can do for your long-term health. It depends entirely on you, and you can get as creative as you want without compromising on the benefits most homecooked meals provide.

Thanks to healthy cooking, we have discovered a new way of how our bodies can operate and, in many cases, like me, even improve my everyday life experience. Though it's difficult at first, things get better quickly and there is no anxiety to go back.

This book contains 600 recipes to help leap to a healthier lifestyle in a quick and interesting way, combining many flavors and variations with classic dishes. Do me a favor, just follow the healthy cooking and you'll see the amazing changes in your life!

Note!!! The cooking times in this cookbook are approximate and may vary depending on the appliances and the exact food proportions you are using. Please do not leave your food unattended throughout cooking and regularly check the food to avoid undercooking, overcooking, or burning!

Happy cooking!

BREAKFAST & BRUNCH

Chorizo & Gruyere Waffles

Ingredients for 6 servings

1 cup Gruyere cheese, shredded
3 chorizo sausages, cooked, chopped
6 eggs   1 tsp Spanish spice mix
6 tbsp milk   Salt and black pepper to taste

Directions and Total Time: approx. 30 minutes

In a bowl, beat the eggs, Spanish spice mix, black pepper, salt, and milk. Add in the Gruyere cheese and chopped sausages. Grease the waffle iron with cooking spray. Working in batches, cook the dough for 5 minutes. Leave to cool completely.

Storage: Place the waffles in airtight containers and keep them in the refrigerator for up to 5 days (or in the freezer for up to 3 months). Reheat in the microwave and serve.

Per Serving: Cal 390; Carbs: 3g; Fat: 30g; Protein: 23g

Sausage & Veggie Omelet

Ingredients for 2 servings

4 tbsp ricotta cheese   4 oz sausages, sliced
2 tbsp olive oil   6 oz roasted squash
4 eggs   Salt and black pepper to taste
2 cups kale, chopped   2 tbsp fresh parsley, chopped

Directions and Total Time: approx. 15 minutes

Beat eggs in a bowl, season with salt and pepper, and stir in kale, ricotta, and parsley. In another bowl, mash the squash. Add the squash to the egg mixture. Heat 1 tbsp of olive oil in a pan and cook sausages for 5 minutes. Drizzle the remaining olive oil. Pour the egg mixture over. Cook for 2 minutes per side. Run a spatula around the edges of the omelet, slide it onto a platter. Let cool completely.

Storage: Place in an airtight container in the refrigerator for up to 5 days (or in the freezer for up to 3 months).

Per serving: Cal 480; Carbs 18g; Fat 38g; Protein 30g

Chia & Coconut Porridge

Ingredients for 2 servings

1 tbsp olive oil   5 tbsp coconut cream
1 egg
1 tbsp flour   1 pinch salt
1 pinch ground chia seeds Strawberries to garnish

Directions and Total Time: approx. 12 minutes

Place a saucepan over low heat and pour in olive oil, egg, flour, chia, coconut cream, and salt. Cook while stirring continuously until the desired consistency is achieved. Top with strawberries. Let cool completely.

Storage: Refrigerate the porridge for up to 4 days.

Per serving: Cal 370; Carbs 9g; Fat 35g; Protein 6g

Morning Almond Shake

Ingredients for 2 servings

3 cups almond milk   1 tsp cinnamon
4 tbsp flax meal   1 scoop collagen peptides
⅛ tsp almond extract   A pinch of salt
3 tbsp almond butter   2 tbsp brown sugar

Directions and Total Time: approx. 2 minutes

Add milk, butter, flax meal, almond extract, collagen, salt, and sugar to the blender. Blitz until uniform and smooth. Place in tightly sealed jars and sprinkle with cinnamon.

Storage: Refrigerate for up to 3 days.

Per serving: Cal 345; Carbs 16g; Fat 27g; Protein 13g

Chessy Vegetable Quiche

Ingredients for 6 servings

2 tbsp heavy cream   10 cherry tomatoes, halved
2 tbsp Parmesan, grated   Salt and black pepper to taste
6 eggs   2 tbsp parsley, chopped
12 oz raw sausage rolls   5 eggplant slices

Directions and Total Time: approx. 55 minutes

Preheat oven to 370 F. Press the sausage roll at the bottom of a greased pie dish. Arrange the eggplant slices on top of the sausage. Top with cherry tomatoes. Whisk together the eggs along with the heavy cream, Parmesan cheese, salt, parsley, and pepper. Spoon the egg mixture over the sausage. Bake for about 40 minutes. Let cool completely.

Storage: Place in an airtight container in the refrigerator for up to 5 days (or in the freezer for up to 3 months).

Per serving: Cal 360; Carbs 8g; Fat 28g; Protein 20g

Pesto & Bacon Muffins in a Mug

Ingredients for 2 servings

2 tbsp heavy cream   ¼ cup flour
2 tbsp cream cheese   ¼ tsp baking soda
¼ cup flax meal   Salt and black pepper to taste
1 egg   4 slices bacon
2 tbsp pesto   ½ avocado, sliced

Directions and Total Time: approx. 10 minutes

Mix together flax meal, flour, and baking soda in a bowl. Add egg, heavy cream, and pesto and whisk well. Season with salt and pepper. Divide the mixture between 2 ramekins. Microwave for 60-90 seconds. Let cool slightly before filling. In a nonstick skillet, cook bacon until crispy; set aside. Invert the muffins onto a plate and cut in half, crosswise. Assemble the sandwiches by spreading cream cheese and topping with bacon and avocado slices. Wrap the muffins in parchment paper to close.

Storage: Place the wraps in the fridge for up to 3 days. To serve, place in the microwave for 1-2 minutes.

Per serving: Cal 540; Carbs 17g; Fat 39g; Protein 23g

Mozzarella & Chorizo Omelet

Ingredients for 2 servings

4 oz mozzarella, grated
1 tbsp butter
4 eggs, beaten

8 thin chorizo slices
1 tomato, sliced
Salt and black pepper to taste

Directions and Total Time: approx. 15 minutes

Whisk the eggs with salt and pepper. Melt butter in a skillet and cook the eggs for 30 seconds. Spread the chorizo slices over. Arrange the sliced tomato and mozzarella over the chorizo. Cook for about 3 minutes. Cover the skillet and continue cooking for 3 more minutes until the omelet is completely set. Run a spatula around the edges of the omelet and flip it onto a plate. Let cool completely.

Storage: Place in airtight containers in the refrigerator for up to 5 days (or in the freezer for up to 3 months).

Per serving: Cal 551; Carbs 5g; Fat 36g; Protein 35g

Buttery Thyme Eggs

Ingredients for 2 servings

1 tbsp olive oil
1 tsp fresh thyme
4 eggs
2 garlic cloves, minced
½ cup chopped parsley

½ cup chopped cilantro
¼ tsp cumin
¼ tsp cayenne pepper
Salt and black pepper to taste

Directions and Total Time: approx. 15 minutes

Warm the olive oil in a skillet and add garlic and thyme; cook for 30 seconds. Sprinkle with parsley, cumin, cayenne, and cilantro. Crack the eggs into the skillet. Lower the heat and cook for 4-6 minutes. Adjust the seasoning. Turn the heat off and leave to cool.

Storage: Place in an airtight container in the refrigerator for up to 5 days (or in the freezer for up to 3 months).

Per serving: Cal 250; Carbs 4g; Fat 16g; Protein 15g

Avocado & Chorizo Eggs

Ingredients for 4 servings

2 tbsp butter
1 yellow onion, sliced
4 oz chorizo, sliced

1 cup chopped collard greens
1 avocado, chopped
4 eggs

Directions and Total Time: approx. 25 minutes

Preheat oven to 370 F. Melt butter in a pan and sauté onion for 2 minutes. Add in chorizo and cook for 2 more minutes, stirring often. Introduce the collard greens with a splash of water to wilt, season with salt, stir, and cook for 3 minutes. Mix in avocado and turn the heat off. Create four holes in the mixture and crack the eggs into each hole. Slide the pan into the preheated oven. Bake for 6 minutes. Allow cooling completely.

Storage: Place in airtight containers in the refrigerator for up to 5 days (or in the freezer for up to 3 months).

Per serving: Cal 379; Carbs 11g; Fat 29g; Protein 16g

Easy Veggie Tart

Ingredients for 6 servings

1 ½ cups mozzarella, grated
12 eggs
1 ½ cups almond milk
½ tsp dried thyme

Salt to taste
1 red bell pepper, sliced
½ cup broccoli, chopped
1 clove garlic, minced

For the Tart

2 oz cold butter
¾ cup flour

1 tbsp cold water
2 eggs

Directions and Total Time: approx. 60 minutes

Preheat oven to 360 F. Make breadcrumbs by rubbing the butter into the flour and a pinch of salt in a bowl. Add the cold water and 2 eggs and mix everything until dough is formed. Press it into a greased baking dish and refrigerate for 25 minutes. Beat the 12 eggs with almond milk, thyme, and salt, then stir in bell pepper, broccoli, and garlic; set aside. Remove dough from the fridge and prick it with a fork. Bake for 20 minutes. Spread mozzarella cheese on the pie crust and top with egg mixture. Bake for 30 minutes until the tart is set. Let cool completely.

Storage: Place in an airtight container in the refrigerator for up to 5 days (or in the freezer for up to 3 months).

Per serving: Cal 520; Carbs 21g; Fat 38g; Protein 24g

Bacon & Egg Topped Zucchini

Ingredients for 1 serving

2 bacon slices
1 tbsp olive oil
1 zucchini, diced

2 eggs
½ small onion, chopped
1 tbsp chopped parsley

Directions and Total Time: approx. 25 minutes

Cook bacon in a skillet for 5 minutes, until crispy; set aside. Warm the oil in the same skillet and cook the onion for 3 minutes. Add in zucchini and parsley and cook for 10 more minutes. Transfer to a plate. Crack the eggs into the same skillet and fry. Top the zucchini mixture with bacon slices and fried eggs. Let Cool completely.

Storage: Put in an airtight container in the refrigerator for up to 5 days (or in the freezer for up to 3 months).

Per serving: Cal 323; Carbs 10g; Fat 21g; Protein 25g

Blue Cheese & Mushrooms Scrambled Eggs

Ingredients for 4 servings

2 tbsp butter
16 oz blue cheese
1 cup sliced white mushrooms

2 cloves garlic, minced
½ cup spinach, sliced
6 fresh eggs

Directions and Total Time: approx. 30 minutes

Melt butter in a skillet over medium heat and sauté mushrooms and garlic for 5 minutes. Crumble blue cheese into the skillet and cook for 6 minutes. Introduce the spinach and sauté for 5 more minutes until wilted.

Crack the eggs into a bowl, whisk until well combined and creamy in color, and pour all over the spinach. Use a spatula to stir the eggs while cooking, until scrambled and no more runny, about 5 minutes. Let cool completely.

Storage: Place in an airtight container in the refrigerator for up to 5 days (or in the freezer for up to 3 months).

Per serving: Cal 469; Carbs 10g; Fat 39g; Protein 25g

Parmesan & Ham Egg Cups

Ingredients for 4 servings

½ chopped onion	2 tbsp flour
1 cup chopped ham	4 eggs
¼ tsp garlic powder	⅓ cup mayonnaise
2 tbsp grated Parmesan	

Directions and Total Time: approx. 35 minutes

Preheat oven to 375 F. Place onion, ham, and garlic in a food processor and pulse until ground. Stir in mayo, flour, and Parmesan. Press this mixture into greased muffin cups. Bake for 5 minutes. Crack an egg into each muffin cup. Return to the oven and bake for 20 minutes until the tops are firm and eggs are cooked. Let cool completely.

Storage: Place in an airtight container in the refrigerator for up to 5 days (or in the freezer for up to 3 months).

Per serving: Cal 380; Carbs 6g; Fat 28g; Protein 20g

Salmon & Egg Omelet Wrap with Avocado

Ingredients for 2 servings

3 tbsp cream cheese	2 oz smoked salmon, sliced
2 tbsp butter	1 spring onion, sliced
1 avocado, sliced	4 eggs, beaten
2 tbsp chopped chives	Salt and black pepper to taste

Directions and Total Time: approx. 15 minutes

In a bowl, combine the chives and cream cheese; set aside. Season the eggs with salt and pepper. Melt butter in a pan and add the eggs; cook for 3 minutes. Flip the omelet over and cook for another 2 minutes until golden. Remove to a plate and spread the chive mixture over. Top with salmon, avocado, and onion. Wrap and allow cooling completely.

Storage: Place in an airtight container in the refrigerator for up to 5 days (or in the freezer for up to 3 months).

Per serving: Cal 485; Carbs 9g; Fat 40g; Protein 16g

Tasty Raspberry Tarts

Ingredients for 8 servings

For the crust:

2 cups flour	1/3 cup brown sugar
6 tbsp butter, melted	1 tsp cinnamon powder

For the filling:

¼ cup butter, melted	½ tsp cinnamon powder
3 cups raspberries, mashed	¼ cup brown sugar
½ tsp fresh lemon juice	

Directions and Total Time: approx. 25 minutes

Preheat oven to 350 F. Lightly grease 4 mini tart tins with cooking spray. In a food processor, blend almond flour, butter, brown sugar, and cinnamon. Divide the dough between the tart tins and bake for 15 minutes. In a bowl, mix raspberries, lemon juice, butter, cinnamon, and brown sugar. Pour filling into the crust, gently tap on a flat surface to release air bubbles, and allow cooling completely.

Storage: Place the tarts in airtight containers and keep in the refrigerator for up to 5 days (or freeze for up to 3 months).

Per serving: Cal 280; Carbs 34g; Fat 14g, Protein 4g

Mozzarella & Pesto Bread Twists

Ingredients for 6 servings

1 egg	
1 ½ cups grated mozzarella	½ cup almond flour
¼ cup butter	1 tsp baking powder
4 tbsp flour	2 tsp pesto

Directions and Total Time: approx. 35 minutes

Preheat oven to 350 F. Line a baking sheet with parchment paper. In a bowl, combine flour, almond flour, and baking powder. Melt 4 tbsp of butter and cheese in a skillet and stir in the egg. Mix in flour mixture until a firm dough forms. Divide the mixture between 2 parchment papers, then use a rolling pin to flatten out the dough of about an inch's thickness. Remove the parchment paper on top and spread pesto all over the dough. Cut the dough into strips, twist each piece, and place it on the baking sheet. Brush with the remaining butter and bake for 15-20 minutes until golden brown. Let cool completely.

Storage: Place the twists in airtight containers in the refrigerator for up to 5 days (or freeze for up to 3 months).

Per serving: Cal 360; Carbs 10g; Fat 27g; Protein 15g

Vanilla Porridge with Walnuts

Ingredients for 2 servings

2 tbsp chia seeds	½ tsp vanilla extract
4 tbsp hemp seeds	4 tbsp shredded coconut
2 tbsp corn flour	¼ tsp brown sugar
4 tbsp almond meal	2 tbsp walnuts, chopped

Directions and Total Time: approx. 10 minutes

Put chia seeds, hemp seeds, corn flour, almond meal, brown sugar, and shredded coconut in a nonstick saucepan and pour over ½ cup water. Simmer, stirring occasionally for about 3-4 minutes. Stir in vanilla. Sprinkle with chopped walnuts and let cool completely.

Storage: Place the porridge in an airtight container in the refrigerator for up to 5 days.

Per serving: Cal 450; Carbs 15g; Fat 33g; Protein 17g

Soft Gruyere Biscuits

Ingredients for 12 servings

½ cup grated Gruyere cheese	¼ cup coconut flakes
¼ cup butter melted	½ tsp xanthan gum
4 eggs	¼ tsp baking powder
¼ tsp salt	2 tsp garlic powder
1/3 cup coconut flour	¼ tsp onion powder

Directions and Total Time: approx. 30 minutes

Preheat oven to 350 F. Line a baking sheet with parchment paper. In a food processor, mix eggs, butter, and salt until smooth. Add coconut flour, coconut flakes, xanthan gum, baking, garlic powder, onion powder, and Gruyere cheese. Combine smoothly. Mold 12 balls out of the mixture and arrange them on the baking sheet at 2-inch intervals. Bake for 25 minutes or until the biscuits are golden brown. Cool.

Storage: Place in an airtight container in the refrigerator for up to 5 days (or in the freezer for up to 3 months).

Per serving: Cal 140; Carbs 5g; Fat 11g, Protein 7g

Ricotta Muffins

Ingredients for 8 servings

8 oz ricotta cheese, softened	2 tsp baking powder
¼ cup butter, melted	1 egg
2 cups flour	1 cup milk

Directions and Total Time: approx. 30 minutes

Preheat oven to 400 F. Grease a muffin tray with cooking spray. Mix flour, baking powder, and salt in a bowl.

In a separate bowl, beat ricotta cheese and butter using a hand mixer and whisk in the egg and milk. Fold in almond flour and spoon the batter into the muffin cups two-thirds way up. Bake for 20 minutes, remove to a wire rack to cool completely before storing.

Storage: Place in an airtight container in the refrigerator for up to 5 days (or in the freezer for up to 3 months).

Per serving: Cal 270; Carbs 29g; Fat 13g; Protein 8g

Light Broccoli Hash Browns

Ingredients for 4 servings

1 egg	1 head broccoli, cut into florets
4 tbsp cheddar, grated	½ white onion, grated

Directions and Total Time: approx. 35 minutes

Preheat oven to 350 F. Pour broccoli into a food processor and pulse until smoothly grated. Transfer to a bowl, add in eggs, cheese, and onion. Mix well. Melt butter in a skillet. Ladle 4 scoops of the broccoli mixture into a greased baking dish, flatten, and bake until golden brown, 15-20 minutes, turning once. Allow cooling completely.

Storage: Place the hash browns in airtight containers in the refrigerator for up to 5 days (or freeze for up to 3 months).

Per serving: Cal 80; Carbs 5g; Fat 4g; Protein 6g

Tri-Color Frittata

Ingredients for 4 servings

8 oz feta cheese, crumbled	8 cherry tomatoes, halved
2 tbsp olive oil	10 eggs
5 oz spinach	4 scallions, diced

Directions and Total Time: approx. 35 minutes

Preheat oven to 350 F. Drizzle the oil in a casserole and place in the oven until heated. In a bowl, whisk eggs and stir in spinach, feta cheese, and scallions. Pour the mixture into the casserole, top with the cherry tomatoes, and place back in the oven. Bake for 25 minutes. Cut the frittata into wedges and let cool completely.

Storage: Place in an airtight container in the refrigerator for up to 5 days (or in the freezer for up to 3 months).

Per serving: Cal 330; Carbs 6g; Fat 25g; Protein 24g

Lemony Beef Patties

Ingredients for 6 servings

¼ cup olive oil	2 tsp fresh lemon juice
6 ground beef patties	6 fresh eggs
2 ripe avocados, pitted	2 tsp red pepper flakes

Directions and Total Time: approx. 25 minutes

In a skillet, warm oil and fry patties for 8 minutes, flipping once. Remove to a plate. Mash the avocado in a bowl and stir in the lemon juice. Spread the mash on the patties. Boil 3 cups of water in a pan over high heat and reduce to simmer (don't boil). Crack an egg into a bowl and put it in the simmering water. Poach for 2-3 minutes. Remove to a plate. Repeat with the remaining eggs. Top patties with eggs and sprinkle with chili flakes. Let the patties cool.

Storage: Keep the cooled patties in an airtight container for up to 5 days (or in the freezer for up to 3 months).

Per serving: Cal 507; Carbs 5g; Fat 38g; Protein 31g

Creamy Coconut Blini with Blackberry Sauce

Ingredients for 6 servings

Pancakes

1 cup coconut flour	1 cup cream cheese
1 tsp salt	¼ cup olive oil
2 tsp sugar	1 ½ cups milk
1 tsp baking soda	1 tsp vanilla extract
1 tsp baking powder	6 large eggs

Blackberry Sauce

3 cups fresh blackberries	½ tsp cornstarch
1 lemon, juiced	A pinch of salt
½ cup sugar	

Directions and Total Time: approx. 40 minutes

Put coconut flour, salt, sugar, baking soda, and baking powder in a bowl and whisk well. Add in milk, cream cheese, vanilla, eggs, and olive oil and whisk until smooth.

Set a pan and pour in a small ladle of batter. Cook on one side for 2 minutes, flip, and cook for 2 minutes. Transfer to a plate and repeat the cooking process until the batter is exhausted. Let cool completely. Pour the berries and ½ cup of water into a saucepan and bring to a boil. Simmer for 12 minutes. Pour in sugar, stir, and continue cooking for 5 minutes. Stir in salt and lemon juice. Mix cornstarch with 1 tbsp of water; pour the mixture into the berries. Stir and continue cooking the sauce until it thickens. Let it cool completely.

Storage: Place the blini in airtight containers and the cooled sauce in a glass jar. Keep in the refrigerator for up to 5 days (or in the freezer for up to 3 months).

Per serving: Cal 433; Carbs 28g; Fat 29g; Protein 15g

Cheesy Nests with Spinach

Ingredients for 4 servings

4 tbsp shredded Pecorino Romano cheese	
2 tbsp shredded fontina	½ lb spinach, chopped
1 tbsp olive oil	4 eggs
1 clove garlic, grated	Salt and black pepper to taste

Directions and Total Time: approx. 30 minutes

Preheat oven to 350 F. Warm oil in a skillet, add garlic and sauté for 2 minutes. Add in spinach to wilt for about 5 minutes and season with salt and pepper. Stir in 2 tbsp of Pecorino Romano cheese and fontina cheese and remove from the heat. Allow cooling. Mold 4 (firm separate) spinach nests on a greased sheet and crack an egg into each nest. Sprinkle with the remaining Pecorino Romano cheese. Bake for 15 minutes. Allow cooling completely.

Storage: Place the nests in airtight containers and keep them in the refrigerator for up to 5 days (or in the freezer for up to 3 months). Reheat in the microwave and serve.

Per serving: Cal 210; Carbs 4g; Fat 15g; Protein 12g

Tangy Herb Biscuits

Ingredients for 4 servings

2 tbsp melted butter	¼ tsp garlic powder
1 cup flour	½ tsp baking soda
1 egg	½ tsp paprika powder
½ tsp salt	½ tbsp plain vinegar
¼ tsp black pepper	½ cup mixed dried herbs

Directions and Total Time: approx. 30 minutes

Preheat oven to 350 F. Line a baking sheet with parchment paper. In a food processor, mix flour, butter, egg, salt, pepper, garlic powder, baking soda, paprika, vinegar, and dried herbs until smoothly combined. Mold 12 balls out of the mixture; arrange them on the baking sheet at 2-inch intervals. Bake for 25 minutes. Allow cooling completely.

Storage: Place the biscuits in airtight containers and keep them in the refrigerator for up to 5 days.

Per serving: Cal 173; Carbs 23g, Fat 9g, Protein 6g

Meatless Loaf

Ingredients for 4 servings

½ cup sour cream	¾ tsp baking powder
1 tbsp olive oil	1 tbsp cinnamon powder
5 large eggs	½ tsp salt
1 cup butternut squash, grated	1 tsp white wine vinegar
1 zucchini, grated	½ tsp nutmeg powder
⅓ cup flour	

Directions and Total Time: approx. 70 minutes

Preheat oven to 360 F. Line a loaf pan with baking parchment. In a bowl, put flour, baking powder, cinnamon powder, salt, and nutmeg. In a separate bowl, whisk eggs, olive oil, sour cream, and vinegar until combined. Add butternut squash and zucchini. Fold the dry mixture into the wet mixture. Pour the batter into the loaf pan and bake for 55 minutes. Let cool before slicing.

Storage: Place the meatloaf in airtight containers and keep in the refrigerator for up to 5 days (or in the freezer for up to 3 months). Reheat in the microwave and serve.

Per serving: Cal 186; Carbs 21g; Fat 8g; Protein 5g

Rosemary Egg Muffins with Sausages

Ingredients for 3 servings

6 eggs, separated into yolks and whites	
1 cup Grana Padano, grated	½ tsp dried rosemary
1 tsp butter, melted	3 beef sausages, chopped

Directions and Total Time: approx. 25 minutes

Set oven to 420 F. Lightly grease a muffin pan with the melted butter. Use an electric mixer to beat the egg whites until there is a formation of stiff peaks. Add in sausages, cheese, and seasonings. Pour into muffin cups and bake for 15 minutes. Place one egg yolk into each cup. Bake for an additional 4 minutes. Let cool before storing.

Storage: Refrigerate the muffins for up to 3 days, or freeze them for up to 3 months.

Per serving: Cal 423; Carbs: 3g; Fat: 31g; Protein: 26g

Geen Frittata with Ricotta

Ingredients for 4 servings

1 cup spinach	8 eggs
8 oz crumbled ricotta cheese	4 green onions, diced
1 pint halved cherry tomatoes	

Directions and Total Time: approx. 35 minutes

Preheat oven to 350 F. In a bowl, whisk the eggs. Stir in spinach, ricotta cheese, and green onions. Pour the mixture into a greased casserole, top with cherry tomatoes, and bake for 25 minutes. Cut into wedges and let cool.

Storage: Place the wedges in airtight containers and keep them in the refrigerator for up to 5 days (or in the freezer for up to 3 months). Reheat in the microwave to serve.

Per serving: Cal 261; Carbs: 10g; Fat: 18g; Protein: 22g

Avocado Shake

Ingredients for 4 servings

1 tbsp cold heavy cream   ¼ cup cold almond milk
4 avocados, halved and pitted   1 tsp vanilla extract
2 tbsp sugar

Directions and Total Time: approx. 5 minutes

In a blender, add avocado, brown sugar, milk, vanilla extract, and heavy cream. Process until smooth. Divide the shake between 4 tightly sealed jars.

Storage: Refrigerate the shake for up to 4 days, or freeze for up to 3 months. Serve cold.

Per serving: Cal 388; Carbs 23g, Fat 32g, Protein 8g

Vegan Seed Bread

Ingredients for 6 servings

1 cup vegan cream cheese   ½ cup chia seeds
½ cup melted coconut oil   1 tsp ground caraway seeds
3 tbsp ground flax seeds   1 tsp hemp seeds
¾ cup coconut flour   ¼ cup psyllium husk powder
1 cup almond flour   1 tsp salt
3 tsp baking powder   ¾ cup coconut cream
5 tbsp sesame seeds   1 tbsp poppy seeds

Directions and Total Time: approx. 60 minutes

Preheat oven to 350 F. Line a loaf pan with parchment paper. For flax egg, whisk flax seed powder with ½ cup water and let the mixture soak for 5 minutes. In a bowl, combine coconut and almond flours, baking powder, sesame, chia, caraway and hemp seeds, psyllium husk powder, and salt. Whisk cream cheese, oil, cream, and flax egg in another bowl. Pour the liquid ingredients into the dry ingredients, and continue whisking until a dough forms. Transfer to the loaf pan, sprinkle with poppy seeds, and bake for 45 minutes. Remove parchment paper with the bread and allow cooling on a rack.

Storage: Place the bread in an airtight container in the refrigerator for up to 5 days (or freeze for up to 3 months).

Per serving: Cal 310; Carbs 13g; Fat 19g; Protein 7g

Almond & Berry Smoothie

Ingredients for 4 servings

½ cup raspberries   Juice from half lemon
1 ½ cups almond milk   ½ tsp almond extract

Directions and Total Time: approx. 5 minutes

In a blender or smoothie maker, pour the almond milk, raspberries, lemon juice, and almond extract. Puree the ingredients at high speed until the raspberries have blended almost entirely into the liquid. Divide the smoothie between 4 tightly sealed jars.

Storage: Refrigerate the smoothie for up to 4 days, or freeze for up to 3 months. Shake well before enjoying.

Per serving: Cal 80; Carbs 7g; Fat 2g; Protein 1g

Croque Madame with Bechamel Sauce

Ingredients for 4 servings

1 (7-oz) can sliced mushrooms, drained
4 tbsp grated Monterey Jack   ½ tsp nutmeg powder
¼ cup grated Parmesan   ½ cup basil leaves
4 slices mozzarella cheese   1/3 cup toasted pine nuts
3 tbsp melted butter   1 garlic clove, peeled
¼ cup + 1 tbsp olive oil   4 slices bread
1 cup milk   3 tomatoes, sliced
2 tbsp flour   4 eggs
Salt and black pepper to taste   Baby arugula for garnishing

Directions and Total Time: approx. 30 minutes

To make the bechamel sauce, place half of the butter and half of the milk in a saucepan over medium heat. Whisk in the remaining milk with flour until smooth roux forms. Season with salt, pepper, and nutmeg. Reduce the heat and stir in Monterey Jack cheese until melted. Set aside the bechamel sauce. For the pesto, in a food processor, puree basil, pine nuts, Parmesan cheese, garlic, and ¼ cup olive oil. Refrigerate the resulting pesto in a glass jar.

Preheat your grill to medium-high heat. Brush both sides of each bread slice with the remaining butter. Toast each on both sides. Remove onto a plate and spread béchamel sauce on one side of each bread, then pesto, and top with tomatoes and mozzarella cheese. One after the other, return each sandwich to the grill and cook until the cheese melts. Heat the remaining olive oil in a skillet and crack in eggs. Cook until the whites set, but the yolks still soft and runny. Place the eggs on the sandwiches. Garnish with arugula. Wrap the sandwiches tightly in aluminum foil and put them in airtight containers.

Storage: Refrigerate the sandwiches for up to 4 days, or freeze for up to 3 months.

Per serving: Cal 567; Carbs 23g; Fat 43g; Protein 26g

Berry & Yogurt Bowls with Toast Sticks

Ingredients for 4 servings

1 tbsp olive oil   ½ cup raspberries
1 ½ tbsp butter   2 eggs
2 cups Greek yogurt   ¼ tsp cinnamon powder
2 tbsp maple syrup   ¼ tsp nutmeg powder
½ cup strawberries, halved   2 tbsp almond milk
½ cup blueberries   4 slices bread

Directions and Total Time: approx. 15 minutes

In a bowl, mix yogurt, maple syrup, and berries. Chill for about 1 hour. In another bowl, whisk eggs, cinnamon, nutmeg, and almond milk. Set aside. Cut each bread slice into four strips. Heat the butter and olive oil in a skillet over medium heat. Dip each strip into the egg mixture and fry in the skillet, flipping once until golden brown on both sides. Transfer to a plate and allow to cool completely.

Storage: Refrigerate the bowls for up to 3 days.

Per serving: Cal 307; Carbs 23g; Fat 19g; Protein 13g

Choco-Mint Milk Shake

Ingredients for 4 servings

3 tsp cocoa powder	4 mint leaves
3 cups flax milk, chilled	3 tbsp brown sugar
1 avocado, sliced	1 scoop protein powder
1 cup milk, chilled	Whipping cream for topping

Directions and Total Time: approx. 5 minutes

Combine flax milk, cocoa powder, avocado, milk, brown sugar, and protein powder into the smoothie maker and blend for 1 minute to smooth. Pour into serving cups, add some whipping cream on top, and garnish with mint. Divide the shake among 4 tightly sealed jars.

Storage: Refrigerate for up to 4 days, or freeze for up to 3 months. Serve cold.

Per serving: Cal 255; Carbs 24g; Fat 15g; Protein 8g

Baked Eggs with Ham & Cauliflower

Ingredients for 4 servings

1 head cauliflower, cut into florets	
1 tbsp butter	1 tsp dried oregano
2 bell peppers, chopped	Salt and black pepper to taste
¼ cup chopped ham	8 eggs

Directions and Total Time: approx. 25 minutes

Preheat oven to 425 F. Melt butter in a pan over medium heat and cook the ham, stirring frequently, about 3 minutes. Arrange cauliflower, bell peppers, and ham on a foil-lined baking sheet. Season with salt, oregano, and pepper. Bake for 10 minutes. Remove, create 8 indentations with a spoon, and crack an egg into each one. Return to the oven and continue baking for 7 more minutes. Allow cooling.

Storage: Place in an airtight container and keep in the refrigerator for up to 5 days (or in the freezer for up to 3 months). Reheat in the microwave and serve.

Per serving: Cal 273; Carbs 12g; Fat 18g; Protein 20g

Salmon & Cottage Cheese Burritos

Ingredients for 4 servings

1 lime, zested and juiced	Salt and black pepper to taste
4 tbsp cottage cheese	4 (7-inch) tortillas
2 tsp chopped fresh dill	8 slices smoked salmon

Directions and Total Time: approx. 10 minutes

In a bowl, mix lime juice, zest, cottage cheese, dill, salt, and black pepper. Lay each tortilla on a plastic wrap (just wide enough to cover the tortilla), spread with cottage cheese mixture, and top each (one) with two salmon slices. Roll up the tortillas and secure both ends by twisting.

Storage: Refrigerate the burritos for up to 4 days, or freeze for up to 3 months. To serve, remove plastic, cut off both ends of each wrap, and cut wraps into half-inch wheels.

Per serving: Cal 232; Carbs 17g; Fat 9g; Protein 15g

Mascarpone & Berry Bowls with Pistachios

Ingredients for 4 servings

4 cups Greek yogurt	1 cup mascarpone cheese
1 ½ cups blueberries and raspberries	
1 tsp sugar	1 cup raw pistachios

Directions and Total Time: approx. 10 minutes

Mix the yogurt, sugar, and mascarpone in a bowl until evenly combined. Divide the mixture into 4 bowls, sprinkle the berries and pistachios on top. Cover.

Storage: Refrigerate the bowls for up to 3 days.

Per serving: Cal 490, Carbs 27g, Fat 35g, Protein 23g

Halloumi Scones with Avocado

Ingredients for 10 servings

1 cup halloumi cheese, grated	
½ cup butter, cold	3 tsp baking powder
1/3 cup buttermilk	1 avocado, pitted and mashed
2 cups flour	1 large egg

Directions and Total Time: approx. 35 minutes

Preheat oven to 350 F. Line a baking sheet with parchment paper. In a bowl, combine flour and baking powder. Add in butter and mix. Stir in halloumi cheese and avocado. Whisk the egg with the buttermilk and stir in the halloumi mix. Mold about 10 scones out to the batter. Place on the baking sheet and bake for 25 minutes or until the scones turn a golden color. Let cool before storing.

Storage: Place the scones in airtight containers in the refrigerator for up to 5 days.

Per serving: Cal 271; Carbs 23g; Fat 15g; Protein 8g

Berry Pancakes with Cinnamon Glaze

Ingredients for 4 servings

1 handful of strawberries and raspberries, mashed
1 handful of fresh strawberries and raspberries for topping

2 tsp butter	A pinch of cinnamon powder
½ cup flour	1 egg
1 tsp baking soda	½ cup milk
A pinch of salt	1 cup Greek yogurt
1 tbsp sugar	

Directions and Total Time: approx. 25 minutes

In a bowl, combine flour, baking soda, salt, sugar, and cinnamon. Whisk in mashed berries, egg, and milk until smooth. Melt ½ tsp of butter in a skillet and pour 1 tbsp of the mixture into the pan. Cook until small bubbles appear, flip, and cook until golden. Transfer to a plate and proceed using up the remaining batter for pancakes. Let the pancakes cool.

Storage: Place the pancakes in airtight containers in the refrigerator for up to 5 days (or in the freezer for up to 3 months). To serve, top pancakes with yogurt and berries.

Per serving: Cal 234; Carbs 26g; Fat 7g; Protein 12g

Simple Garlic Naan Bread

Ingredients for 6 servings

8 oz butter	1 tsp salt
¼ cup olive oil	½ tsp baking powder
¾ cup almond flour	2 cups boiling water
2 tbsp cornstarch	2 garlic cloves, minced

Directions and Total Time: approx. 25 minutes

In a bowl, mix almond flour, cornstarch, ½ teaspoon of salt, and baking powder. Mix in olive oil and boiling water to combine the ingredients like a thick porridge. Stir and allow the dough to rise for 5 minutes. Divide the dough into 6 balls. Place the balls on parchment paper and roll them into 8-inch circles using a rolling spin. Melt half of the butter in a frying pan over medium heat and fry the dough on both sides to have a golden color. Transfer to a plate and let cool. Add the remaining butter to the pan and sauté garlic until fragrant, about 1 minute. Pour the garlic butter into a mason jar and let it cool completely. Place the naan bread in airtight containers.

Storage: Keep the naan bread and butter in the refrigerator for up to 5 days (or in the freezer for up to 3 months). Melt the garlic butter and reheat the bread before serving.

Per serving: Cal 224; Carbs 7g; Fat 16g; Protein 4g

Berry & Greek Yogurt Parfait

Ingredients for 4 servings

3 cups Greek yogurt	1 cup low-sugar granola
2 cups mixed berries	1 tsp vanilla extract

Directions and Total Time: approx. 10 minutes

In a bowl, mix Greek yogurt with vanilla extract. In individual jars, layer Greek yogurt, mixed berries, and granola. Repeat the layers, finishing with a layer of berries on top. Seal the jars and place in the refrigerator.

Storage: Keep in the refrigerator for up to 3 days.

Per serving: Cal 243; Carbs 31g; Fat 11g; Protein 10g

School-Style Cookies

Ingredients for 20 servings

1 egg	¼ cup brown sugar
1 tbsp butter	½ tsp baking soda
2 cups ground pecans	20 pecan halves

Directions and Total Time: approx. 25 minutes

Preheat oven to 350 F. Mix all the ingredients except for the pecans until combined. Make 20 balls out of the mixture and press them with your thumb onto a lined cookie sheet. Top the cookie with pecan halves. Bake for about 12 minutes. Let cool completely.

Storage: Place in airtight containers in the refrigerator for up to 5 days (or in the freezer for up to 3 months).

Per serving: Cal 63; Carbs 3g; Fat 4g; Protein 3g

Strawberry Donuts

Ingredients for 8 servings

For the donuts:

2 oz cream cheese	2 tsp lemon juice
¼ cup sour cream	2 tsp water
½ cup butter	2 egg whites
1 ½ tsp vanilla extract	2 cups flour
½ cup brown sugar	2 tbsp protein powder
10 fresh strawberries, mashed	2 tsp baking powder

For the glaze:

2 tbsp whipping cream	2 tbsp brown sugar
4 fresh strawberries, mashed	2 tsp water

Directions and Total Time: approx. 25 minutes

Preheat oven to 350 F. For the donuts, in a bowl, whisk butter, cream cheese, sour cream, vanilla, brown sugar, strawberries, lemon juice, water, and egg whites until smooth. In another bowl, mix flour, protein, and baking powder. Combine both mixtures until smooth. Pour the batter into 8 greased donut cups and bake for 15 minutes. Flip the donuts onto a wire rack to cool. In a bowl, combine strawberries, whipping cream, sugar, and water until smooth. Swirl the glaze over the donuts. Cool.

Storage: Place the donuts in airtight containers in the refrigerator for up to 5 days (or freeze for up to 3 months).

Per serving: Cal 290; Carbs 29g, Fat 17g, Protein 6g

Coconut & Blueberry Squares

Ingredients for 6 servings

1 cup butter	2 cups fresh blueberries
2 cups coconut cream	4 tbsp lemon juice
5 tbsp flax seed powder	1 tsp vanilla extract
1 cup dark chocolate	4 oz walnuts, chopped
1 pinch salt	½ cup toasted coconut flakes
1 tsp vanilla extract	

Directions and Total Time: approx. 40 minutes

Preheat oven to 320 F. Line a springform pan with parchment paper. In a bowl, mix the flax seed powder with 2/3 cup water and allow thickening for 5 minutes. Break chocolate and butter into a bowl and microwave for 2 minutes. Share the flax egg into 2 bowls; whisk the salt into one portion, and then vanilla. Pour the chocolate mixture into the vanilla mixture and combine well. Fold into the other flax egg mixture. Pour the batter into the springform pan and bake for 20 minutes. Let the cake cool and slice it into squares. Place them in airtight containers.

Storage: Refrigerate the bowls for up to 3 days. Before serving, pour the blueberries and lemon juice into a small bowl. Break the blueberries and let sit for a few minutes. Whip the coconut cream with a whisk until a soft peak forms. Spoon the cream on the cakes, top with blueberry mixture, and sprinkle with walnuts and coconut flakes.

Per serving: Cal 345; Carbs 7g; Fat 31g; Protein 6g

Cranberry Waffles

Ingredients for 4 servings

1/3 tbsp unsalted butter, melted and cooled slightly
2/3 cup flour   ¼ cup fresh cranberries
2 ½ tsp baking powder   2/3 cup brown sugar
A pinch of salt   1 tsp lemon zest
2 eggs   ½ tsp vanilla extract
1 ½ cups milk

Directions and Total Time: approx. 40 minutes

Add cranberries, brown sugar, 3/4 cup water, vanilla, and lemon zest in a saucepan. Bring to a boil and reduce the temperature; simmer for 15 minutes or until the cranberries break and a sauce forms; set aside. In a bowl, mix flour, baking powder, and salt. In another bowl, whisk eggs, milk, and butter and pour the mixture into the flour mixture. Combine until a smooth batter forms. Preheat the waffle iron and brush it with butter. Pour some of the batter and cook until golden and crisp, 4 minutes. Repeat with the remaining batter. Let the waffles cool.

Storage: Place the waffles in airtight containers and the cooled sauce in a glass jar. Keep in the refrigerator for up to 5 days (or in the freezer for up to 3 months).

Per serving: Cal 267; Carbs 49g; Fat 6g; Protein 9g

Pumpkin & Sausage Omelet

Ingredients for 2 servings

4 tbsp cotija cheese   1 cup spinach, chopped
1 tbsp olive oil   4 oz sausage, chopped
6 eggs   2 oz pumpkin puree

Directions and Total Time: approx. 10 minutes

Whisk eggs in a bowl. Stir in spinach, cotija cheese, and pumpkin puree. Heat olive oil in a pan over medium heat and add the sausage to cook for 5 minutes, stirring often. Pour in eggs. Cook for 2 minutes or until the eggs are cooked. Fold in half and allow cooling completely.

Storage: Place the omelet in airtight containers and keep in the refrigerator for up to 5 days (or in the freezer for up to 3 months). Reheat in the microwave and serve.

Per serving: Cal 467; Carbs 7g; Fat 38g; Protein 33g

Citrus Blueberry Soufflé

Ingredients for 4 servings

1 cup frozen blueberries   4 egg yolks
2 tsp olive oil   3 egg whites
2 tbsp sugar   ½ lemon, zested

Directions and Total Time: approx. 35 minutes

Pour blueberries, 2 tbsp brown sugar, and 1 tbsp water in a saucepan. Cook until the berries soften and become syrupy, 8-10 minutes. Set aside. Preheat oven to 350 F. In a bowl, beat egg yolks and 1 tbsp of sugar until thick and pale. In another bowl, whisk egg whites until foamy.

Add in remaining brown sugar and whisk until soft peak forms, 3-4 minutes. Fold the egg white mixture into the egg yolk mixture. Heat olive oil in a pan over low heat. Pour in the egg mixture; swirl to spread. Cook for 3 minutes and transfer to the oven; bake for 2-3 minutes or until puffed and set. Let cool completely.

Storage: Place the soufflé in an airtight container and the cooled sauce in a glass jar. Refrigerate for up to 5 days. To serve, spoon blueberry sauce all over the soufflé. Sprinkle with lemon zest.

Per serving: Cal 150; Carbs 18g; Fat 8g; Protein 5g

Mixed Seed Coconut Loaf

Ingredients for 8 servings

4 tbsp sesame oil   5 tbsp sesame seeds
1 cup cream cheese, softened   ¼ cup corn flour
¾ cup heavy cream   ¼ cup hemp seeds
¾ cup coconut flour   1 tsp ground caraway seeds
1 cup almond flour   1 tbsp poppy seeds
3 tbsp baking powder   1 tsp salt
2 tbsp cornstarch   1 tsp allspice
2 tbsp desiccated coconut   6 eggs

Directions and Total Time: approx. 55 minutes

Preheat oven to 350 F. In a bowl, mix coconut and almond flour, baking powder, psyllium husk, desiccated coconut, sesame seeds, corn flour, hemp seeds, ground caraway and poppy seeds, salt, and allspice. Whisk eggs, cream cheese, heavy cream, and sesame oil in another bowl. Pour the mixture into the dry ingredients and combine both into a smooth dough. Pour the dough into a greased loaf pan. Bake for 45 minutes. Remove onto a rack and let cool.

Storage: Put the loaf in an airtight container and refrigerate for up to 5 days, or freeze for up to 3 months.

Per serving: Cal 430; Carbs 21g; Fat 34g; Protein 12g

Spanish Eggs with Goat Cheese

Ingredients for 4 servings

2 green onions, thinly sliced diagonally
2 tbsp olive oil   3 oz chorizo, diced
½ cup crumbled goat cheese   8 eggs
1 tsp smoked paprika   2 tbsp fresh parsley, chopped

Directions and Total Time: approx. 15 minutes

Preheat oven to 350 F. Heat the olive oil and paprika in a pan for 30 seconds. Add the chorizo and cook until lightly browned; set aside. Crack the eggs into the pan and cook them for 2 minutes. Sprinkle the chorizo, green onions, parsley, and goat cheese around the egg whites but not on the yolks. Transfer the pan to the oven and bake for 2 more minutes until the yolks are quite set but still runny within. Let cool before storing.

Storage: Place in airtight containers in the refrigerator for up to 5 days (or in the freezer for up to 3 months).

Per serving: Cal 357; Carbs 9g; Fat 23g; Protein 26g

Spicy Bacon Egg Muffins

Ingredients for 6 servings

12 eggs	Salt and black pepper to taste
1 cup Colby cheese, grated	12 slices bacon
¼ cup milk	4 jalapeño peppers, minced

Directions and Total Time: approx. 30 minutes

Preheat oven to 370 F. Crack the eggs into a bowl and whisk with milk until combined. Season with salt and pepper and stir in the Colby cheese. Line each muffin tin hole with a bacon slice and fill each two-thirds of the way up with the egg mixture. Top with the jalapeños and bake in the oven for 18-20 minutes or until puffed and golden. Remove and let cool completely.

Storage: Place the muffins in airtight containers and keep them in the refrigerator for up to 5 days.

Per serving: Cal 360; Carbs 4g; Fat 27g; Protein 22g

Chili Tofu Casserole

Ingredients for 4 servings

3 oz grated Parmesan cheese	1 tomato, finely chopped
2 tbsp butter	2 tbsp chopped scallions
8 oz tofu, scrambled	Salt and black pepper to taste
1 green bell pepper, chopped	1 tsp Mexican chili powder

Directions and Total Time: approx. 45 minutes

Melt butter in a skillet over medium heat. Fry the tofu until golden brown, stirring occasionally, about 5 minutes.

Stir in the bell pepper, tomato, and scallions and cook until the vegetables are soft, 4 minutes. Season with salt, pepper, and chili powder, and stir in the Parmesan cheese for about 2 minutes. Let cool completely.

Storage: Place in airtight containers and keep in the refrigerator for up to 5 days (or freeze for up to 3 months).

Per serving: Cal 254; Carbs 7g; Fat 19g; Protein 16g

Chia Pudding with Almonds & Blackberries

Ingredients for 4 servings

½ cup Greek yogurt	7 tbsp chia seeds
1 ½ cups coconut milk	1 cup fresh blackberries
4 tsp maple syrup	3 tbsp chopped almonds
1 tsp vanilla extract	Mint leaves to garnish

Directions and Total Time: approx. 45 minutes

Combine Greek yogurt, coconut milk, sugar-free maple syrup, and vanilla extract until evenly combined. Mix in the chia seeds. Puree half the blackberries in a bowl using a fork and stir them into the yogurt mixture. Divide the mixture evenly among medium mason jars.

Storage: Refrigerate the pudding for up to 3 days. To serve, stir the mixture. Garnish with remaining blackberries, almonds, and some mint leaves.

Per serving: Cal 309; Carbs 13g; Fat 26g; Protein 7g

Walnut & Chia Pudding with Blueberries

Ingredients for 4 servings

1 cup blueberries	4 tbsp chia seeds
1 ½ cups milk	2 tbsp chopped walnuts
1 tsp vanilla extract	

Directions and Total Time: approx. 10 minutes

Pour half of the blueberries, coconut milk, and vanilla extract into a blender. Blend the ingredients quickly until the blueberries are incorporated into the liquid. Mix in the chia seeds. Divide the mixture among 4 breakfast jars.

Storage: Refrigerate the pudding for 4 days. To serve, garnish with the remaining blueberries and walnuts.

Per serving: Cal 230; Carbs 21g; Fat 13g; Protein 8g

Pancetta & Zucchini Quiche

Ingredients for 4 servings

6 pancetta slices	4 eggs
1 tbsp olive oil	1 yellow onion, chopped
2 medium zucchinis, diced	1 tbsp cilantro, chopped

Directions and Total Time: approx. 25 minutes

Warm olive oil in a skillet over medium heat. Place in the pancetta in a skillet and cook for 5 minutes, until crispy; reserve. Stir-fry the onion in the same skillet for 3 minutes. Add in zucchini and cook for 10 more minutes. Transfer to a plate. Fry the eggs in the same skillet. Top the zucchini mixture with pancetta, fried eggs, and cilantro. Let cool.

Storage: Place the quiche in an airtight container and keep it in the refrigerator for up to 5 days (or in the freezer for up to 3 months). Reheat in the microwave and serve.

Per serving: Cal 270; Carbs: 7g; Fat: 23g; Protein: 15g

Cheese & Sesame Seed Bread

Ingredients for 6 servings

5 tbsp sesame oil	2 tbsp psyllium husk powder
1 cup cream cheese	1 tsp salt
4 tbsp flax seed powder	1 tsp baking powder
1 cup flour	1 tbsp sesame seeds

Directions and Total Time: approx. 50 minutes

In a bowl, mix flax seed powder with 1 ½ cups water until smoothly combined and set aside to soak for 5 minutes. Preheat oven to 400 F. When the flax egg is ready, beat in cream cheese and 4 tbsp sesame oil until mixed. Whisk in flour, psyllium husk powder, salt, and baking powder until adequately blended. Spread the dough on a greased baking tray. Allow to stand for 5 minutes and then brush with remaining sesame oil. Sprinkle with sesame seeds and bake for 30 minutes. Let cool and slice.

Storage: Put the bread slices in airtight containers and refrigerate for up to 5 days, or freeze for up to 3 months.

Per serving: Cal 410; Carbs 21g; Fat 29g; Protein 12g

Berry & Coconut Smoothie

Ingredients for 4 servings

2 cups coconut milk	¼ tsp vanilla extract
2 cup water	4 oz protein powder
4 cups fresh blueberries	

Directions and Total Time: approx. 5 minutes

Combine all ingredients in a blender until you attain a uniform and creamy consistency. Pour the smoothie into 4 tightly sealed jars.

Storage: Refrigerate the smoothie for up to 4 days, or freeze for up to 3 months. Shake thoroughly before consuming.

Per serving: Cal 330; Carbs: 23g; Fat: 13g; Protein: 24g

Cheddar & Zucchini Muffins with Olives

Ingredients for 6 servings

5 tbsp olive oil	1/3 cup almond milk
½ cup grated cheddar cheese	1 large egg
½ cup almond flour	2 zucchini, grated
1 tsp baking powder	6 green olives, sliced
½ tsp baking soda	1 spring onion, chopped
1 ½ tsp mustard powder	1 red bell pepper, chopped
Salt and black pepper to taste	1 tbsp freshly chopped thyme

Directions and Total Time: approx. 40 minutes

Preheat oven to 325 F. In a bowl, combine flour, baking powder, baking soda, mustard powder, salt, and pepper. In another bowl, whisk milk, egg, and olive oil. Mix the wet and dry ingredients and add cheese, zucchini, olives, spring onion, bell pepper, and thyme; mix well. Spoon the batter into 6 greased muffin cups and bake for 30 minutes or until golden brown. After, let them cool.

Storage: Place in airtight containers in the refrigerator for up to 5 days (or in the freezer for up to 3 months).

Per serving: Cal 243; Carbs 8g; Fat 19g; Protein 10g

Mozzarella Scrambled Eggs with Bresaola

Ingredients for 2 servings

1 tbsp butter	1 tbsp water
2 tbsp mozzarella, grated	4 bresaola slices, chopped
6 eggs	Salt and black pepper to taste
2 tbsp chives, chopped	

Directions and Total Time: approx. 15 minutes

Crack the eggs into a large bowl and whisk in water, salt, and pepper. Melt the butter in a skillet over medium heat and cook the eggs, stirring constantly for 30 seconds.

Spread the bresaola over and top with grated mozzarella cheese and chives. Stir and cook for 3 minutes until the omelet is set. Let cool completely.

Storage: Put the omelet in an airtight container and refrigerate for up to 4 days, or freeze for up to 3 months.

Per serving: Cal 341; Carbs 2g; Fat 25g; Protein 25g

Vanilla Muffins

Ingredients for 12 servings

For the muffins:

½ cup butter, softened	½ cup coconut flour
1 cup sour cream	2 tsp baking powder
¾ cup sugar	¼ tsp cornstarch
3 large eggs	½ tsp vanilla extract
1 lemon, zested and juiced	A pinch of salt
1 ½ cups almond flour	

For the topping:

3 tbsp butter, melted	1 tsp lemon zest
¾ cup almond flour	1 tbsp coconut flour
2 tbsp sugar	

For the lemon glaze:

½ cup confectioner's sugar
3 tbsp lemon juice

Directions and Total Time: approx. 40 minutes

For the muffins:

Preheat oven to 350 F. Line a 12-cup muffin pan with paper liners. In a bowl, mix butter, sugar, eggs, lemon zest, and lemon juice until smooth. In another bowl, combine coconut flour, baking powder, and cornstarch. Combine both mixtures and mix in vanilla, sour cream, and salt until smooth. Fill the cups two-thirds way up.

For the topping:

In a bowl, mix melted butter, almond flour, sugar, lemon zest, and coconut flour until well combined. Spoon the mixture onto the muffin batter and bake for 25 minutes or until a toothpick inserted comes out clean. Remove the muffins from the oven and let them cool.

Storage: Place the muffins in airtight containers in the refrigerator for up to 5 days (or in the freezer for up to 3 months). To serve, in a bowl, whisk the confectioner's sugar and lemon juice until smooth and semi-thick. Drizzle over the muffins.

Per serving: Cal 272; Carbs 15g; Fat 19g; Protein 7g

Minty Pistachio & Blueberry Shake

Ingredients for 4 servings

2 cups fresh blueberries	2 tbsp sesame seeds
½ cup heavy cream	2 tbsp chopped pistachios
2 cups almond milk	1 tbsp chopped mint leaves
1 tbsp maple syrup	

Directions and Total Time: approx. 10 minutes

Combine blueberries, milk, heavy cream, and syrup in a blender. Process until smooth and pour into glasses. Top with sesame seeds, pistachios, and mint leaves. Divide the shake between 4 tightly sealed jars.

Storage: Refrigerate the shake for up to 4 days, or freeze for up to 3 months. Shake well before enjoying.

Per serving: Cal 228, Carbs 14g, Fat 17g, Protein 5g

Easy Pumpkin Donuts

Ingredients for 4 servings

1 egg	¼ cup maple syrup
½ cup heavy cream	1 cup almond flour
2 egg yolks	¼ cup coconut flour
½ tsp vanilla extract	1 tsp baking powder
2 tsp pumpkin pie spice	A pinch of salt
½ cup pumpkin puree	1 cup confectioner's sugar

Directions and Total Time: approx. 30 minutes

Preheat oven to 350 F. In a bowl, beat egg, heavy cream, egg yolks, vanilla, pumpkin spice, pumpkin puree, and maple syrup. One after another, smoothly mix in almond and coconut flour, baking powder, and salt. Pour the batter into greased donut cups and bake for 18 minutes or until set. Remove, flip onto a wire rack and let cool. In a bowl, whisk the confectioner's sugar and 4 tbsp of water until smooth. Swirl the glaze over the donuts. Let cool.

Storage: Refrigerate the donuts for up to 3 days or freeze them for up to 3 months.

Per serving: Cal 405; Carbs 48g, Fat 18g, Protein 11g

Cinnamon Protein Bars

Ingredients for 4 servings

2 tbsp unsweetened chocolate chips	
2 tbsp coconut oil	¼ cup maple syrup
½ cup butter	1 tsp cinnamon powder
2 oz of vanilla protein	1 tbsp chopped toasted peanuts

Directions and Total Time: approx. 65 minutes

Line a baking sheet with parchment paper. In a bowl, mix the butter, coconut oil, vanilla protein, maple syrup, 2 tbsp chocolate chips, and cinnamon. Spread the mixture onto the sheet and scatter the remaining chocolate and peanuts on top. Refrigerate until firm, at least 1 hour. Cut into bars.

Storage: Refrigerate the bars for up to 3 days.

Per serving: Cal 411; Carbs 22g, Fat 28g, Protein 15g

Quick Cheddar Biscuits

Ingredients for 12 servings

3 tbsp melted butter	2 tsp baking powder
¾ cup grated cheddar cheese	2 eggs beaten
2 ½ cups flour	

Directions and Total Time: approx. 30 minutes

Preheat oven to 350 F. Line a baking sheet with parchment paper. In a bowl, mix flour, baking powder, and eggs until smooth. Whisk in the melted butter and cheddar cheese until well combined. Mold 12 balls out of the mixture and arrange on the sheet at 2-inch intervals. Bake for 25 minutes until golden brown. Let cool completely.

Storage: Put the biscuits in airtight containers and refrigerate for up to 5 days, or freeze for up to 3 months.

Per serving: Cal 132; Carbs 12g, Fat 7g, Protein 4g

Mozzarella & Avocado Lettuce Sandwiches

Ingredients for 4 servings

½ tbsp butter, softened	4 little gem lettuce leaves
1 avocado, sliced	8 fresh mozzarella slices
1 large red tomato, sliced	1 tsp chopped parsley

Directions and Total Time: approx. 10 minutes

Arrange the lettuce leaves on a flat serving plate. Smear each leaf with butter and arrange 2 cheese slices on each leaf. Top with avocado and tomato. Wrap the sandwiches tightly in aluminum foil.

Storage: Keep the sandwiches in the fridge for up to 4 days.

Per serving: Cal 60; Carbs 6g; Fat 13g; Protein 7g

Almond Mascarpone Cups

Ingredients for 8 servings

¼ cup olive oil	2 tsp baking soda
1 cup mascarpone cheese	1 egg
2 cups almond flour	1 cup almond milk

Directions and Total Time: approx. 30 minutes

Preheat oven to 380 F. Grease an 8-hole muffin tray with cooking spray. In a bowl, mix almond flour and baking soda. In a separate bowl, beat mascarpone cheese and olive oil and whisk in egg and almond milk. Fold in flour and spoon 2 tbsp of the batter into each muffin cup. Bake for 20 minutes, remove to a wire rack and cool completely.

Storage: Place the cups in airtight containers in the refrigerator for up to 5 days (or freeze for up to 3 months).

Per serving: Cal 331; Carbs 9g; Fat 28g; Protein 11g

Cinnamon Strawberry Porridge with Nuts

Ingredients for 6 servings

1 cup steel-cut oats	2 tbsp flour
2 cups dairy milk	1 tsp cornstarch
1 tsp cinnamon powder	2 eggs, beaten
6 fresh strawberries, sliced	2 tbsp lemon juice
6 tbsp heavy whipping cream	4 tbsp chopped walnuts
1 oz butter	2 tbsp chopped pecans

Directions and Total Time: approx. 55 minutes

Bring steel-cut oats, 4 cups of water, and milk to boil in a saucepan over medium heat. Cook for 20-25 minutes or until oats are tender. Stir in cinnamon and strawberries. In another saucepan, melt butter. To make a roux, stir in flour and cornstarch for 1-2 minutes. Gradually whisk in heavy cream until smooth. In a separate bowl, mix eggs and lemon juice. Slowly add this mixture to the saucepan, stirring continuously. Cook until the mixture thickens. Remove and let it cool slightly. Divide the porridge into 6 serving containers. Sprinkle with walnuts and pecans.

Storage: Refrigerate the porridge in the refrigerator for up to 4 days, keeping the nut topping separately.

Per serving: Cal 387; Carbs 35g; Fat 25g; Protein 10g

SNACKS & SIDE DISHES

Tex-Mex Chicken Wings

Ingredients for 8 servings

2 cups shredded Mexican cheese blend
16 chicken wings, halved   2 tbsp chopped green chilies
½ cup butter, melted   1 cup chopped scallions
1 cup corn flour   1 jalapeño pepper, sliced

Directions and Total Time: approx. 45 minutes

Preheat oven to 350 F. Brush the chicken with butter. Spread the corn flour on a wide plate and roll in each chicken wing. Place on a baking sheet and bake for 30-35 minutes or until golden brown and cooked within. Sprinkle with the cheese blend, green chilies, scallions, and jalapeño pepper on top. Let cool completely.

Storage: Place in airtight containers in the refrigerator for up to 5 days (or in the freezer for up to 2 months).

Per serving: Cal 342; Carbs 9g; Fat 23g; Protein 17g

Herby Bacon & Eggplant Gratin

Ingredients for 4 servings

½ cup crumbled feta cheese   3 large eggplants, sliced
½ cup shredded Parmesan   1 tbsp dried oregano
¾ cup heavy cream   2 tbsp chopped parsley
6 bacon slices, chopped   Salt and black pepper to taste

Directions and Total Time: approx. 40 minutes

Preheat oven to 400 F. Put bacon in a skillet and fry over medium heat until brown and crispy, 6 minutes; transfer to a plate. Arrange half of the eggplants in a greased baking sheet and season with oregano, parsley, salt, and pepper. Scatter half of bacon and half of feta cheese on top and repeat the remaining ingredients' layering process. In a bowl, combine heavy cream with half of the Parmesan cheese, and spread on top of the layered ingredients. Sprinkle with the remaining Parmesan. Bake until the cream is bubbly and the gratin golden, 20 minutes. Cool.

Storage: Place in airtight containers in the refrigerator for up to 5 days (or in the freezer for up to 2 months).

Per serving: Cal 441; Carbs 17g; Fat 35g; Protein 14g

Bacon-Wrapped Halloumi

Ingredients for 16 servings

½ lb halloumi cheese, cut into 16 cubes
16 bacon strips   ½ cup mayonnaise
½ cup brown sugar   ¼ cup hot sauce

Directions and Total Time: approx. 25 minutes

Lay bacon in a skillet and cook over medium heat on both sides until crisp, 5 minutes; transfer to a plate. Wrap each halloumi cheese with a bacon strip and secure with a toothpick each. Place on a baking sheet.

In a bowl, combine brown sugar, mayonnaise, and hot sauce. Pour the mixture all over the bacon-halloumi pieces and bake in the oven at 350 F for 10 minutes. Cool.

Storage: Place in airtight containers in the refrigerator for up to 5 days (or in the freezer for up to 2 months).

Per serving: Cal 175; Carbs 8g; Fat 13g; Protein 5g

Mustard Mini Sausages

Ingredients for 4 servings

3 tbsp almond flour   ¼ cup white wine vinegar
1 cup Brown sugar   1 tsp tamari sauce
2 tsp mustard powder   2 lb mini smoked sausages
¼ cup lemon juice

Directions and Total Time: approx. 15 minutes

In a pot, combine almond flour, brown sugar, and mustard. Gradually stir in lemon juice, vinegar, and tamari sauce. Bring to a boil over medium heat while stirring until thickened, 2 minutes. Mix in sausages until properly coated. Cook them for 5 minutes. Let cool completely.

Storage: Place in airtight containers in the refrigerator for up to 5 days (or in the freezer for up to 2 months).

Per serving: Cal 527; Carbs 37g; Fat 33g; Protein 21g

Roasted Broccoli with Pancetta

Ingredients for 3 servings

1 lb broccoli rabe, halved   6 pancetta slices, chopped
2 tbsp olive oil   ¼ tsp red chili flakes

Directions and Total Time: approx. 40 minutes

Preheat oven to 425 F. Place broccoli rabe in a greased baking sheet and top with pancetta. Drizzle with olive oil and sprinkle with chili flakes. Roast for 30 minutes. Cool.

Storage: Share among 3 airtight containers in the refrigerator for up to 5 days (or in the freezer for up to 2 months).

Per serving: Cal 184; Carbs 7g; Fat 13g; Protein 9g

Pancetta-Wrapped Strawberries

Ingredients for 4 servings

1 cup mascarpone cheese   12 fresh strawberries
1/8 tsp white pepper   12 thin pancetta slices
2 tbsp confectioner's sugar

Directions and Total Time: approx. 30 minutes

In a bowl, combine mascarpone, confectioner's brown sugar, and white pepper. Coat strawberries in the mixture, wrap each strawberry in a pancetta slice, and place on an ungreased baking sheet. Bake in the oven at 425 F for 15-20 minutes until pancetta browns. Let cool completely.

Storage: Place in airtight containers in the refrigerator for up to 5 days.

Per serving: Cal 255; Carbs 8g; Fat 19g; Protein 8g

Minute Steak & Radish Stir-Fry

Ingredients for 4 servings

1 ½ lb oz minute steak, cut into small pieces
3 tbsp butter   1 garlic clove, minced
1 ½ lb radishes, quartered   2 tbsp freshly chopped thyme

Directions and Total Time: approx. 30 minutes

Melt butter in a skillet over medium heat and brown the meat until brown on all sides, 12 minutes; transfer to a plate. Add and sauté radishes, garlic, and thyme until the radishes are cooked, 10 minutes. Let cool completely.

Storage: Place in airtight containers in the refrigerator for up to 5 days (or in the freezer for up to 2 months).

Per serving: Cal 390; Carbs 8g; Fat 25g; Protein 33g

Crunchy Parsnip Chips

Ingredients for 4 servings

4 large parsnips, sliced   3 tbsp ground pork rinds
3 tbsp olive oil   ¼ tsp red chili flakes

Directions and Total Time: approx. 55 minutes

Preheat oven to 425 F. Pour parsnips into a baking dish and add in the pork rinds. Toss to coat. Drizzle with olive oil and sprinkle with chili flakes. Bake until crispy, 40-45 minutes, tossing halfway. Let cool completely.

Storage: Place in airtight containers in the refrigerator for up to 5 days (or in the freezer for up to 2 months).

Per serving: Cal 211; Carbs 22g; Fat 11g; Protein 3g

Baked Celeriac with Cheese & Bacon

Ingredients for 8 servings

2 cups shredded cheddar   1 cup chicken broth
1 cup whipping cream   Salt and black pepper to taste
3 tbsp butter   1 lb celeriac, peeled and
6 bacon slices, chopped   sliced
3 garlic cloves, minced   ¼ cup chopped scallions
3 tbsp flour

Directions and Total Time: approx. 50 minutes

Preheat oven to 400 F. Add bacon to a skillet and fry over medium heat until brown and crispy. Spoon onto a plate. Melt butter in the same skillet and sauté garlic for 1 minute. Mix in flour and cook for another minute. Whisk in whipping cream, chicken broth, salt, and black pepper. Simmer for 5 minutes. Spread a layer of the sauce in a greased casserole dish and arrange celeriac slices on top. Cover with more sauce, top with some bacon and cheddar cheese, and scatter scallions on top. Repeat the layering process until the ingredients are exhausted. Bake for 35 minutes. Let cool completely and cut into 8 portions.

Storage: Place in airtight containers in the refrigerator for up to 5 days (or in the freezer for up to 2 months).

Per serving: Cal 279; Carbs 7g; Fat 25g; Protein 10g

Stuffed Mini Bell Peppers

Ingredients for 12 servings

12 mini green bell peppers, halved and deseeded
1 cup shredded Gruyere   4 oz chicken ham, chopped
8 oz cream cheese   1 tbsp chopped parsley
2 tbsp melted butter   ½ tbsp hot sauce

Directions and Total Time: approx. 30 minutes

Preheat oven to 400 F. Place the peppers in a greased baking dish and set aside. In a bowl, combine ham, parsley, cream cheese, hot sauce, and butter. Spoon the mixture into the peppers and sprinkle Gruyere cheese on top. Bake until the cheese melts, about 20 minutes. Let cool.

Storage: Place in airtight containers in the refrigerator for up to 5 days (or in the freezer for up to 2 months).

Per serving: Cal 122; Carbs 2g; Fat 9g; Protein 5g

Spanish-Style Asparagus Bake

Ingredients for 4 servings

1 cup grated Pecorino Romano cheese
1 cup grated mozzarella   3 garlic cloves, minced
¾ cup coconut cream   1 cup crushed pork rinds
4 oz Serrano ham, chopped   ½ tsp sweet paprika
2 lb asparagus, stalks trimmed

Directions and Total Time: approx. 40 minutes

Preheat oven to 400 F. Arrange asparagus on a greased baking dish and pour coconut cream on top. Scatter the garlic, serrano ham, and pork rinds on top and sprinkle with Pecorino cheese, mozzarella cheese, and paprika. Bake until the cheese melts and is golden and asparagus tender, 30 minutes. Let cool completely.

Storage: Place in airtight containers in the refrigerator for up to 5 days (or in the freezer for up to 2 months).

Per serving: Cal 392; Carbs 11g; Fat 26g; Protein 28g

Cheddar & Salami Kabobs

Ingredients for 12 servings

12 oz cheddar cheese, cubed   1 tsp Italian herb blend
¼ cup olive oil   4 oz hard salami, cubed
1 tbsp plain vinegar   ¼ cup pitted Kalamata olives
2 garlic cloves, minced   1 tsp chopped parsley

Directions and Total Time: approx. 1 hour 10 minutes

In a bowl, mix olive oil, vinegar, garlic, and herb blend. Add in salami, olives, and cheddar cheese. Mix until well coated. Cover the bowl with plastic wrap and marinate in the refrigerator for 1 hour. Remove, drain the marinade and thread one salami cube, one olive, and one cheese cube on a skewer. Repeat making more skewers with the remaining ingredients. Garnish with parsley. Let cool.

Storage: Place in airtight containers in the refrigerator for up to 5 days (or in the freezer for up to 2 months).

Per serving: Cal 194; Carbs 2g; Fat 17g; Protein 10g

One Pot Bacon & Cauliflower

Ingredients for 6 servings

1 large head cauliflower, cut into florets
10 oz bacon, chopped   Salt and black pepper to taste
1 garlic clove, minced   2 tbsp parsley, finely chopped

Directions and Total Time: approx. 15 minutes

Pour cauliflower in salted boiling water over medium heat and cook for 5 minutes or until soft; drain and set aside. In a skillet, fry bacon until brown and crispy, 5 minutes. Add cauliflower and garlic and sauté until the cauliflower browns slightly. Season with salt and pepper. Garnish with parsley. Let cool completely.

Storage: Place in airtight containers in the refrigerator for up to 5 days (or in the freezer for up to 2 months).

Per serving: Cal 183; Carbs 6g; Fat 14g; Protein 9g

Chili Cheese & Bacon Balls

Ingredients for 6 servings

6 oz shredded Gruyere cheese   6 bacon slices
6 oz cream cheese   ½ tsp red chili flakes
2 tbsp butter, softened

Directions and Total Time: approx. 30 minutes

Put the bacon in a skillet and fry over medium heat until crispy, 5 minutes. Transfer to a plate to cool and crumble it. Pour the bacon grease into a bowl and mix in cream cheese, Gruyere cheese, butter, and red chili flakes. Refrigerate to set for 15 minutes. Remove and mold into 6 walnut-sized balls. Roll in the crumbled bacon.

Storage: Keep in the refrigerator for up to 5 days.

Per serving: Cal 294; Carbs 2g; Fat 25g; Protein 14g

Cheese-Crusted Zucchini Strips with Aioli

Ingredients for 4 servings

¼ cup Pecorino Romano cheese, shredded
¼ cup breadcrumbs   Juice from half lemon
1 tsp sweet paprika   2 garlic cloves, minced
Salt and chili pepper to taste   3 fresh eggs
1 cup low-fat mayonnaise   2 zucchinis, cut into strips

Directions and Total Time: approx. 25 minutes

Preheat oven to 425 F. Line a baking sheet with foil. In a bowl, mix the crumbs, paprika, Pecorino Romano cheese, salt, and chili pepper. Beat the eggs in another bowl. Coat zucchini strips in eggs, then in the cheese mixture, and arrange on the sheet. Grease lightly with cooking spray and bake for 15 minutes. Let cool. Combine in a bowl mayonnaise, lemon juice, and garlic, and gently stir until everything is well incorporated. Place in a glass jar.

Storage: Keep the zucchini sticks and aioli in the refrigerator for up to 5 days.

Per serving: Cal 269; Carbs 6g; Fat 18g; Protein 10g

Cheesy Green Beans with Bacon

Ingredients for 4 servings

5 tbsp grated mozzarella   1 egg, beaten
2 tbsp olive oil   15 oz fresh green beans
1 tsp onion powder   4 bacon slices, chopped

Directions and Total Time: approx. 30 minutes

Preheat oven to 350 F. Line a baking sheet with parchment paper. In a bowl, mix olive oil, onion powder, and egg. Add in green beans and mozzarella cheese and toss to coat. Pour the mixture onto the baking sheet and bake until the green beans brown slightly and cheese melts, 20 minutes. Fry bacon in a skillet until crispy and brown. Remove green beans and divide between airtight containers. Top with bacon. Let cool completely.

Storage: Keep in the refrigerator for up to 5 days (or in the freezer for up to 2 months).

Per serving: Cal 163; Carbs 28g; Fat 11g; Protein 8g

Artichoke & Cauli Rice Gratin with Bacon

Ingredients for 6 servings

¼ cup grated Parmesan   ¼ cup sour cream
1 ½ cups grated mozzarella   1 tbsp olive oil
8 oz cream cheese, softened
1 cup canned artichoke hearts, drained and chopped
6 bacon slices, chopped   1 garlic clove, minced
2 cups cauliflower rice   Salt and black pepper to taste
3 cups baby spinach, chopped

Directions and Total Time: approx. 30 minutes

Preheat oven to 350 F. Cook bacon in a skillet over medium heat until brown and crispy, 5 minutes. Spoon onto a plate. In a bowl, mix cauli rice, artichokes, spinach, garlic, olive oil, salt, pepper, sour cream, cream cheese, bacon, and half of Parmesan cheese. Spread the mixture onto a baking dish and top with the remaining Parmesan and mozzarella cheese Bake for 15 minutes. Let cool.

Storage: Place in airtight containers in the refrigerator for up to 5 days (or in the freezer for up to 2 months).

Per serving: Cal 332; Carbs 7g; Fat 27g; Protein 13g

Ham & Radish Roast

Ingredients for 3 servings

1 lb radishes, halved   Salt and black pepper to taste
1 tbsp butter, melted   3 slices deli ham, chopped

Directions and Total Time: approx. 30 minutes

Preheat oven to 375 F. Arrange the radishes on a greased baking sheet. Season with salt and pepper and sprinkle with butter and ham. Bake for 25 minutes. Let cool.

Storage: Place in airtight containers in the refrigerator for up to 5 days (or in the freezer for up to 2 months).

Per serving: Cal 78; Carbs 7g; Fat 5g; Protein 5g

Oregano Parsnip Mash with Ham

Ingredients for 6 servings

4 tbsp heavy cream	2 tsp garlic powder
2 tbsp olive oil, divided	¾ cup almond milk
4 tbsp butter	6 slices deli ham, chopped
1 lb parsnips, diced	2 tsp freshly chopped oregano

Directions and Total Time: approx. 50 minutes

Preheat oven to 400 F. Spread parsnips on a baking sheet and drizzle with 2 tbsp olive oil. Cover tightly with aluminum foil and bake until the parsnips are tender, 40 minutes. Remove from the oven, take off the foil, and transfer to a bowl. Add in garlic powder, almond milk, heavy cream, and butter. With an immersion blender, puree the ingredients until smooth. Fold in the ham and sprinkle with oregano. Let cool completely.

Storage: Place in airtight containers in the refrigerator for up to 5 days.

Per serving: Cal 477; Carbs 8g; Fat 21g; Protein 5g

Cheesy Chips with Guacamole

Ingredients for 4 servings

1 cup Grana Padano, grated	¼ tsp garlic powder
1 tbsp rosemary, chopped	2 avocados, pitted and scooped
¼ tsp sweet paprika	1 tomato, chopped

Directions and Total Time: approx. 15 minutes

Preheat oven to 350 F. Line a baking sheet with parchment paper. Mix Grana Padano cheese, paprika, rosemary, and garlic powder evenly. Spoon 6-8 teaspoons on the baking sheet, creating spaces between each mound; flatten mounds. Bake for 5 minutes. Let cool. Place in airtight containers. To make the guacamole, mash avocados with a fork in a bowl, add in tomato and continue to mash until mostly smooth; season. Transfer to a glass jar.

Storage: Keep the chips and guacamole in the refrigerator for up to 5 days.

Per serving: Cal 271; Carbs 10g; Fat 22g; Protein 11g

Bacon-Wrapped Brussels Sprouts

Ingredients for 4 servings

8 bacon slices	1/8 teaspoon chili pepper
16 Brussels sprouts, trimmed	

Directions and Total Time: approx. 40 minutes

Preheat oven to 420 F. Line a baking sheet with parchment paper. Cut the bacon slices in half. Wrap each Brussels sprout with a bacon strip. Transfer the wraps to the baking sheet and bake in the oven for 25-30 until crispy. Sprinkle with chili powder. Let cool completely.

Storage: Place in airtight containers in the refrigerator for up to 5 days (or in the freezer for up to 2 months).

Per serving: Cal 90; Carbs 5g; Fat 9g; Protein 5g

Blackberry & Prosciutto Appetizer

Ingredients for 4 servings

1 cup crumbled goat cheese	1 cup fresh blackberries
4 bread slices	¼ tsp dry Italian seasoning
¾ cup balsamic vinegar	1 tbsp almond milk
1 tbsp sugar	4 thin prosciutto slices

Directions and Total Time: approx. 20 minutes

Cut the bread into 3 pieces each and arrange on a baking sheet. Place under the broiler and toast for 1-2 minutes on each side or until golden brown; set aside. In a saucepan, add balsamic vinegar and stir in sugar until dissolved. Boil the mixture over medium heat until reduced by half, 5 minutes. Turn the heat off and carefully stir in the blackberries. Make sure they do not break open. Set aside. In a bowl, add goat cheese, Italian seasoning, and almond milk. Mix until smooth. Brush one side of the toasted bread with the balsamic reduction and top with the cheese mixture. Cut each prosciutto slice into 3 pieces and place on the bread. Top with some of the whole blackberries from the balsamic mixture. Let cool completely.

Storage: Place in airtight containers in the refrigerator for up to 5 days (or in the freezer for up to 2 months).

Per serving: Cal 380; Carbs 34g; Fat 14g; Protein 20g

Cheese & Ham Rolls

Ingredients for 6 servings

16 thin deli ham slices, cut in half lengthwise	
1 medium sweet red pepper, cut into 16 strips	
8 oz Havarti cheese, cut into 16 strips	
2 tbsp salted butter	16 fresh green beans
1 ½ cups water	16 whole chives

Directions and Total Time: approx. 15 minutes

Bring the water to a boil in a saucepan over medium heat. Add in green beans, cover, and cook for 3 minutes or until softened; drain. Melt butter in a skillet and sauté green beans for 2 minutes; transfer to a plate. Assemble 1 green bean, 1 strip of red pepper, 1 cheese strip, and wrap with a ham slice. Tie with one chive. Repeat the assembling process with the remaining ingredients.

Storage: Place in airtight containers in the refrigerator for up to 4 days.

Per serving: Cal 172; Carbs 3g; Fat 13g; Protein 12g

Goat Cheese & Rutabaga Puffs

Ingredients for 4 servings

½ oz goat cheese, crumbled	1 rutabaga, peeled and diced
2 tbsp melted butter	¼ cup breadcrumbs

Directions and Total Time: approx. 35 minutes

Preheat oven to 400 F. Spread rutabaga on a baking sheet and drizzle with the butter. Bake until tender, 15 minutes. Transfer to a bowl. Allow cooling and add in goat cheese.

Using a fork, mash and mix the ingredients. Pour the crumbs onto a plate. Mold 1-inch balls out of the rutabaga mixture and roll properly in the crumbs while pressing gently to stick. Place in the same baking sheet and bake for 10 minutes until golden. Let cool completely.

Storage: Place in airtight containers in the refrigerator for up to 5 days.

Per serving: Cal 139; Carbs 11g; Fat 9g; Protein 3g

Roasted Butternut Squash with Pancetta

Ingredients for 4 servings

2 butternut squash, cubed	½ tsp garlic powder
2 tbsp olive oil	8 pancetta slices, chopped
1 tsp turmeric powder	1 tbsp chopped cilantro

Directions and Total Time: approx. 25 minutes

Preheat oven to 425 F. In a bowl, add butternut squash, turmeric, garlic powder, pancetta, and olive oil. Toss until well-coated. Spread the mixture onto a greased baking sheet and roast for 10-15 minutes. Transfer the veggies to a bowl and garnish with cilantro. Let cool completely.

Storage: Place in airtight containers in the refrigerator for up to 5 days (or in the freezer for up to 2 months).

Per serving: Cal 243; Carbs 26g; Fat 12g; Protein 5g

Dilled Deviled Eggs

Ingredients for 8 servings

8 large eggs	3 tbsp sriracha sauce
1 tsp dill, chopped	4 tbsp mayonnaise
3 cups water	¼ tsp sweet paprika

Directions and Total Time: approx. 20 minutes

Boil the eggs in salted water for 10 minutes. Transfer to an ice-water bath, cool completely, and peel the shells. Slice the eggs in half lengthwise and empty the yolks into a bowl. Smash with a fork and mix in the sriracha sauce, mayonnaise, and paprika until smooth. Spoon the filling into a piping bag and fill the egg whites slightly above the brim. Garnish with dill. Let cool.

Storage: Place in airtight containers in the refrigerator for up to 5 days.

Per serving: Cal 82; Carbs 0g; Fat 7g; Protein 7g

Roasted Eggplants with Almonds

Ingredients for 4 servings

2 large eggplants	1 tsp red chili flakes
2 tbsp butter	4 oz raw ground almonds

Directions and Total Time: approx. 30 minutes

Preheat oven to 400 F. Cut off the head of the eggplants and slice the body into rounds. Arrange on a parchment paper-lined baking sheet. Drop thin slices of butter on each eggplant slice and sprinkle with chili flakes.

Bake for 20 minutes. Slide out and sprinkle with almonds. Roast further for 5 minutes. Let cool completely.

Storage: Place in airtight containers in the refrigerator for up to 5 days (or in the freezer for up to 2 months).

Per serving: Cal 231; Carbs 14g; Fat 16g; Protein 10g

Crab Stuffed Dill Pickles

Ingredients for 4 servings

2 tbsp mayonnaise	1 tbsp lemon juice
6 oz canned crab meat	1 tbsp onion flakes
2 tsp Dijon mustard	
4 dill pickles, sliced lengthwise	

Directions and Total Time: approx. 15 minutes

Combine the mayonnaise, crab meat, mustard, and lemon juice in a bowl. With a spoon, scoop out the seeds from the pickles to create boats. Fill them with the crab mixture and sprinkle with onion flakes. Place in airtight containers.

Storage: Keep in the refrigerator for up to 5 days.

Per serving: Cal 114; Carbs 4g; Fat 10g; Protein 7g

Hot Stuffed Eggs

Ingredients for 6 servings

6 eggs	¼ cup mayonnaise
1 tbsp green tabasco	2 tbsp black olives, sliced

Directions and Total Time: approx. 20 minutes

Place eggs in salted boiling water and cook for 10 minutes. Remove the eggs to an ice bath and let cool. Peel and slice in half lengthwise. Scoop out the yolks to a bowl; mash with a fork. Whisk together the tabasco, mayonnaise, and mashed yolks in a bowl. Spoon this mixture into egg whites. Garnish with olives. Place in airtight containers.

Storage: Keep in the refrigerator for up to 5 days.

Per serving: Cal 126; Carbs: 1g; Fat: 11g; Protein: 6g

Delicious Cheese Bread

Ingredients for 12 servings

¼ cup grated Pecorino Romano cheese	
2 cups grated mozzarella	1 cup breadcrumbs
8 oz cream cheese	3 large eggs
1 tbsp baking powder	1 tbsp Italian mixed herbs

Directions and Total Time: approx. 30 minutes

Preheat oven to 375 F. Line a baking sheet with parchment paper. Microwave cream and mozzarella cheese for 1 minute or until melted. Whisk in baking powder, crumbs, eggs, Pecorino Romano cheese, and Italian mixed herbs. Spread the mixture on the baking sheet and bake for 20 minutes until lightly brown. Let cool completely.

Storage: Place in airtight containers in the refrigerator for up to 5 days (or in the freezer for up to 2 months).

Per serving: Cal 192; Carbs 4g; Fat 15g; Protein 11g

Crispy Green Beans with Parmesan

Ingredients for 4 servings

¼ cup breadcrumbs	2 eggs
¼ cup Parmesan, shredded	1 lb green beans
1 tsp minced garlic	Salt and black pepper to taste

Directions and Total Time: approx. 25 minutes

Preheat oven to 425 F. Line a baking sheet with foil. Mix breadcrumbs, Parmesan, garlic, salt, and pepper in a bowl. Beat the eggs in another bowl. Coat green beans in the eggs, then the cheese mixture, and arrange them on the baking sheet. Lightly grease the sheet with cooking spray and bake for 15 minutes. Transfer to a wire rack to cool.

Storage: Place in airtight containers in the refrigerator for up to 6 days.

Per serving: Cal 95; Carbs 5g; Fat 6g; Protein 8g

Garlicky Cheese Crackers

Ingredients for 6 servings

1 ¼ cups Pecorino Romano cheese, grated	
½ cup heavy cream	Salt and black pepper to taste
¼ cup ghee, softened	1 tsp garlic powder
1 ¼ cups coconut flour	¼ tsp sweet paprika

Directions and Total Time: approx. 30 minutes

Preheat oven to 350 F. Mix coconut flour, Pecorino Romano cheese, salt, pepper, garlic, and paprika in a bowl. Add in ghee and mix well. Top with heavy cream and mix again until a thick mixture has formed. Cover the dough with plastic wrap. Use a rolling pin to spread out the dough into a light rectangle. Cut into cracker squares and arrange them on a baking sheet. Bake for 20 minutes. Let cool completely. Place in airtight containers.

Storage: Keep in the refrigerator for up to 5 days.

Per serving: Cal 384; Carbs 10g; Fat 34g; Protein 10g

Cheese & Spinach Puffs

Ingredients for 4 servings

3 tbsp Parmesan cheese	¼ tsp garlic powder
¼ cup crumbled ricotta	¼ tsp onion powder
2 tbsp heavy cream	1 egg
1 tbsp butter, melted	4 oz spinach
¼ tsp nutmeg	½ cup almond flour
¼ tsp black pepper	

Directions and Total Time: approx. 30 minutes

Place all ingredients in a food processor. Process until smooth. Place in the freezer for 10 minutes. Make balls out of the mixture and arrange them on a lined baking sheet. Bake in the oven at 350 F for 10-12 minutes. Cool.

Storage: Place in airtight containers in the refrigerator for up to 4 days.

Per serving: Cal 189; Carbs 6g; Fat 15g; Protein 10g

Prosciutto-Wrapped Piquillo Peppers

Ingredients for 4 servings

4 oz goat cheese, crumbled	2 tbsp chopped parsley
2 tbsp heavy cream	1 garlic clove, minced
2 tbsp olive oil	1 tbsp chopped mint
4 canned roasted piquillo peppers	
2 prosciutto slices, cut into thin strips	

Directions and Total Time: approx. 15 minutes

Combine goat cheese, heavy cream, parsley, garlic, and mint in a bowl. Place the mixture in a freezer bag, press down, squeeze, and cut off the bottom. Drain and deseed the peppers. Squeeze about 2 tbsp of the filling into each pepper. Wrap a prosciutto slice onto each pepper. Secure with toothpicks. Arrange them on a serving platter. Sprinkle the olive oil over. Let cool.

Storage: Place in airtight containers in the refrigerator for up to 5 days (or in the freezer for up to 2 months).

Per serving: Cal 211; Carbs 4g; Fat 19g; Protein 8g

Cheesy Chicken Wraps

Ingredients for 4 servings

4 oz fontina cheese	4 raw chicken tenders
¼ tsp garlic powder	4 prosciutto slices

Directions and Total Time: approx. 15 minutes

Pound the chicken until it is half an inch thick. Season with garlic powder. Cut the cheese into 8 strips. Place a slice of prosciutto on a flat surface. Top with a chicken tender. Add a fontina strip. Roll the chicken and secure it with skewers. Grill the wraps for 3 minutes per side. Let cool.

Storage: Place in airtight containers in the refrigerator for up to 5 days (or in the freezer for up to 2 months).

Per serving: Cal 234; Carbs: 2g; Fat: 14g; Protein: 33g

Ham & Cheese Waffle Sandwiches

Ingredients for 4 servings

½ cup Gruyère cheese, grated	½ tsp baking powder
4 tbsp butter, softened	½ tsp dried thyme
4 oz smoked ham, chopped	4 tomato slices
6 eggs	

Directions and Total Time: approx. 30 minutes

In a bowl, mix eggs, baking powder, thyme, and butter. Set a waffle iron over medium heat, add in ¼ cup of the batter, and cook for 6 minutes until golden. Do the same with the remaining batter until you have 8 thin waffles. Lay a tomato slice on top of a waffle, followed by a ham slice, then top with ¼ of the grated cheese. Cover with another waffle, place the sandwich in the waffle iron and cook until the cheese melts. Repeat with the remaining ingredients. Let cool completely. Place in airtight containers.

Storage: Keep in the refrigerator for up to 3 days.

Per serving: Cal 350; Carbs 3g; Fat 27g; Protein 23g

Simple Fried Baby Artichokes

Ingredients for 4 servings

12 fresh baby artichokes
2 tbsp olive oil

2 tbsp lime juice
Salt to taste

Directions and Total Time: approx. 20 minutes

Slice artichokes vertically into narrow wedges. Drain on paper towels before frying. Heat olive oil in a skillet over medium heat and fry the artichokes until browned and crispy. Sprinkle with salt. Let cool completely.

Storage: Place in airtight containers in the refrigerator for up to 5 days. Before serving, reheat in the microwave for 1-2 minutes. Drizzle with lime juice and enjoy!

Per serving: Cal 55; Carbs: 8g; Fat: 4g; Protein: 2g

Cottage Cheese & Chorizo Bake

Ingredients for 4 servings

4 oz cottage cheese, crumbled
7 oz Spanish chorizo, sliced
¼ cup chopped parsley

Directions and Total Time: approx. 20 minutes

Preheat the oven to 325 F. Spread the chorizo on a parchment-lined baking dish and bake for 15 minutes until crispy. Remove from the oven and let cool. Arrange on a serving platter. Top with cottage cheese and parsley. Let cool completely.

Storage: Place in airtight containers in the refrigerator for up to 5 days (or in the freezer for up to 2 months).

Per serving: Cal 274; Carbs: 3g; Fat: 23g; Protein: 18g

Liverwurst & Bacon Balls

Ingredients for 12 servings

6 oz cream cheese
8 oz liverwurst
8 bacon slices, cooked and crumbled
¼ cup chopped pistachios
1 tsp Dijon mustard

Directions and Total Time: approx. 45 minutes

Combine liverwurst and pistachios in a food processor. Pulse until smooth. Whisk cream cheese and mustard in another bowl. Form 12 balls out of the liverwurst mixture. Make a thin cream cheese layer over it. Roll in bacon. Place in airtight containers.

Storage: Keep in the refrigerator for up to 5 days.

Per serving: Cal 187; Carbs 2g; Fat 15g; Protein 7g

Cauliflower Crackers with Cheese Dip

Ingredients for 6 servings

8 oz cream cheese, softened
1 ½ tbsp almond flour
1 tbsp flax seeds
1 head cauliflower, cut into florets
¾ cup dried cranberries, chopped
½ cup toasted pecans, chopped
4 tbsp chia seeds
2 tbsp maple syrup
1 tbsp lemon zest

Directions and Total Time: approx. 55 minutes

Preheat oven to 350 F. Pour cauliflower and 2 cups salted water into a pot and boil for 5 minutes. Drain and transfer to a food processor; pulse until smooth. Pour into a bowl and stir in flour. Mix in flax seeds and 1 tbsp chia seeds. Line a baking sheet with parchment paper and spread in the batter. Cover with plastic wrap and use a rolling pin to flatten and level the mixture. Take off the plastic wrap and cut it into squares. Bake for 30-35 minutes until brown on the edges, flipping once. Let cool completely.

Storage: Place in airtight containers in the refrigerator for up to 5 days. Before serving, mix cream cheese with maple syrup. Add in cranberries, pecans, remaining chia seeds, and lemon zest in a bowl. Reheat the cauliflower chips in the microwave for 1-2 minutes. Enjoy the dip!

Per serving: Cal 323; Carbs 16g; Fat 25g; Protein 6g

Baby Spinach Crisps with Avocado Dip

Ingredients for 4 servings

½ cup baby spinach
1 tbsp olive oil
½ cup butter
½ tsp plain vinegar
3 avocados, chopped
½ cup chopped parsley
¼ cup pumpkin seeds
¼ cup sesame paste
Juice from ½ lemon
1 garlic clove, minced
½ tsp coriander powder
Salt and black pepper to taste

Directions and Total Time: approx. 25 minutes

Preheat oven to 300 F. Put spinach in a bowl and toss with olive oil, plain vinegar, and salt. Arrange on a parchment paper-lined baking sheet and bake until the leaves are crispy but not burned, 15 minutes. Cool. Place avocados in a food processor. Add in butter, pumpkin seeds, sesame paste, lemon juice, garlic, coriander, parsley, salt, and pepper; puree until smooth. Spoon into a glass jar.

Storage: Keep the spinach crisps and avocado dip in the refrigerator for up to 5 days.

Per serving: Cal 318; Carbs 13g; Fat 27g; Protein 6g

Fiery Cheese-Nut Balls

Ingredients for 6 servings

1 ½ cups feta, crumbled
½ cream cheese
2 tbsp butter, softened
1 cup ground walnuts
1 habanero pepper, chopped
¼ tsp parsley flakes
½ tsp hot paprika

Directions and Total Time: approx. 40 minutes

In a bowl, combine all ingredients except the walnuts. Cover with foil and refrigerate for 30 minutes to firm. Remove from the fridge and form the mixture into balls. Place the ground walnuts on a plate and roll the balls to coat all sides.

Storage: Place in airtight containers in the refrigerator for up to 5 days (or in the freezer for up to 2 months).

Per serving: Cal 232; Carbs 5g; Fat 19g; Protein 7g

Baked Salami Bites

Ingredients for 6 servings

4 oz cream cheese   ¼ cup chopped parsley
7 oz dried salami

Directions and Total Time: approx. 20 minutes

Preheat oven to 325 F. Slice the salami into 30 slices. Line a baking dish with waxed paper. Bake the salami for 15 minutes until crispy. Remove from the oven and let cool. Top each slice with cream cheese. Top with parsley.

Storage: Place in airtight containers in the refrigerator for up to 5 days.

Per serving: Cal 237; Carbs 2g; Fat 19g; Protein 12g

Garlic-Butter Broccoli

Ingredients for 6 servings

1 head broccoli, florets only 1 tsp garlic flakes
¼ cup butter, melted   Salt and black pepper to taste

Directions and Total Time: approx. 15 minutes

Place the broccoli in a pot filled with salted water and bring to a boil. Cook for about 3 minutes, or until tender. Drain. Drizzle the butter over and season with salt and pepper. Top with garlic flakes. Let cool completely.

Storage: Place in airtight containers in the refrigerator for up to 5 days (or in the freezer for up to 2 months).

Per serving: Cal 81; Carbs 5g; Fat 8g; Protein 4g

Cauliflower Popcorn

Ingredients for 4 servings

¼ cup Parmesan, grated 1 tsp turmeric
1 tbsp olive oil   1 tsp fresh parsley, chopped
1 cup walnuts, halved   1 tsp chili pepper powder
1 tsp garlic, smashed   Salt to taste
1 head cauliflower, broken into florets

Directions and Total Time: approx. 35 minutes

Preheat oven to 390 F. Coat the florets with olive oil, salt, chili pepper powder, garlic, and turmeric. Pour in a baking dish and add in walnuts and parsley. Bake for 25 minutes until crisp. Sprinkle with Parmesan cheese and bake for another 2-3 minutes until the cheese melts. Cool.

Storage: Place in airtight containers in the refrigerator for up to 5 days (or in the freezer for up to 2 months).

Per serving: Cal 312; Carbs 7g; Fat 28g; Protein 8g

Greek-Style Deviled Eggs

Ingredients for 6 servings

2 tbsp crumbled feta cheese 1 tsp white wine vinegar
6 large eggs   ¼ tsp turmeric powder
Ice water bath   1 red chili, minced
1 tsp Dijon mustard   1 tbsp chopped parsley
3 tbsp mayonnaise   1 tbsp smoked paprika

Directions and Total Time: approx. 25 minutes

Boil eggs in salted water for 10 minutes. Transfer to an ice-water bath. Let cool for 5 minutes. Peel, and slice in half. Remove the yolks to a bowl and put the whites on a plate. Mash the yolks with a fork and mix in mustard, mayonnaise, vinegar, feta, turmeric, and chili until evenly combined. Spoon the mixture into a piping bag and fill it into the egg whites. Garnish with parsley and paprika.

Storage: Place in airtight containers in the refrigerator for up to 5 days.

Per serving: Cal 144; Carbs 1g, Fat 12g, Protein 7g

Parmesan Cauliflower Patties

Ingredients for 4 servings

½ cup Parmesan cheese ½ tsp baking powder
4 tbsp olive oil   ½ cup almond flour
1 pound grated cauliflower 3 eggs
1 chopped onion   ½ tsp lemon juice

Directions and Total Time: approx. 15 minutes

Combine cauliflower, Parmesan cheese, onion, baking powder, almond flour, and eggs in a bowl. Heat olive oil in a skillet over medium heat. Form the cauliflower mixture into patties. Fry for 3 minutes per side. Let cool. Drizzle with lemon juice.

Storage: Place in airtight containers in the refrigerator for up to 5 days.

Per serving: Cal 316; Carbs 13g; Fat 25g; Protein 14g

Prosciutto Chicken Wraps

Ingredients for 8 servings

8 oz provolone cheese 8 chicken tenders
¼ tsp garlic powder   8 prosciutto slices

Directions and Total Time: approx. 30 minutes

Pound the chicken until half an inch thick. Season with garlic powder. Cut the provolone cheese into 8 strips. Place a slice of prosciutto on a flat surface. Place one chicken tender on top. Top with a provolone strip. Roll the chicken and secure with previously soaked skewers. Grill the wraps for about 3 minutes per side. Let cool.

Storage: Place in airtight containers in the refrigerator for up to 5 days (or in the freezer for up to 2 months).

Per serving: Cal 174; Carbs 0.7g; Fat 10g; Protein 17g

Crudités with Dill Yogurt Dip

Ingredients for 4 servings

1 cup radishes, cut into matchsticks
2 celery stalks, cut into matchsticks
1 tbsp olive oil   Salt and black pepper to taste
1 cup Greek yogurt   2 cups baby carrots
¼ cup chopped fresh dill 1 cup cherry tomatoes
1 garlic clove, minced   1 yellow bell pepper, sliced

Directions and Total Time: approx. 15 minutes

In a small bowl, add the olive oil, Greek yogurt, dill, garlic, salt, and black pepper. Stir to combine. Transfer to a glass jar. Place the vegetables in airtight containers.

Storage: Keep the vegetables and yogurt dip in the refrigerator for up to 5 days.

Per serving: Cal 115; Carbs 9g; Fat 5g; Protein 7g

Lazy Onion Rings with Green Dip

Ingredients for 4 servings

½ cup grated Parmesan	½ tbsp sweet paprika
4 tbsp coconut cream	2 oz chopped kale
2 tbsp olive oil	2 tbsp dried cilantro
1 onion, sliced in rings	1 tbsp dried oregano
1 egg, beaten	Salt and black pepper to taste
1 cup almond flour	1 cup mayonnaise
1 tsp garlic powder	Juice of ½ lemon

Directions and Total Time: approx. 30 minutes

Preheat oven to 400 F. In a bowl, combine almond flour, Parmesan cheese, garlic powder, paprika, and salt. Line a baking sheet with parchment paper. Dip in the onion rings one after another in the egg, then into the almond flour mixture. Place the rings on the sheet and spray with cooking spray. Bake for 20 minutes. Let cool completely.

Storage: Place in airtight containers in the refrigerator for up to 5 days. Before serving, reheat the onion rings in the microwave for 1-2 minutes. Blend the kale, olive oil, cilantro, oregano, salt, pepper, mayonnaise, coconut cream, and lemon juice until mixed well. Enjoy the onion with dip.

Per serving: Cal 385; Carbs 11g; Fat 29g; Protein 14g

Poached Egg Cups with Bacon

Ingredients for 6 servings

½ cup mozzarella, shredded	6 eggs
4 tbsp sour cream	2 tbsp chives, chopped
4 oz smoked bacon, sliced	Salt and black pepper, to taste

Directions and Total Time: approx. 30 minutes

Fry bacon slices on both sides over medium heat for 5 minutes. Using the bacon fat, grease 6 ramekins, then line 2 bacon slices inside each cup. Divide the sour cream and mozzarella, and crack an egg in each cup. Sprinkle with salt, pepper, and chives. Bake for 15 minutes in a preheated oven at 400 F until the eggs are set. Let cool.

Storage: Place in airtight containers in the refrigerator for up to 5 days.

Per serving: Cal 212; Carbs 2g; Fat 16g; Protein 13g

Tasty Roasted Nuts

Ingredients for 8 servings

8 oz walnuts and pecans	1 tsp cumin powder
2 tbsp coconut oil	Salt and paprika to taste

Directions and Total Time: approx. 15 minutes

In a bowl, mix walnuts, pecans, salt, coconut oil, cumin powder, and paprika until the nuts are well coated. Pour the mixture into a preheated dry pan and toast over medium heat while stirring continually until fragrant and brown. Let cool completely. Place in a resealable container.

Storage: Keep the nuts at room temperature for up to 5 days.

Per serving: Cal 193; Carbs 5g; Fat 14g; Protein 6g

Hot Edamame

Ingredients for 4 servings

1 lb edamame in pods	½ tbsp chili garlic sauce
1 tbsp soy sauce	1 tsp toasted sesame oil

Directions and Total Time: approx. 5 minutes

Bring 4 cups of water to a boil in a pot over medium heat, add in edamame, and cook for 5 minutes. Drain and place the edamame in a large bowl. Set aside to cool.

In a bowl, combine the soy sauce, chili garlic sauce, and sesame oil. Pour the sauce over the edamame and toss to coat. Divide the mixture between 4 airtight containers.

Storage: Keep the containers in the refrigerator for up to 5 days. To reheat, microwave for 1 minute or serve cold.

Per serving: Cal 153; Carbs 8g; Fat 7g; Protein 12g

Basil-Mozzarella Prosciutto Wraps

Ingredients for 6 servings

6 thin prosciutto slices	18 mozzarella cheese ciliegine
18 basil leaves	

Directions and Total Time: approx. 10 minutes

Cut the prosciutto slices into three strips. Place basil leaves at the end of each strip. Top with mozzarella. Wrap the mozzarella in prosciutto. Secure with toothpicks.

Storage: Keep in the refrigerator for up to 5 days.

Per serving: Cal 102; Carbs 1g; Fat 8g; Protein 7g

Roasted Tamari Almonds

Ingredients for 10 servings

2 tbsp olive oil	1 tbsp nutritional yeast
3 tbsp tamari sauce	1 tsp chili powder
1 lb raw almonds	Salt to taste

Directions and Total Time: approx. 20 minutes

Preheat oven to 400 F. In a bowl, whisk the olive oil and tamari sauce and add the almonds; toss to coat. Spread the almonds on a parchment-lined baking sheet and roast for 12-15 minutes until browned. Let cool for 5 minutes. Sprinkle with salt, nutritional yeast, and chili powder. Pour in a glass jar and close tightly with a lid.

Storage: Keep in the refrigerator for up to 5 days.

Per serving: Cal 195; Carbs 6g; Fat 17g; Protein 7g

Vegetarian Pinwheels

Ingredients for 24 servings

1 cup grated cheddar cheese	3 tbsp brown sugar
4 tbsp cream cheese, softened	1 ½ tsp vanilla extract
¼ cup butter, cold	1 whole egg, beaten
¼ cup almond flour	1 cup mushrooms, chopped
3 tbsp coconut flour	1 cup basil pesto
½ tsp xanthan gum	2 cups baby spinach
¼ tsp yogurt	Salt and black pepper to taste
3 whole eggs	

Directions and Total Time: approx. 1 hour 45 minutes

In a bowl, mix almond and coconut flour, xanthan gum, and ½ tsp salt. Add in yogurt, cream cheese, and butter; mix until crumbly. Add in brown sugar and vanilla until mixed. Pour in 3 eggs one after another while mixing until formed into a ball. Flatten the dough on a clean, flat surface, cover it in plastic wrap, and refrigerate it for 1 hour.

Dust a clean flat surface with almond flour, unwrap the dough, and roll out into 15x12 inches. Spread pesto on top with a spatula, leaving a 2-inch border on one end.

In a bowl, combine baby spinach and mushrooms, season with salt and pepper, and spread the mixture over the pesto. Sprinkle with cheddar cheese and roll up as tightly as possible from the shorter end. Refrigerate.

Preheat oven to 380 F. Roll the pastry out on a flat surface and cut into 24 slim discs with a sharp knife. Arrange on the baking sheet, brush with the beaten egg, and bake for 25 minutes until golden. Let cool completely.

Storage: Place in airtight containers in the refrigerator for up to 5 days (or in the freezer for up to 2 months).

Per serving: Cal 87; Carbs 2g; Fat 8g; Protein 5g

Easy Mixed Seed Crackers

Ingredients for 6 servings

1/3 cup sesame seed flour	¼ cup butter, melted
1/3 cup pumpkin seeds	1 tbsp cornstarch
1/3 cup sunflower seeds	1 tsp salt
1/3 cup chia seeds	

Directions and Total Time: approx. 45 minutes

Preheat oven to 300 F. Combine sesame seed flour with pumpkin, chia, sunflower seeds, cornstarch, and salt. Add butter and 1 cup of boiling water and mix until a dough with a gel-like consistency forms. Line a baking sheet with parchment paper and place the dough on it. Cover with another piece of parchment paper and flatten with a rolling pin. Remove the top piece of parchment paper. Bake for 25 minutes. Turn off the oven and allow the crackers to cool and dry in the oven for 10 minutes. Break and let cool completely.

Storage: Keep in the refrigerator for up to 5 days.

Per serving: Cal 165; Carbs 5g; Fat 15g; Protein 4g

Roasted Broccoli & Cauliflower Steaks

Ingredients for 6 servings

1 cauliflower head, cut into steaks	
1 broccoli head, cut into steaks	
2 tbsp olive oil	1 tsp ground coriander
Salt and chili pepper to taste	

Directions and Total Time: approx. 20 minutes

Preheat oven to 400 F. Line a baking sheet with foil. Brush the broccoli and cauliflower steaks with olive oil and season with chili pepper, coriander, and salt. Spread on the baking sheet in one layer. Roast in the oven for 10 minutes until tender and lightly browned. Let cool.

Storage: Place in airtight containers in the refrigerator for up to 5 days (or in the freezer for up to 2 months).

Per serving: Cal 85; Carbs 7g; Fat 6g; Protein 3g

Cauliflower & Chorizo Stuffed Cabbage Rolls

Ingredients for 8 servings

¼ cup coconut oil	1 cup canned tomato sauce
1 onion, chopped	1 tsp dried oregano
3 cloves garlic, minced	1 tsp dried basil
1 cup crumbled chorizo	Salt and black pepper to taste
1 cup cauliflower rice	8 green cabbage leaves

Directions and Total Time: approx. 35 minutes

Heat coconut oil in a saucepan and sauté onion, garlic, and chorizo for 5 minutes. Stir in cauli rice, season with salt and pepper, and cook for 4 minutes; set aside. In the saucepan, pour tomato sauce, oregano, and basil. Add ¼ cup water and simmer for 10 minutes. Lay cabbage leaves on a flat surface and spoon the chorizo mixture into the middle of each leaf. Roll the leaves to secure the filling. Put the cabbage rolls in tomato sauce and cook for 10 minutes. Let cool completely. Place in airtight containers.

Storage: Keep in the refrigerator for up to 5 days.

Per serving: Cal 163; Carbs 10g; Fat 12g; Protein 5g

Yum-Yum Cheese Sticks

Ingredients for 10 servings

1 lb halloumi cheese, cut into 10 strips	2 tsp smoked paprika
	2 tbsp chopped parsley
½ cup grated cheddar cheese	½ tsp cayenne powder
1/3 cup almond flour	

Directions and Total Time: approx. 15 minutes

Preheat oven to 350 F. In a bowl, mix almond flour with paprika and lightly dredge in the halloumi cheese strips. Arrange them on a greased baking sheet. In a bowl, combine parsley, cheddar cheese, and cayenne powder. Sprinkle the mixture on the cheese and grease with cooking spray. Bake for 10 minutes until golden brown. Let cool.

Storage: Place in airtight containers in the refrigerator for up to 5 days (or in the freezer for up to 2 months).

Per serving: Cal 145; Carbs 2g; Fat 7g; Protein 9g

No-Bake Salami & Olive Egg Balls

Ingredients for 12 servings

2 hard-boiled eggs, chopped	8 black olives, chopped
½ cup butter, softened	1 oz salami, chopped
Salt and pepper flakes to taste	2 tbsp flax seeds
3 tbsp mayonnaise	

Directions and Total Time: approx. 30 minutes

Throw the eggs, olives, pepper flakes, mayonnaise, butter, and salt in a food processor and blitz until everything is combined. Stir in the chopped salami. Refrigerate for 20 minutes. Make 12 balls from the mixture. Pour the flax seeds on a large plate; roll the balls through to coat.

Storage: Put in airtight containers and chill for up to 5 days.

Per serving: Cal 133; Carbs 1g; Fat 13g; Protein 4g

Baked Chili Zucchini Chips

Ingredients for 4 servings

4 zucchinis, sliced into rounds	2 tbsp hemp seeds
4 tbsp olive oil	Salt and black pepper to taste
1 tsp smoked paprika	1 tsp red chili flakes

Directions and Total Time: approx. 45 minutes

Preheat oven to 400 F. Drizzle zucchini with olive oil and sprinkle with paprika. Scatter with hemp seeds and chili flakes. Season with salt and pepper, and bake for 30-35 minutes or until crispy and golden brown. Let cool.

Storage: Keep in the fridge for up to 5 days.

Per serving: Cal 140; Carbs 4g; Fat 11g; Protein 2g

Quick Snickerdoodles

Ingredients for 16 servings

2 cups almond flour	¾ cup sugar
½ tsp baking soda	2 tbsp brown sugar
½ cup butter, softened	1 tsp cinnamon

Directions and Total Time: approx. 25 minutes

Preheat oven to 350 F. Combine almond flour, baking soda, sugar, and butter in a bowl. Make 16 balls out of the mixture; flatten them. Combine the cinnamon and brown sugar into a bowl. Dip in the cookies and arrange them on a cookie sheet. Bake for 15 minutes. Let cool.

Storage: Place in airtight containers in the refrigerator for up to 5 days (or in the freezer for up to 2 months).

Per serving: Cal 133; Carbs 5g; Fat 11g; Protein 3g

Multi-Seed Flapjacks

Ingredients for 16 servings

6 tbsp salted butter	3 tbsp chia seeds
8 tbsp maple syrup	3 tbsp hemp seeds
8 tbsp sugar	3 tbsp sunflower seeds
3 tbsp sesame seeds	1 tbsp poppy seeds
4 tbsp dried goji berries, chopped	

Directions and Total Time: approx. 30 minutes

Preheat oven to 350 F. Put butter and maple syrup in a saucepan over low heat. Stir in the sugar until it dissolves. Remove the pan and stir in the seeds and goji berries. Spread the mixture on a baking sheet lined with wax paper. Bake for 20 minutes. Slice the flapjacks into 16 strips. Cool.

Storage: Place in airtight containers in the refrigerator for up to 5 days (or in the freezer for up to 2 months).

Per serving: Cal 75; Carbs 7g; Fat 5g; Protein 1g

Cheesy Mushroom Broccoli Noodles

Ingredients for 8 servings

1 cup grated Gruyere cheese	2 tbsp almond flour
2 tbsp olive oil	1 ½ cups almond milk
4 large broccoli	Salt and black pepper to taste
2 garlic cloves, minced	¼ cup chopped fresh parsley
4 scallions, chopped	
1 cup sliced cremini mushrooms	

Directions and Total Time: approx. 20 minutes

Cut off the florets of the broccoli heads, leaving only the stems. Cut the ends of the stem flatly and evenly. Run the stems through a spiralizer to make the noodles. Heat olive oil in a skillet and sauté the broccoli noodles, mushrooms, garlic, and scallions until softened, 5 minutes. In a bowl, combine almond flour and almond milk and pour the mixture over the vegetables. Stir and allow thickening for 2-3 minutes. Whisk in half of the Gruyere cheese to melt and adjust the taste with salt and black pepper. Garnish with the remaining Gruyere cheese and parsley. Let cool.

Storage: Place in airtight containers in the refrigerator for up to 5 days (or in the freezer for up to 2 months).

Per serving: Cal 120; Carbs 6g; Fats 9g; Protein 6g

Italian-Style Zoodles

Ingredients for 4 servings

1 cup grated Parmesan cheese	2 garlic cloves, minced
2 tbsp olive oil	¼ tsp red pepper flakes
4 zucchinis, spiralized	1 cup chopped kale
4 shallots, finely chopped	2 tbsp balsamic vinegar
Salt and black pepper to taste	½ lemon, juiced
1 head broccoli, cut into florets	
1 cup sliced mixed bell peppers	

Directions and Total Time: approx. 20 minutes

Heat oil in a skillet and sauté broccoli, bell peppers, and shallots until softened, 7 minutes. Mix in garlic and red pepper flakes and cook until fragrant, 30 seconds. Stir in kale and zucchini spaghetti; cook until tender, 3 minutes. Mix in vinegar and lemon juice and adjust the taste with salt and pepper. Garnish with Parmesan cheese. Let cool.

Storage: Place in airtight containers in the refrigerator for up to 5 days (or in the freezer for up to 2 months).

Per serving: Cal 168; Carbs 15g; Fats 9g; Protein 5g

Baked Nut & Seed Granola

Ingredients for 6 servings

¼ cup sunflower seeds	¼ cup chopped cashews
¼ cup pepitas seeds	2 tablespoons cinnamon
2 tbsp sesame seeds	¼ cup maple syrup
¼ cup chopped walnuts	1 tbsp vanilla extract
¼ cup chopped pecans	2 tbsp coconut oil

Directions and Total Time: approx. 40 minutes

Preheat the oven to 300 F. In a large bowl, combine all the ingredients and toss well to coat. Pour the mixture onto a wax paper-lined baking sheet and spread it out evenly. Bake for 25-30 minutes, stirring halfway through the cooking time, until golden and lightly toasted. Let cool.

Storage: Place the granola in airtight containers and keep it at room temperature for up to 14 days.

Per serving: Cal 293; Carbs 18g; Fat 18g; Protein 4g

Cheese & Tofu Stuffed Peppers

Ingredients for 4 servings

1 cup grated Parmesan	4 oz tofu, chopped
1 cup cream cheese	1 tbsp fresh parsley, chopped
2 tbsp melted butter	1 tbsp chili paste, mild
4 red bell peppers	

Directions and Total Time: approx. 30 minutes

Preheat oven to 400 F. Cut bell peppers into two, lengthwise, and remove the core and seeds. In a bowl, mix tofu with parsley, cream cheese, chili paste, and melted butter until smooth. Spoon the cheese mixture into the bell peppers. Arrange peppers on a greased sheet. Sprinkle Parmesan on top and bake for 20 minutes. Cool.

Storage: Place in airtight containers in the refrigerator for up to 5 days (or in the freezer for up to 2 months).

Per serving: Cal 374; Carbs 10g; Fat 28g; Protein 17g

Nutty Chocolate Bars

Ingredients for 8 servings

¼ cup walnuts	1 egg, beaten
¼ cup cashew nuts	¼ cup dark chocolate chips
¼ cup almonds	¼ cup hemp seeds
¼ cup coconut chips	Salt to taste
½ cup butter, melted	1 cup mixed dried berries

Directions and Total Time: approx. 25 minutes

Preheat oven to 350 F. Line a baking sheet with wax paper. In a food processor, pulse nuts until roughly chopped. Place in a bowl and stir in coconut chips, chocolate chips, egg, butter, hemp seeds, salt, and berries. Spread the mixture on the sheet and bake for 18 minutes. Let cool.

Storage: Place in airtight containers in the refrigerator for up to 5 days.

Per serving: Cal 283; Carbs 11g; Fat 25g; Protein 6g

Homemade Yellow Squash Nachos

Ingredients for 4 servings

½ cup coconut oil	Salt to taste
1 yellow squash, sliced	1 tbsp taco seasoning

Directions and Total Time: approx. 20 minutes

Heat coconut oil in a skillet over medium heat. Add in squash slices and fry until crispy and golden brown, 15 minutes. Remove to a paper towel-lined plate. Sprinkle the slices with taco seasoning and salt. Let cool completely.

Storage: Place in airtight containers in the refrigerator for up to 5 days (or in the freezer for up to 2 months).

Per serving: Cal 233; Carbs 22g; Fat 18g; Protein 2g

Vegetable Penne with Walnuts

Ingredients for 4 servings

1 cup grated Parmigiano-Reggiano cheese	
1 cup shredded mozzarella	1 red bell pepper, sliced
3 tbsp olive oil	2 garlic cloves, minced
1 head broccoli, cut into florets	Salt and black pepper to taste
1 egg yolk	1 tsp dried oregano
1 red onion, thinly sliced	3 tbsp balsamic vinegar
1 lb green beans, halved	2 tbsp chopped walnuts

Directions and Total Time: approx. 2 hours 30 minutes

Microwave mozzarella cheese for 2 minutes. Let cool for 1 minute and mix in egg yolk until well combined. Lay a parchment paper on a flat surface, pour the cheese mixture on top and cover with another parchment paper. Flatten the dough into 1/8-inch thickness. Take off the parchment paper and cut the dough into mimicked penne-size pieces. Place in a bowl and refrigerate for 2 hours. Bring 2 cups of water to a boil and add in penne. Cook for 1 minute and drain; set aside. Heat olive oil in a skillet and sauté onion, garlic, green beans, broccoli, and bell pepper for 5 minutes. Season with salt, pepper, and oregano. Mix in balsamic vinegar, cook for 1 minute and toss in the pasta. Top with Parmigiano-Reggiano cheese and walnuts. Cool.

Storage: Keep in the refrigerator for up to 5 days.

Per serving: Cal 271; Carbs 14g; Fats 21g; Protein 13g

Dijon Broccoli Slaw

Ingredients for 6 servings

1 tbsp olive oil	⅓ cup mayonnaise
2 tbsp brown sugar	1 tsp celery seeds
1 tbsp Dijon mustard	1 ½ tbsp apple cider vinegar
4 cups broccoli slaw	Salt and black pepper to taste

Directions and Total Time: approx. 10 minutes

Whisk together all ingredients except for the broccoli. Transfer to a glass jar. Place broccoli in an airtight container.

Storage: Keep in the refrigerator for up to 5 days. Before serving, pour the dressing over the broccoli. Mix well.

Per serving: Cal 167; Carbs 6g; Fat 13g; Protein 1g

SALADS & SOUPS

Bok Choy & Chicken Caesar Salad

Ingredients for 4 servings

2 tbsp shaved Parmesan
4 tbsp olive oil
½ lb chicken breasts, thinly sliced
4 bok choy heads, cut lengthwise
¼ cup lemon juice
½ cup Caesar salad dressing

Directions and Total Time: approx. 1 hour 25 minutes

Preheat your grill to medium-high heat. Combine the chicken slices, lemon juice, and 2 tbsp olive oil in a bowl and toss to coat. Grill the chicken for 4 minutes per side. Brush bok choy with the remaining olive oil and grill for 3 minutes. Remove to a serving platter. Top with the chicken and leave to cool completely.

Storage: Place in airtight containers in the refrigerator for up to 3 days. To serve, drizzle the Caesar dressing over and finish with Parmesan cheese.

Per serving: Cal 465; Carbs 13g; Fat 31g; Protein 30g

Favorite Greek Salad

Ingredients for 4 servings

7 oz feta cheese, chopped
4 tbsp olive oil
5 tomatoes, chopped
1 cucumber, chopped
1 green bell pepper, chopped
1 small red onion, sliced
16 kalamata olives, chopped
4 tbsp capers
1 tsp oregano, dried
2 tbsp lemon juice

Directions and Total Time: approx. 10 minutes

Place tomatoes, bell pepper, cucumber, onion, capers, feta cheese, and olives in an airtight container. Mix well.

Storage: Keep in the refrigerator for up to 5 days. To serve, combine the olive oil, lemon juice, and oregano in a bowl. Drizzle the dressing over the salad and enjoy!

Per serving: Cal 343; Carbs 12g; Fat 28g; Protein 11g

Coconut Collard Green Salad

Ingredients for 2 servings

4 oz tofu cheese
¾ cup coconut cream
1 tbsp butter
2 tbsp mayonnaise
1 tsp mustard powder
Salt and black pepper to taste
1 garlic clove, minced
1 cup collard greens, rinsed

Directions and Total Time: approx. 10 minutes

In a glass jar, whisk coconut cream, mayonnaise, mustard powder, garlic, salt, and pepper until well mixed; set aside. Melt butter in a skillet over medium heat and sauté collard greens until wilted and brownish. Let cool completely.

Storage: Keep in the refrigerator for up to 3 days. To serve, pour the dressing over the greens. Mix the salad well and crumble the tofu cheese over. Serve and enjoy

Per serving: Cal 371; Carbs 6g; Fat 33g; Protein 9g

Fennel & Squash Salad

Ingredients for 4 servings

2 tbsp butter
1 fennel bulb, sliced
2 lb green squash, cubed
2 oz chopped green onions
1 cup mayonnaise
2 tbsp chives, finely chopped
A pinch of mustard powder
2 tbsp chopped dill

Directions and Total Time: approx. 20 minutes

Put a pan over medium heat and melt butter. Fry squash until slightly softened, about 7 minutes; let cool. In an airtight container, mix squash, fennel slices, green onions, mayonnaise, chives, dill, and mustard powder.

Storage: Keep in the refrigerator for up to 7 days.

Per serving: Cal 317; Carbs 23g; Fat 27g; Protein 4g

Tofu & Beet Salad

Ingredients for 4 servings

2 tbsp butter
8 oz red beets, washed
2 oz tofu, cubed
½ red onion, sliced
1 cup mayonnaise
1 small romaine lettuce, torn
Salt and black pepper to taste
2 tbsp chopped chives

Directions and Total Time: approx. 55 minutes

Put beets in a pot over medium heat, cover with salted water, and boil for 40 minutes or until soft. Drain and allow cooling. Slip the skin off and slice the beets. Melt butter over medium heat and fry tofu until browned, 3-4 minutes. Remove to a plate and let cool. Combine beets, tofu, red onion, lettuce, salt, pepper, chives, and mayonnaise in an airtight container.

Storage: Keep in the refrigerator for up to 7 days.

Per serving: Cal 320; Carbs 10g; Fat 30g; Protein 3g

Mushroom & Bell Pepper Salad

Ingredients for 4 servings

2 tbsp sesame oil
2 yellow bell peppers, sliced
1 garlic clove, minced
2 tbsp tamarind sauce
½ tsp hot sauce
1 cup mixed mushrooms, chopped
1 tsp maple syrup
½ tsp ginger paste
Salt and black pepper to taste
Chopped toasted pecans
Sesame seeds to garnish

Directions and Total Time: approx. 20 minutes

Heat half of the sesame oil in a skillet over medium heat and sauté bell peppers and mushrooms for 8-10 minutes. Season with salt and pepper. In a bowl, mix garlic, tamarind sauce, hot sauce, maple syrup, and ginger paste. Stir the mix into the vegetables and stir-fry for 2-3 minutes; let cool. Place in airtight containers.

Storage: Keep in the refrigerator for up to 5 days. To serve, drizzle the salad with the remaining sesame oil and garnish with pecans and sesame seeds. Enjoy!

Per serving: Cal 295; Carbs 14g; Fat 21g; Protein 7g

Chorizo & Cherry Tomato Salad

Ingredients for 4 servings

2 tbsp olive oil
2 ½ cups cherry tomatoes
1 head romaine lettuce, torn
4 chorizo sausages, chopped
2 tsp red wine vinegar
1 small red onion, sliced
2 tbsp chopped cilantro
Salt and black pepper to taste
8 sliced Kalamata olives

Directions and Total Time: approx. 10 minutes

Heat 1 tbsp of olive oil in a skillet and fry the chorizo until golden; remove and let it cool. Cut in half cherry tomatoes. In an airtight container, add the lettuce, onion, tomatoes, cilantro, and chorizo. Top with olives.

Storage: Keep in the refrigerator for up to 3 days. To serve, in a small bowl, whisk the remaining olive oil, vinegar, salt, and pepper. Drizzle over the salad and toss to coat.

Per serving: Cal 370; Carbs 14g; Fat 29g; Protein 15g

Bacon & Zoodle Caprese

Ingredients for 4 servings

8 mozzarella cheese slices
2 tsp olive oil
2 zucchinis, spiralized
6 cherry tomatoes, halved
4 basil leaves
3 oz bacon, chopped
1 tsp balsamic vinegar

Directions and Total Time: approx. 30 minutes

Place the bacon in a skillet over medium heat and cook until crispy, 5 minutes; set aside. Add the cherry tomatoes to the skillet and cook for 5-8 minutes until softened. Stir in zoodles for 3-4 minutes. Divide the mixture between two containers and arrange the mozzarella slices on top. Scatter basil leaves and top with the bacon. Drizzle with olive oil and balsamic vinegar.

Storage: Refrigerate for up to 3 days.

Per serving: Cal 285; Carbs 7g; Fat 19g; Protein 15g

Walnut & Sweet Beet Salad

Ingredients for 4 servings

4 tbsp avocado oil-based dressing
½ cup chopped walnuts
8 oz mixed lettuce greens
2 cooked beets, sliced
1 Granny Smith apple, diced
2 tbsp dried cranberries
2 tbsp goat cheese, crumbled

Directions and Total Time: approx. 20 minutes

Preheat oven to 400 F. Spread the walnuts over a foil-lined baking sheet and toast for 5 minutes, shaking once until golden brown. Set aside to cool. Evenly divide the lettuce greens between 4 glass containers with tight-fitting lids. Top with beet slices, apple, walnuts, dried cranberries, and goat cheese. Cover and place in the refrigerator.

Storage: Refrigerate for up to 5 days. Before serving, pour the avocado oil-based dressing over the salad, secure the lid, and shake well to coat and combine.

Per serving: Cal 253; Carbs 14g; Fat 19g; Protein 6g

Summer Salad with Artichoke & Capers

Ingredients for 4 servings

4 tbsp olive oil
¼ cup pitted green olives, sliced
6 baby artichokes
¼ cup cherry peppers, halved
¼ tsp lemon zest
2 tsp balsamic vinegar
1 tbsp chopped dill
Salt and black pepper to taste
2 tbsp capers

Directions and Total Time: approx. 35 minutes

Trim and halve the artichokes. Cover them in a pot over medium heat with salted water. Bring to a boil, lower the heat, and let simmer for 20 minutes until tender. Combine the remaining ingredients, except for olives, in a glass jar. Drain the artichokes and let them cool. Place them in airtight containers.

Storage: Keep the artichokes in the refrigerator for up to 5 days. To serve, pour the prepared dressing over the artichokes and toss to combine. Top with olives.

Per serving: Cal 186; Carbs 3g; Fat 18g; Protein 1g

Spinach & Avocado Salad with Bacon

Ingredients for 4 servings

4 cooked bacon slices, crumbled
2 avocados, 1 chopped and 1 sliced
3 tbsp olive oil
1 spring onion, sliced
2 cups spinach, chopped
1 lettuce head, chopped
2 hard-boiled eggs, chopped
1 tsp Dijon mustard
1 tbsp apple cider vinegar
Salt and black pepper to taste

Directions and Total Time: approx. 20 minutes

Combine the spinach, lettuce, eggs, chopped avocado, and spring onion in a large, airtight container. Whisk the olive oil, mustard, vinegar, salt, and pepper in a glass jar.

Storage: Keep the salad in the refrigerator for up to 3 days. Before serving, pour the dressing over and toss to combine. Top with sliced avocado and bacon. Enjoy!

Per serving: Cal 316; Carbs 11g; Fat 26g; Protein 7g

Anchovy Caprese Salad

Ingredients for 4 servings

12 fresh mozzarella slices
4 red tomato slices
4 yellow tomato slices
1 cup basil pesto
4 anchovy fillets in oil

Directions and Total Time: approx. 10 minutes

On an airtight container, alternately stack a tomato slice, a mozzarella slice, a yellow tomato slice, another mozzarella slice, a red tomato slice, and then a mozzarella slice. Repeat making 3 more stacks in the same way. Spoon pesto all over. Top with anchovies.

Storage: Keep in the refrigerator for up to 3 days.

Per serving: Cal 321; Carbs 9g; Fat 23g; Protein 12g

Brussels Sprouts with Seeds & Nuts

Ingredients for 4 servings

½ cup olive oil	1 tsp chili paste
1 tbsp butter	2 oz pecans
1 lb Brussels sprouts, grated	1 oz pumpkin seeds
1 lemon, juice and zest	1 oz sunflower seeds
Salt and black pepper to taste	½ tsp cumin powder

Directions and Total Time: approx. 20 minutes

Place Brussels sprouts in a salad bowl. In a bowl, mix lemon juice, zest, olive oil, salt, and pepper, and drizzle the dressing over Brussels sprouts. Toss and let marinate for 10 minutes. Melt butter in a pan. Stir in chili paste, pecans, pumpkin and sunflower seeds, cumin powder, and salt. Cook on low heat for 4 minutes just to heat up; let cool. Mix nuts and seeds with Brussels sprouts.

Storage: Place in airtight containers in the refrigerator for up to 3 days.

Per serving: Cal 422; Carbs 16g; Fat 27g; Protein 12g

Power Green Salad with Feta

Ingredients for 4 servings

2 cups broccoli slaw	2 cups chopped spinach
2 tbsp olive oil	1/3 cup chopped walnuts
1 tbsp white wine vinegar	1/3 cup sunflower seeds
2 tbsp poppy seeds	1/3 cup blueberries
Salt and black pepper to taste	2/3 cup crumbled feta cheese

Directions and Total Time: approx. 15 minutes

In an airtight container, combine the broccoli slaw, spinach, walnuts, sunflower seeds, blueberries, and feta. Drizzle the dressing on top and toss to coat.

Storage: Keep in the refrigerator for up to 3 days. To serve, In a bowl, whisk the olive oil, vinegar, poppy seeds, salt, and pepper. Pour over the salad and toss to coat.

Per serving: Cal 397; Carbs 11g; Fat 23g; Protein 10g

Summertime Cheese Salad

Ingredients for 2 servings

½ cup colby cheese, cubed	½ red onion, sliced thinly
4 tbsp olive oil	10 green olives, pitted
½ yellow bell pepper, sliced	½ tbsp red wine vinegar
2 tomatoes, sliced	Salt and black pepper to taste
½ cucumber, sliced	½ tsp dried oregano

Directions and Total Time: approx. 10 minutes

Pour bell pepper, tomatoes, cucumber, red onion, and colby cheese in an airtight container.

Storage: Place in airtight containers in the refrigerator for up to 3 days. To serve, drizzle red wine vinegar and olive oil all over and season with salt, pepper, and oregano; toss to coat. Top with olives, and enjoy!

Per serving: Cal 383; Carbs 8g; Fat 35g; Protein 10g

Roasted Bell Pepper Salad with Cheese

Ingredients for 4 servings

½ cup goat cheese, crumbled	1 tbsp mint leaves
2 tbsp olive oil	3 tbsp chopped walnuts
½ tsp brown sugar	½ tbsp balsamic vinegar
1/3 cup arugula	1 tbsp toasted pine nuts
4 tbsp pitted Kalamata olives	Salt and black pepper to taste
4 large red bell peppers, deseeded and cut in wedges	

Directions and Total Time: approx. 30 minutes

Preheat oven to 400 F. Throw bell peppers on a roasting pan; season with brown sugar and drizzle with half of the olive oil. Roast for 20 minutes or until slightly charred; set aside to cool. Put the arugula in an airtight container and top with roasted bell peppers, olives, mint, and walnuts.

Storage: Keep in the refrigerator for up to 3 days. To serve, drizzle with vinegar and olive oil. Season with salt and pepper. Toss, top with goat cheese and pine nuts.

Per serving: Cal 217; Carbs 7g; Fat 15g; Protein 5g

Green Bean & Asparagus Mix

Ingredients for 4 servings

6 oz Swiss cheese, cubed	1 cup asparagus, halved
2 tbsp olive oil	Salt and black pepper to taste
2 tbsp butter	½ lemon, juiced
1 cup green beans, trimmed	4 tbsp chopped almonds

Directions and Total Time: approx. 25 minutes

Heat butter in a skillet over medium heat and pour in green beans and asparagus. Season with salt and pepper and cook until softened, about 5-8 minutes. Let cool.

Storage: Place in airtight containers in the refrigerator for up to 5 days. To serve, drizzle with lemon juice and olive oil and scatter almonds and Swiss cheese on top.

Per serving: Cal 343; Carbs 9g; Fat 25g; Protein 16g

Cotija Cheese & Arugula Salad

Ingredients for 4 servings

4 tbsp crumbled cotija cheese	½ tsp sesame seeds
2 tbsp olive oil	1 tbsp maple syrup
1 lb asparagus, halved	½ cup arugula
½ tsp dried tarragon	2 tbsp hazelnuts, chopped
½ tsp dried oregano	Salt and black pepper to taste

Directions and Total Time: approx. 30 minutes

Preheat oven to 350 F. our asparagus on a baking tray and drizzle with olive oil, tarragon, oregano, salt, pepper, and sesame seeds. Toss and roast for 15 minutes. Remove and drizzle with the maple syrup and continue cooking for 5 minutes or until slightly charred; let cool. Spread the arugula in an airtight container and spoon the asparagus on top. Scatter with cotija cheese and hazelnuts and cover.

Storage: Keep in the refrigerator for up to 5 days.

Per serving: Cal 166; Carbs 10g; Fat 13g; Protein 4g

Fresh Gazpacho with Avocado

Ingredients for 6 servings

7 oz goat cheese	2 spring onions, chopped
1 cup olive oil	1 cucumber, chopped
2 green peppers, roasted	2 tbsp lemon juice
2 large red peppers, roasted	4 tomatoes, chopped
2 avocados, flesh scoped out	1 red onion, coarsely chopped
2 garlic cloves	2 tbsp apple cider vinegar

Directions and Total Time: approx. 10 minutes

Place peppers, tomatoes, avocados, spring onions, garlic, lemon juice, olive oil, vinegar, and salt in a food processor. Pulse until slightly chunky but smooth. Adjust the seasoning and transfer to a pot. Stir in cucumbers and red onion. Place in airtight containers.

Storage: Keep in the refrigerator for up to 5 days (or in the freezer for up to 2 months). To serve, top with goat cheese and a drizzle of olive oil. Enjoy!

Per serving: Cal 311; Carbs 13g; Fat 23g, Protein 8g

Thai-Style Cream Soup

Ingredients for 4 servings

1 tbsp ghee	5 oz watercress
1 broccoli head, chopped	4 cups vegetable stock
7 oz spinach	1 cup coconut milk
1 onion, chopped	1 bay leaf
2 garlic cloves, minced	Salt and black pepper to taste

Directions and Total Time: approx. 20 minutes

Melt ghee in a pot over medium heat. Add onion and garlic and cook for 3 minutes. Stir in broccoli and cook for an additional 5 minutes. Pour in vegetable stock and bay leaf. Bring to a boil, reduce the heat, and simmer for 3 minutes. Add spinach and watercress and cook for 3 minutes. Stir in coconut milk, salt, and pepper. Discard the bay leaf and blend the soup with a hand blender. Let cool completely.

Storage: Place in airtight containers in the refrigerator for up to 5 days (or in the freezer for up to 2 months).

Per serving: Cal 14; Carbs 18g; Fat 12g, Protein 5g

Green Leafy Soup

Ingredients for 4 servings

3 ½ cups coconut cream	3 tbsp chopped mint leaves
3 tbsp butter	Juice from 1 lime
1 cup spinach, coarsely	1 cup collard greens, chopped
1 cup kale, coarsely	3 garlic cloves, minced
1 large avocado	3 tbsp cardamom powder
1 cup vegetable broth	2 tbsp toasted pistachios

Directions and Total Time: approx. 20 minutes

Set a saucepan over medium heat and melt 2 tbsp of the butter. Add the spinach and kale and sauté for 5 minutes. Transfer to a food processor. Add the avocado, coconut cream, broth, mint, lime juice, and puree until smooth; reserve the soup. Reheat the saucepan with the remaining butter, add the collard greens, garlic, cardamom powder, and sauté for 4 minutes. Spoon the soup into airtight containers and let it cool completely.

Storage: This soup can be kept in the refrigerator for up to five days (or in the freezer for up to two months). To serve, microwave the soup for 1-2 minutes, stirring once, and top with collards and pistachios. Enjoy!

Per serving: Cal 470; Carbs 15g; Fat 31g; Protein 6g

Basil Mushroom Soup

Ingredients for 4 servings

5 oz white button mushrooms, chopped	
5 oz cremini mushrooms, chopped	
5 oz shiitake mushrooms, chopped	
1 vegetable stock cube, crushed	
1 cup coconut cream	½ lb celery root, chopped
4 oz unsalted butter	½ tsp dried rosemary
1 small onion, finely chopped	1 tbsp plain vinegar
1 clove garlic, minced	6 leaves basil, chopped

Directions and Total Time: approx. 35 minutes

Melt butter in a saucepan over medium heat. Sauté onion, garlic, mushrooms, and celery until fragrant, 6 minutes. Reserve some mushrooms for garnishing. Add in rosemary, 4 cups of water, stock cube, and vinegar. Stir and bring to a boil; reduce the heat and simmer for 20 minutes. Mix in coconut cream and puree. Garnish with the reserved mushrooms and basil and let cool completely.

Storage: Place in airtight containers in the refrigerator for up to 5 days (or in the freezer for up to 2 months).

Per serving: Cal 373; Carbs 12g; Fat 32g; Protein 4g

Green Egg Benedict Soup

Ingredients for 4 servings

2 tbsp butter	2 cups baby spinach, chopped
1 tbsp sesame oil	2 cups chopped green beans
1 small onion, finely sliced	4 cups vegetable stock
3 garlic cloves, minced	3 tbsp chopped cilantro
2 tsp ginger paste	4 eggs

Directions and Total Time: approx. 35 minutes

Melt butter in a pot and sauté onion, garlic, and ginger for 4 minutes, stirring frequently. Stir in spinach, allowing wilting, and pour in green beans and vegetable stock. Bring to a boil and simmer for 10 minutes. Transfer the soup to a blender and puree until smooth. Divide the soup between airtight containers and let it cool completely.

Storage: Keep in the refrigerator for up to 5 days (or in the freezer for up to 2 months). Before serving, bring 3 cups of vinegared water to simmer. When hot, slide in an egg to poach for 3 minutes; remove with a perforated spoon. Repeat the process with the remaining eggs. Top the soup with poached eggs and drizzle with sesame oil and cilantro.

Per serving: Cal 245; Carbs 8g; Fat 17g, Protein 8g

Daikon & Bell Pepper Soup

Ingredients for 4 servings

1 cup grated Parmesan cheese	1 daikon radish, chopped
1 tbsp butter	2 parsnips, chopped
1 tbsp olive oil	3 cups chopped tomatoes
1 large red onion, chopped	4 cups vegetable stock
4 garlic cloves, minced	1 cup milk
6 red bell peppers, sliced	1 cup chopped walnuts

Directions and Total Time: approx. 40 minutes

Heat butter and olive oil in a pot over medium heat and sauté onion and garlic for 3 minutes. Stir in bell peppers, daikon radish, and parsnips; cook for 10 minutes. Pour in tomatoes and vegetable stock; simmer for 20 minutes. Puree the soup with an immersion blender. Mix in milk. Let cool completely. Place in airtight containers.

Storage: Keep in the refrigerator for up to 5 days (or in the freezer for up to 2 months). To serve, reheat the soup in the microwave for 1-2 minutes, stirring once, and top with walnuts and Parmesan cheese. Enjoy!

Per serving: Cal 454; Carbs 27g; Fat 33g, Protein 12g

Bacon & Cheddar Soup

Ingredients for 4 servings

1 cup grated cheddar cheese	1 tbsp chopped fresh tarragon
1 tbsp butter	1 tbsp chopped fresh oregano
1 tbsp olive oil	2 cups cubed parsnips
6 slices bacon, chopped	4 cups vegetable broth
1 small white onion, chopped	Salt and black pepper to taste
3 garlic cloves, minced	1 cup almond milk
2 tbsp finely chopped thyme	2 tbsp chopped scallions

Directions and Total Time: approx. 30 minutes

Heat olive oil in a saucepan over medium heat and fry bacon until browned and crunchy, 5 minutes; set aside. Melt butter in the saucepan. Sauté onion, garlic, thyme, tarragon, and oregano for 3 minutes. Add the parsnips and broth, season with salt and pepper, and cook for 15 minutes until the parsnips soften. Using an immersion blender, process the soup until smooth. Stir in almond milk and cheddar cheese and simmer with continuous stirring until the cheese melts. Top with bacon and scallions and cool.

Storage: Place in airtight containers in the refrigerator for up to 5 days (or in the freezer for up to 2 months).

Per serving: Cal 337; Carbs 13g; Fat 27g, Protein 11g

White Cream Soup with Walnuts

Ingredients for 4 servings

1 cup feta cheese, crumbled	1 tbsp olive oil
1 cup cremini mushrooms, sliced and pre-cooked	
1 garlic clove, minced	Salt and black pepper to taste
1 white onion, finely chopped	2 cups almond milk
1 tsp ginger puree	1 tbsp chopped basil
1 cup vegetable stock	Finely chopped parsley
2 turnips, peeled and chopped	Chopped walnuts for topping

Directions and Total Time: approx. 25 minutes

Heat olive oil in a saucepan over medium heat and sauté garlic, onion, and ginger puree until fragrant and soft, about 3 minutes. Pour in vegetable stock, turnips, salt, and pepper, cook for 6 minutes. Use an immersion blender to puree the ingredients until smooth. Stir in mushrooms and simmer covered for 7 minutes. Add in almond milk and heat for 2 minutes. Stir in basil and parsley. Let cool.

Storage: Place in airtight containers in the refrigerator for up to 5 days (or in the freezer for up to 2 months). To serve, reheat the soup in the microwave for 1-2 minutes, stirring once, and top with feta cheese and walnuts. Enjoy!

Per serving: Cal 253; Carbs 13g; Fat 17g, Protein 9g

Gourmet Reuben Soup

Ingredients for 6 servings

1 ½ cups Swiss cheese, grated	2 celery stalks, diced
2 cups heavy cream	2 garlic cloves, minced
3 tbsp butter	1 cup sauerkraut
1 onion, diced	1 lb corned beef, chopped
7 cups beef stock	Salt and black pepper to taste
1 tsp caraway seeds	

Directions and Total Time: approx. 30 minutes

Melt butter in a large pot. Add in onion, garlic, and celery and fry for 3 minutes until tender. Pour the broth over and stir in sauerkraut, salt, caraway seeds, and pepper. Bring to a boil. Reduce the heat to low and add the corned beef. Cook for about 15 minutes. Stir in heavy cream and Swiss cheese and cook for 1 minute. Let cool completely.

Storage: Place in airtight containers in the refrigerator for up to 5 days (or in the freezer for up to 2 months).

Per serving: Cal 487; Carbs 10g; Fat 39g, Protein 22g

Herby Onion Soup

Ingredients for 4 servings

1 cup grated Parmesan cheese	2 tsp almond flour
2 tbsp butter	½ cup dry white wine
1 tbsp olive oil	2 sprigs chopped rosemary
3 sliced white onions	Salt and black pepper to taste
2 garlic cloves, thinly sliced	2 cups almond milk

Directions and Total Time: approx. 35 minutes

Heat butter and olive oil in a pot over medium heat. Sauté onions and garlic for 6-7 minutes. Reduce the heat to low and cook for 10 minutes. Stir in almond flour, white wine, salt, pepper, and rosemary and pour in 2 cups water. Bring to a boil and simmer for 10 minutes. Pour in almond milk and half of the Parmesan cheese.Stir the cheese to melt it and spoon it into airtight containers. Let cool.

Storage: Keep in the refrigerator for up to 5 days (or in the freezer for up to 2 months). To serve, reheat the soup in the microwave for 1-2 minutes, stirring once, and top with the remaining Parmesan cheese. Enjoy!

Per serving: Cal 305; Carbs 17g; Fat 23g, Protein 13g

POULTRY

Stuffed Chicken Breasts

Ingredients for 8 servings

½ cup mozzarella, shredded	A pinch of nutmeg
1 cup Parmesan, grated	½ tsp minced garlic
6 ounces cream cheese	2 eggs, beaten in a bowl
4 tbsp olive oil	Salt and black pepper to taste
4 chicken breasts	½ tsp parsley
2 cups spinach, chopped	A pinch of onion powder

Directions and Total Time: approx. 45 minutes

Pound the chicken until it doubles in size. Mix the cream cheese, spinach, mozzarella cheese, nutmeg, salt, pepper, and half of Parmesan cheese in a bowl. Divide the mixture between the chicken breasts and spread it out evenly. Wrap the chicken in plastic foil. Refrigerate for 15 minutes. Combine 2 tbsp olive oil, parsley, the remaining Parmesan cheese, and onion powder in a bowl. Dip the chicken in egg first, then in the breading mixture. Heat the remaining olive oil in a pan over medium heat. Cook the chicken until browned. Place on a lined baking sheet and bake in the oven at 370 F for 20 minutes. Let cool completely.

Storage: Place in airtight containers in the refrigerator for up to 5 days (or in the freezer for up to 2 months).

Per serving: Cal 365; Carbs 3g; Fat 26g; Protein 31g

Chicken with Homemade Linguine

Ingredients for 8 servings

¾ cup grated Pecorino Romano cheese

1 cup sun-dried tomatoes in oil, drained and chopped	1 white onion, chopped
	1 red bell pepper, chopped
1 cup shredded mozzarella	2 garlic cloves, minced
1 cup heavy cream	1 tsp dried oregano
2 tbsp olive oil	¾ cup chicken broth
1 egg yolk	1 cup baby kale, chopped
4 chicken breasts	

Directions and Total Time: approx. 2 hours 35 minutes

Microwave mozzarella cheese for 2 minutes. Take out the bowl and allow it to cool for 1 minute. Mix in egg yolk until well combined. Lay a parchment paper on a flat surface, pour the cheese mixture on top and cover with another parchment paper. Flatten the dough into 1/8-inch thickness. Take off the parchment paper and cut the dough into linguine-like strands. Place in a bowl and refrigerate for 2 hours. Bring 2 cups of water to a boil and add the linguine. Cook for 1 minute and drain; set aside.

Heat olive oil in a skillet over medium heat. Cook the chicken in the skillet for 7-8 minutes on both sides. Transfer to a plate and cut into 4 slices each; set aside. Add onion, sundried tomatoes, bell pepper, garlic, and oregano to the skillet and sauté for 5 minutes. Deglaze the skillet with chicken broth and mix in heavy cream.

Simmer for 2 minutes and stir in Pecorino Romano cheese for 2 minutes. Stir in kale to wilt. Mix in linguine and chicken. Let cool completely.

Storage: Place in airtight containers in the refrigerator for up to 5 days (or in the freezer for up to 2 months).

Per serving: Cal 395; Carbs 9g; Fats 27g; Protein 30g

Weekend Chicken Thighs in Peanut Sauce

Ingredients for 6 servings

1 tbsp soy sauce	1 tsp minced ginger
1 tbsp fish sauce	1 tbsp rice wine vinegar
1 tbsp olive oil	1 tsp cayenne pepper
1 tbsp lime juice	1 tbsp brown sugar
1 tsp coriander	6 chicken thighs
1 tsp minced garlic	

Peanut Sauce

½ cup peanut butter	1 tbsp chopped Jalapeno
1 tsp minced garlic	2 tbsp rice wine vinegar
1 tbsp lime juice	2 tbsp brown sugar
1 tsp minced ginger	1 tbsp fish sauce

Directions and Total Time: approx. 1 hour 20 minutes

Combine all chicken ingredients in a large Ziploc bag. Seal the bag and shake to combine. Refrigerate for 1 hour. Remove from fridge 15 minutes before cooking. Preheat the grill to medium and grill the chicken for 7 minutes per side. Whisk together all sauce ingredients with 2 tbsp water in a bowl. Drizzled with peanut sauce. Let cool.

Storage: Place in airtight containers in the refrigerator for up to 5 days (or in the freezer for up to 2 months).

Per serving: Cal 432; Carbs 13g; Fat 29g; Protein 30g

Chicken Puffs

Ingredients for 4 servings

1 ½ cups chopped chicken thighs, boneless and skinless

½ cup olive oil	Salt and black pepper to taste
1/3 cup peanuts, crushed	1 tsp celery seeds
1 cup chicken broth	¼ tsp cayenne pepper
2 tsp Worcestershire sauce	1 cup almond flour
1 tbsp dried parsley	4 eggs

Directions and Total Time: approx. 30 minutes

In a bowl, combine chicken and peanuts; set aside. In a saucepan over medium heat, mix broth, olive oil, Worcestershire sauce, parsley, salt, pepper, celery seeds, and cayenne pepper. Bring to a boil and stir in almond flour until smooth ball forms. Allow resting for 5 minutes. Add eggs into the batter one after the other and beat until smooth. Mix in chicken and peanuts until well combined. Drop tbsp heaps of the mixture onto a greased baking sheet and bake in the oven at 450 F for 15 minutes. Cool.

Storage: Place in airtight containers in the refrigerator for up to 5 days (or in the freezer for up to 2 months).

Per serving: Cal 577. Carbs 6g; Fat 47g; Protein 32g

Italian-Style Chicken with Fettuccine

Ingredients for 8 servings

1 cup grated mozzarella	1 tsp Italian seasoning
½ cup grated cheddar cheese	¼ tsp red chili flakes
2 tbsp olive oil	¼ tsp cayenne pepper
4 chicken breasts, cubed	1 cup marinara sauce
1 yellow onion, minced	Salt and black pepper to taste
3 garlic cloves, minced	2 tbsp chopped parsley
2 (8 oz) packs shirataki fettuccine	

Directions and Total Time: approx. 35 minutes

Boil 2 cups of water in a pot over medium heat. Strain the shirataki pasta and rinse well under hot running water. Allow draining and pour the shirataki pasta into the boiling water. Cook for 3 minutes and strain again. Place a dry skillet and stir-fry the pasta until visibly dry, 1 to 2 minutes; set aside. Heat olive oil in a pot, season the chicken with salt and pepper. Cook for 10 minutes; set aside.

Add onion and garlic to the pan and cook for 3 minutes. Season with Italian seasoning, red chili flakes, and cayenne pepper. Stir in marinara sauce and simmer for 5 minutes. Add the chicken, shirataki fettuccine, mozzarella and cheddar cheeses. Stir until the cheeses melt. Garnish with parsley. Let cool completely.

Storage: Place in airtight containers in the refrigerator for up to 5 days (or in the freezer for up to 2 months).

Per serving: Cal 424; Carbs 11g; Fat 17g; Protein 37g

Bacon & Chicken Tart

Ingredients for 4 servings

¾ cup mozzarella, shredded	1 carrot, chopped
3 tbsp butter	3 garlic cloves, minced
¾ cup Greek yogurt	Salt and black pepper, to taste
1 sweet onion, chopped	½ cup chicken stock
3 oz bacon, chopped	½ lb chicken breasts, cubed

For the dough

2 tbsp cottage cheese	1 egg
2 cups mozzarella, shredded	1 tsp onion powder
¾ cup almond flour	1 tsp garlic powder

Directions and Total Time: approx. 50 minutes

Preheat oven to 370 F. Warm butter in a pan over medium heat. Sauté onion, garlic, bacon, carrot, salt, and pepper for 5 minutes. Add in chicken and cook for 3 minutes. Stir in yogurt and stock; cook for 7 minutes. Stir in ¾ cup mozzarella cheese; reserve. Microwave the mozzarella and cottage cheeses from the dough ingredients for 1 minute. Stir in garlic powder, almond flour, onion powder, and egg. Knead the dough. Split into 4 pieces and flatten each into a circle. Set the chicken mixture into 4 ramekins, top each with a dough circle, and bake for 25 minutes. Cool.

Storage: Place in airtight containers in the refrigerator for up to 5 days (or in the freezer for up to 2 months).

Per serving: Cal 577; Carbs 11g; Fat 45g; Protein 38g

Cheesy Hasselback Chicken

Ingredients for 6 servings

3 oz mozzarella cheese slices	10 oz spinach
⅓ cup shredded mozzarella	⅔ cup tomato-basil sauce
4 oz cream cheese	3 chicken breasts
1 tbsp olive oil	

Directions and Total Time: approx. 40 minutes

Preheat oven to 400 F. Mix cream cheese, shredded mozzarella cheese, and spinach, and microwave the mixture until the cheese melts. Cut the chicken a couple of times horizontally. Stuff with the spinach mixture. Brush the top with olive oil. Place on a lined baking dish and bake in the oven for 25 minutes. Pour the tomato-basil sauce over and top with mozzarella slices. Return to the oven and bake for 5 more minutes. Let cool completely.

Storage: Place in airtight containers in the refrigerator for up to 5 days (or in the freezer for up to 2 months).

Per serving: Cal 308; Carbs 5g; Fat 18g; Protein 27g

Creamy Mustard Chicken

Ingredients for 4 servings

¼ cup heavy cream	1 lb chicken breasts, halved
2 tbsp olive oil	2 tbsp Dijon mustard
½ cup chicken stock	1 tsp thyme
½ cup chopped onions	1 tsp garlic powder

Directions and Total Time: approx. 25 minutes

Heat olive oil in a pan over medium heat. Cook the chicken for about 4 minutes per side; set aside. Sauté the onions in the same pan for 3 minutes, add the stock, and simmer for 5 minutes. Stir in mustard, heavy cream, thyme, and garlic powder. Pour the sauce over the chicken. Let cool.

Storage: Place in airtight containers in the refrigerator for up to 5 days (or in the freezer for up to 2 months).

Per serving: Cal 284; Carbs 4g; Fat 18g; Protein 30g

One-Pan Chicken with Mushrooms

Ingredients for 4 servings

4 chicken thighs	½ tsp garlic powder
¼ cup butter	1 tsp Dijon mustard
2 cups sliced mushrooms	1 tbsp tarragon, chopped
½ tsp onion powder	Salt and black pepper to taste

Directions and Total Time: approx. 30 minutes

Season the thighs with salt, pepper, garlic, and onion powder. Melt butter in a skillet and cook the chicken until browned; set aside. Add mushrooms to the skillet and cook for 5 minutes. Stir in mustard and ½ cup of water. Return the chicken and reduce the heat. Cover and let simmer for 15 minutes. Stir in tarragon and let cool completely.

Storage: Place in airtight containers in the refrigerator for up to 5 days (or in the freezer for up to 2 months).

Per serving: Cal 392; Carbs 3g; Fat 32g; Protein 23g

Bell Pepper & Chicken Skewers

Ingredients for 6 servings

1 tbsp olive oil	2 tbsp five-spice powder
1 tsp sesame oil	2 tbsp brown sugar
2 lb chicken breasts, cubed	1 tbsp fish sauce
1 cup red bell pepper pieces	Salt and black pepper to taste

Directions and Total Time: approx. 80 minutes

Combine all the ingredients, except the chicken, in a bowl. Add in chicken, and let marinate for 1 hour in the fridge. Preheat the grill. Take 12 skewers and thread the chicken and bell peppers. Grill for about 3 minutes per side. Cool.

Storage: Place in airtight containers in the refrigerator for up to 5 days (or in the freezer for up to 2 months).

Per serving: Cal 282; Carbs 8g; Fat 9g; Protein 41g

Chicken & Shiitake Stir-Fry

Ingredients for 4 servings

4 tbsp coconut oil	1 tsp Dijon mustard
4 green onions, sliced	1 tbsp fresh cilantro, chopped
2 garlic cloves, minced	1 lb chicken thighs
1 cup shiitake mushrooms, sliced	

Directions and Total Time: approx. 35 minutes

Melt coconut oil in a pan over medium heat and cook chicken until browned, about 6-8 minutes; set aside. Add mushrooms, garlic, and green onions to the pan and stir-fry for 5 minutes. Stir in mustard and ½ cup water. Return chicken to the pan, reduce the heat and simmer for 15 minutes. Sprinkle with cilantro. Let cool completely.

Storage: Place in airtight containers in the refrigerator for up to 5 days (or in the freezer for up to 2 months).

Per serving: Cal 333; Carbs 3g; Fat 23g; Protein 23g

Braised Chicken with Eggplants

Ingredients for 4 servings

1 lb chicken thighs	2 cloves garlic, minced
2 tbsp butter	Salt and black pepper to taste
2 cups canned tomatoes	1 cup eggplants, cubed
2 green onions, chopped	2 tbsp fresh basil, chopped

Directions and Total Time: approx. 40 minutes

Season the chicken with salt and pepper. Melt butter in a saucepan and fry chicken, skin side down, for 4 minutes. Flip and cook for another 2 minutes; remove to a plate. In the same saucepan, sauté garlic and green onions for 3 minutes. Add in the eggplants and cook for 5 minutes. Stir in tomatoes and cook for 10 minutes. Season the sauce with salt and pepper, stir, and add back the chicken. Simmer for 15 minutes. Garnish with fresh basil. Let cool.

Storage: Place in airtight containers in the refrigerator for up to 5 days (or in the freezer for up to 2 months).

Per serving: Cal 274; Carbs 9g; Fat 15g; Protein 21g

Beer Lemony Chicken Wings

Ingredients for 6 servings

1 lemon, juiced and zested	2 tbsp butter
1 tbsp fish sauce	¼ tsp xanthan gum
1 cup beer	12 chicken wings
3 tbsp brown sugar	Salt and black pepper to taste
A pinch of garlic powder	

Directions and Total Time: approx. 30 minutes

Combine lemon juice and zest, fish sauce, beer, brown sugar, and garlic powder in a saucepan. Bring to a boil, lower the heat, and let simmer for 10 minutes. Stir in butter and xanthan gum; set aside. Season the wings with salt and pepper. Preheat the grill and cook the wings for 5 minutes per side. Top with the sauce. Let cool completely.

Storage: Place in airtight containers in the refrigerator for up to 5 days (or in the freezer for up to 2 months).

Per serving: Cal 212; Carbs 6g; Fat 14g; Protein 12g

Garam Masala Chicken with Spinach

Ingredients for 8 servings

1 ¼ cups coconut cream	2 ½ tbsp garam masala
3 tbsp ghee	1 cup baby spinach, pressed
4 chicken breasts, cubed	1 tbsp cilantro, finely chopped

Directions and Total Time: approx. 35 minutes

Preheat oven to 350 F. Heat ghee in a skillet, season the chicken with garam masala, and cook until golden, about 6 minutes. Transfer the chicken with juices to a greased baking dish. Add spinach and cilantro and spread coconut cream on top. Bake for 20 minutes or until the cream is bubbly. Let cool completely.

Storage: Place in airtight containers in the refrigerator for up to 5 days (or in the freezer for up to 2 months).

Per serving: Cal 321; Carbs 4g; Fat 18g; Protein 27g

Oregano Chicken with Leafy Greens

Ingredients for 4 servings

1 cup heavy cream	2 tbsp flour
2 tbsp olive oil	2 carp dark leafy greens
2 tbsp butter, melted	1 tsp oregano
1 lb chicken thighs	1 cup chicken broth

Directions and Total Time: approx. 30 minutes

Melt olive oil in a skillet over medium heat and brown the chicken for 7-9 minutes; set aside. Melt butter in the same skillet and whisk in the flour. Whisk in the chicken broth and bring to a boil. Stir in oregano, leafy greens, and heavy cream for 1 minute. Add in the thighs back and cook for an additional 10 minutes. Let cool.

Storage: Place in airtight containers in the refrigerator for up to 5 days (or in the freezer for up to 2 months).

Per serving: Cal 446; Carbs 6g; Fat 33g; Protein 28g

Dijon Chicken & Pancetta Pot

Ingredients for 4 servings

5 tbsp Dijon mustard	Salt and black pepper to taste
2 tbsp olive oil	1 cup chicken stock
3 oz smoked and smoked pancetta	1 lb chicken breasts
1 fennel bulb, sliced	¼ tsp sweet paprika

Directions and Total Time: approx. 35 minutes

Put mustard in a bowl and add in the paprika, salt, and pepper; stir to combine. Massage the mixture onto all sides of the chicken. Warm 1 tbsp olive oil in a pot over medium heat and cook the chicken for 3 minutes per side or until golden; set aside. To the same pot, add the remaining olive oil and cook pancetta and fennel for 5 minutes. Return chicken, pour in stock and simmer for 20 minutes. Cool.

Storage: Place in airtight containers in the refrigerator for up to 5 days (or in the freezer for up to 2 months).

Per serving: Cal 388; Carbs 5g; Fat 24g; Protein 31g

Lemony Chicken Thighs

Ingredients for 4 servings

1 tsp salt	1 tsp lemon zest
2 tbsp olive oil	1 tbsp chopped thyme
8 chicken thighs	¼ tsp black pepper
2 tbsp lemon juice	1 garlic cloves, minced

Directions and Total Time: approx. 1 hour 20 minutes

Combine all ingredients in a bowl. Cover and place to marinate in the fridge for 1 hour. Heat a skillet over medium heat. Add the marinated chicken and their juices and cook until crispy, 7 minutes per side. Let cool.

Storage: Place in airtight containers in the refrigerator for up to 5 days (or in the freezer for up to 2 months).

Per serving: Cal 351; Carbs 1g; Fat 25g; Protein 32g

Whole Chicken Roast with Brussels Sprouts

Ingredients for 6 servings

4 lb whole chicken	1 bunch thyme
3 tbsp olive oil	1 tbsp parsley
4 tbsp butter	2 lb Brussels sprouts
1 bunch oregano	1 lemon

Directions and Total Time: approx. 80 minutes

Preheat oven to 450 F. Stuff the chicken with oregano, thyme, and lemon. Make sure the wings are tucked over and behind. Brush with olive oil and roast in the oven for 15 minutes. Reduce the heat to 325 F and cook for 20 minutes. Spread the butter over the chicken and sprinkle with parsley. Add the Brussels sprouts. Bake for 25 more minutes. Let sit for 10 minutes before carving. Let cool.

Storage: Place in airtight containers in the refrigerator for up to 5 days (or in the freezer for up to 2 months).

Per serving: Cal 523; Carbs 15g; Fat 27g; Protein 38g

Chicken Linguine with Kale

Ingredients for 4 servings

1 cup grated Parmigiano-Reggiano cheese for serving	
1 cup shredded mozzarella	3 tbsp olive oil
4 chicken thighs, cut into 1-inch pieces	
1 cup cherry tomatoes, halved	4 garlic cloves, minced
1 egg yolk	½ cup chicken broth
Salt and black pepper to taste	2 cups baby kale, chopped
1 yellow onion, chopped	2 tbsp pine nuts for topping

Directions and Total Time: approx. 2 hours 40 minutes

Microwave mozzarella cheese for 2 minutes. Take out the bowl and allow cooling for 1 minute. Mix in egg yolk until well combined. Lay a parchment paper on a flat surface, pour the cheese mixture on top and cover with another parchment paper. Flatten the dough into 1/8-inch thickness. Take off the parchment paper and cut the dough into linguine strands. Place in a bowl and refrigerate for 2 hours. Bring 2 cups of water to a boil and add in linguine. Cook for 1 minute and drain; set aside.

Heat olive oil in a pot, season the chicken with salt and pepper, and sear it for 6-8 minutes; set aside. Add onion and garlic to the pot and cook for 3 minutes. Mix in tomatoes and broth and return the chicken; cook until the liquid reduces by half, about 10 minutes. Stir in kale for 5 minutes. Divide linguine between serving plates, pour in the chicken/kale mixture and sprinkle with Parmigianino-Reggiano cheese. Garnish with pine nuts. Let cool.

Storage: Place in airtight containers in the refrigerator for up to 5 days (or in the freezer for up to 2 months).

Per serving: Cal 543; Carbs 18g; Fat 33g; Protein 42g

Kale & Chicken Pie

Ingredients for 4 servings

1 cup shredded provolone cheese	
2 cups powdered Parmesan	½ cup tomato sauce
1 lb ground chicken	1 tsp white wine vinegar
¼ tsp onion powder	½ tsp smoked paprika
¼ tsp garlic powder	¼ cup baby kale, chopped

Directions and Total Time: approx. 30 minutes

Preheat oven to 400 F. Line a pizza pan with parchment paper and grease with cooking spray. In a bowl, combine chicken and Parmesan cheese. Spread the mixture on the pan to fit. Bake for 15 minutes until the chicken cooks. In a bowl, mix onion and garlic powder, tomato sauce, white wine vinegar, and smoked paprika. Remove the meat crust from the oven and spread the tomato mixture on top. Add kale and sprinkle with provolone cheese. Bake for 7 minutes or until the cheese melts. Let cool completely.

Storage: Place in airtight containers in the refrigerator for up to 5 days (or in the freezer for up to 2 months).

Per serving: Cal 231; Carbs 6g; Fat 12g; Protein 23g

Pesto Chicken Bake

Ingredients for 6 servings

½ cup shredded Pepper Jack	3 tbsp basil pesto
¾ cup heavy cream	2 lb chicken breasts, cubed
½ cup cream cheese, softened	1 celery, chopped
3 tbsp butter	¼ cup chopped tomatoes
½ lemon, juiced	1 lb radishes, sliced

Directions and Total Time: approx. 50 minutes

Preheat oven to 400 F. In a bowl, combine lemon juice, pesto, heavy cream, and cream cheese; set aside. Melt butter in a skillet and cook the chicken until no longer pink, 8 minutes. Transfer to a greased casserole and spread the pesto mixture on top. Cover with celery, tomatoes, and radishes. Sprinkle with Pepper Jack cheese and bake for 30 minutes or until the cheese melts. Let cool completely.

Storage: Place in airtight containers in the refrigerator for up to 5 days (or in the freezer for up to 2 months).

Per serving: Cal 523; Carbs 13g; Fat 37g; Protein 48g

Easy Chargrilled Chili Chicken

Ingredients for 4 servings

1 tsp chili powder	Salt and garlic powder to taste
2 tbsp olive oil	1 ½ lb chicken breasts

Directions and Total Time: approx. 20 minutes

Grease grill grate with cooking spray and preheat to 400 F. Combine chili, salt, and garlic powder in a bowl. Brush chicken with olive oil, sprinkle with the spice mixture, and massage with your hands. Grill for 7 minutes per side until well done or to your preference. Let cool completely.

Storage: Place in airtight containers in the refrigerator for up to 5 days (or in the freezer for up to 2 months).

Per serving: Cal 283; Carbs 1g; Fat 11g; Protein 44g

Cubed Chicken with Mushrooms

Ingredients for 8 servings

1 cup heavy cream	1 tbsp sweet paprika
2 tbsp olive oil	1 cup chicken stock
2 garlic cloves, minced	¼ cup dry white wine
1 onion, sliced into half-moons	4 chicken breasts, sliced
1 cup mushrooms, chopped	2 tbsp fresh parsley, chopped

Directions and Total Time: approx. 40 minutes

Heat olive oil in a saucepan and sauté onion and garlic for 3 minutes. Add in chicken and fry for 5 minutes, stirring often. Pour in white wine, mushrooms, and paprika and cook for 4 minutes until the liquid is reduced by half. Pour in the chicken stock and parsley. Cook for 20 minutes, stir in heavy cream and cook for 2 more minutes. Let cool.

Storage: Place in airtight containers in the refrigerator for up to 5 days (or in the freezer for up to 2 months).

Per serving: Cal 341; Carbs 3.4g; Fat 18g; Protein 30g

Green Chicken Thighs

Ingredients for 4 servings

4 tbsp butter	½ cup Swiss chard, chopped
4 chicken thighs	1 tbsp fresh parsley, chopped
1 cup spinach, chopped	1 cup half-and-half
4 green onions, chopped	1 cup vegetable broth

Directions and Total Time: approx. 40 minutes

Melt butter in a skillet and brown the chicken on all sides, about 8 minutes; set aside. Add in green onions and sauté for 2 minutes. Pour in the vegetable broth, return the chicken and bring to a boil. Simmer for 15 minutes. Add in spinach, Swiss chard, and parsley and cook until wilted. Stir in half-and-half for 3-4 minutes. Let cool completely.

Storage: Place in airtight containers in the refrigerator for up to 5 days (or in the freezer for up to 2 months).

Per serving: Cal 458; Carbs 5g; Fat 23g; Protein 35g

Chicken Bake with Blue Cheese & Squash

Ingredients for 8 servings

1 cup blue cheese, crumbled	1 lb acorn squash, sliced
2 tbsp olive oil	Salt and black pepper to taste
4 chicken breasts	2 tbsp parsley, chopped

Directions and Total Time: approx. 45 minutes

Preheat oven to 420 F. Grease a baking dish, add in chicken breasts, salt, pepper, and squash, and drizzle with olive oil. Bake for 20 minutes. Scatter the blue cheese and bake for 15 more minutes. Top with parsley. Let cool.

Storage: Place in airtight containers in the refrigerator for up to 5 days (or in the freezer for up to 2 months).

Per serving: Cal 275, Carbs 7g, Fat 12g, Protein 32g

Baked Chicken with Veggies

Ingredients for 4 servings

8 oz mozzarella, sliced	1 onion, chopped
1 tbsp butter	1 zucchini, sliced
1 lb chicken breasts, sliced	2 garlic cloves, minced
2 green bell peppers, sliced	2 tsp Italian seasoning
1 turnip, chopped	Salt and black pepper to taste

Directions and Total Time: approx. 50 minutes

Grease a baking dish with cooking spray and place in the chicken slices. Melt butter in a pan over medium heat and sauté onion, zucchini, garlic, bell peppers, turnip, salt, pepper, and Italian seasoning.

Cook until tender, 8 minutes. Spread the vegetables over the chicken and cover with cheese slices. Set into the oven and cook until browned for 30 minutes at 370 F. Let cool.

Storage: Place in airtight containers in the refrigerator for up to 5 days (or in the freezer for up to 2 months).

Per serving: Cal 388; Carbs 14g; Fat 19g; Protein 43g

Easy Chicken Gratin

Ingredients for 6 servings

3 cups Monterey Jack, grated   ½ cup breadcrumbs, crushed
3 tbsp olive oil   1 lb chicken breasts, boneless
2 eggs   Salt to taste

Directions and Total Time: approx. 40 minutes

Line a baking sheet with parchment paper. Whisk the eggs with the olive oil in a bowl. Mix the Monterey Jack cheese and breadcrumbs in another bowl. Season the chicken with salt, dip in egg mixture, and coat in the cheese mixture.

Place on a baking sheet, cover with aluminium foil and bake in the oven for 25 minutes at 350 F. Remove foil and bake further for 12 minutes until golden brown. Let cool.

Storage: Place in airtight containers in the refrigerator for up to 5 days (or in the freezer for up to 2 months).

Per serving: Cal 434; Carbs 2g; Fat 32g; Protein 36g

Chicken & Caper Casserole

Ingredients for 6 servings

1 cup crème fraîche   1 ½ lb chicken thighs
8 oz cream cheese   1/3 cup capers
2 tbsp butter, melted   1 tbsp tamari sauce

Directions and Total Time: approx. 25 minutes

Preheat oven to 350 F. Place the chicken on a baking sheet, season with salt and pepper, and brush with butter. Pour in ½ cup of water, cover with foil; bake for 25-30 minutes. Take off the foil and bake for 5 minutes until golden.

Place a saucepan over low heat and mix in crème fraiche and cream cheese. Simmer until the sauce thickens, 2-3 minutes. Mix in capers and tamari sauce and cook for 1 minute. Drizzle the sauce all over the chicken. Let cool.

Storage: Place in airtight containers in the refrigerator for up to 5 days (or in the freezer for up to 2 months).

Per serving: Cal 423; Carbs 2g; Fat 35g; Protein 23g

Lemon-Butter Roasted Whole Chicken

Ingredients for 6 servings

4-lb chicken, whole bird   1 large lemon, juiced
8 tbsp butter, melted   2 large lemons, thinly sliced

Directions and Total Time: approx. 1 hour 40 minutes

Preheat oven to 400 F. Put the whole chicken, breast side up, in a baking dish. In a bowl, combine butter and lemon juice. Spread the mixture all over the chicken. Arrange lemon slices at the bottom of the dish and bake for 1 to 1 ½ hours. Baste the chicken with the juice every 20 minutes. Let cool completely before carving.

Storage: Place in airtight containers in the refrigerator for up to 5 days (or in the freezer for up to 2 months).

Per serving: Cal 393; Carbs 1g; Fat 22g; Protein 46g

Chicken & Vegetable Stir-Fry

Ingredients for 4 servings

3 zucchinis, cut into 1-inch dices
2 tbsp olive oil   ¼ cup chopped fresh parsley
1 tbsp unsalted butter   1 tsp dried thyme
1 lb chicken chunks   Salt and black pepper to taste
1 finely chopped onion

Directions and Total Time: approx. 25 minutes

Heat olive oil and butter in a skillet over medium heat and sauté chicken for 5 minutes. Add in onion and parsley and cook further for 3 minutes. Stir in zucchini and thyme, season with salt and pepper, cover, and cook for 8-10 minutes or until the vegetables soften. Let cool completely.

Storage: Place in airtight containers in the refrigerator for up to 5 days (or in the freezer for up to 2 months).

Per serving: Cal 257; Carbs 12g; Fat 12g; Protein 18g

Chicken Roast with Yogurt Sauce

Ingredients for 8 servings

2 tbsp butter   Salt and black pepper, to taste
4 scallions, chopped   6 ounces plain yogurt
4 chicken breasts   2 tbsp fresh dill, chopped

Directions and Total Time: approx. 35 minutes

Melt butter in a pan, add in chicken, season with pepper and salt, and fry for 2-3 minutes per side. Transfer to a greased baking dish and bake for 15 minutes at 390 F. To the pan, add scallions and cook for 2 minutes. Pour in yogurt and dill and warm without boil. Slice the chicken and pour the sauce over. Let cool completely.

Storage: Place in airtight containers in the refrigerator for up to 5 days (or in the freezer for up to 2 months).

Per serving: Cal 276, Carbs 6g, Fat 10g, Protein 31g

Cheddar Chicken & Cauliflower Steaks

Ingredients for 4 servings

4 slices chicken luncheon meat
½ cup grated cheddar cheese   4 tbsp ranch dressing
2 tbsp olive oil   2 tbsp chopped parsley
1 large head cauliflower   Salt and black pepper to taste
½ tsp smoked paprika

Directions and Total Time: approx. 20 minutes

Stand cauliflower on a flat surface and into 4 steaks from top to bottom. Season with paprika, salt, and pepper, and drizzle with olive oil. Heat a grill pan over medium heat and cook in the cauliflower on both sides until softened, 4 minutes. Top one side with chicken and sprinkle with cheddar cheese. Heat to melt the cheese. Drizzle with ranch dressing and garnish with parsley. Let cool completely.

Storage: Place in airtight containers in the refrigerator for up to 5 days (or in the freezer for up to 2 months).

Per serving: Cal 323; Carbs 11g; Fat 19g; Protein 16g

Broccoli & Chicken Casserole

Ingredients for 4 servings

1 cup grated Parmesan cheese 2 garlic cloves, minced
3 tbsp butter 1 lb ground chicken
1 small white onion, chopped 1 lb broccoli rabe, chopped

Directions and Total Time: approx. 40 minutes

Preheat oven to 350 F. Melt butter in a skillet and sauté onion and garlic for 3 minutes. Put in chicken and cook until no longer pink, 8 minutes. Add chicken and broccoli rabe to a greased baking dish and mix evenly. Top with butter from the skillet and sprinkle with Parmesan cheese. Bake for 20 minutes until the cheese melts. Let cool.

Storage: Place in airtight containers in the refrigerator for up to 5 days (or in the freezer for up to 2 months).

Per serving: Cal 410; Carbs 43g; Fat 24g; Protein 33g

Moroccan-Style Chicken Tenders

Ingredients for 4 servings

1 tbsp harissa paste ½ cup white wine
3 tbsp butter, melted 1 lb chicken tenders
1 tsp garlic powder 2 tbsp fresh mint, chopped
1 tsp smoked paprika Salt and black pepper to taste

Directions and Total Time: approx. 95 minutes

In a large bowl, combine harissa, butter, garlic powder, paprika, salt, and pepper. Add in the chicken and mix well to coat. Cover with plastic wrap and refrigerate for 1 hour.

Preheat oven to 360 F. Remove the chicken and transfer to a greased baking dish. Add in the white wine and ½ cup water. Bake until the chicken is well done, about 20-25 minutes. Top with mint. Let cool completely.

Storage: Place in airtight containers in the refrigerator for up to 5 days (or in the freezer for up to 2 months).

Per serving: Cal 354, Carbs 2g, Fat 19g, Protein 36g

Chicken, Bell Pepper & Cauliflower Skillet

Ingredients for 4 servings

1 large head cauliflower, cut into florets
2 tbsp olive oil 1 yellow bell pepper, diced
2 chicken breasts, sliced 3 tbsp chicken broth
1 red bell pepper, diced 2 tbsp chopped parsley

Directions and Total Time: approx. 25 minutes

Heat olive oil in a skillet and brown the chicken until brown on all sides, 8 minutes. Transfer to a plate. Pour bell peppers into the pan and sauté until softened, 5 minutes. Add in cauliflower and chicken broth and mix. Cover the pan and cook for 5 minutes or until cauliflower is tender. Mix in chicken and parsley. Let cool completely.

Storage: Place in airtight containers in the refrigerator for up to 5 days (or in the freezer for up to 2 months).

Per serving: Cal 272; Carbs 15g; Fat 8g; Protein 30g

Buffalo Chicken Bake

Ingredients for 6 servings

6 oz cottage cheese, grated 1 lb ground chicken
2 cups Monterey Jack, grated ½ cup buffalo sauce
2 tbsp olive oil ½ cup ranch dressing

Directions and Total Time: approx. 35 minutes

Preheat oven to 350 F. Warm olive oil in a skillet and brown chicken for 2-3 minutes; set aside. Spread cottage cheese on a greased sheet, top with chicken, pour in buffalo sauce, add ranch dressing, and sprinkle with Monterey Jack cheese. Bake for 23 minutes. Let cool.

Storage: Place in airtight containers in the refrigerator for up to 5 days (or in the freezer for up to 2 months).

Per serving: Cal 569; Carbs 4g; Fat 43g; Protein 41g

Baked Chicken with Pumpkin & Olives

Ingredients for 4 servings

1 lb chicken thighs ½ tsp ground cinnamon
4 tbsp olive oil ¼ tsp ground nutmeg
1 lb pumpkin, cubed 5 garlic cloves, sliced
½ cup black olives, pitted 1 tbsp dried rosemary
3 onion springs, sliced Salt and black pepper to taste

Directions and Total Time: approx. 55 minutes

Set oven to 400 F. Place the chicken, skin down in a greased baking dish. Arrange garlic, olives, onions, and pumpkin around the chicken. Drizzle with olive oil. Season with pepper, salt, cinnamon, nutmeg, and rosemary. Bake in the oven for 45 minutes. Let cool completely.

Storage: Place in airtight containers in the refrigerator for up to 5 days (or in the freezer for up to 2 months).

Per serving: Cal 431; Carbs 13g; Fat 27g; Protein 28g

Trick-or-Treat Chicken Meatballs

Ingredients for 4 servings

1 cup Pecorino cheese, grated 2 tbsp breadcrumbs, crushed
2 tbsp olive oil 2 garlic cloves, minced
1 large egg 2 shallots, chopped
1 lb ground chicken Salt and black pepper to taste
1 cup celery, chopped 2 tbsp fresh parsley, chopped

Directions and Total Time: approx. 20 minutes

Put ground chicken, egg, shallots, garlic, celery, parsley, black pepper, and salt in a bowl and mix to combine. Form meatballs from the mixture. Spread the breadcrumbs on a large plate and roll the meatballs in them. Fry the meatballs in warm olive oil over medium heat on all sides until lightly golden, about 5-6 minutes. Transfer to a baking dish. Scatter the grated cheese over and bake for 5 minutes or until the cheese melts. Let cool completely.

Storage: Place in airtight containers in the refrigerator for up to 5 days (or in the freezer for up to 2 months).

Per serving: Cal 426; Carbs 4g; Fat 29g; Protein 32g

Pecorino Chicken Sausages with Broccoli

Ingredients for 4 servings

½ cup Pecorino Romano
2 tbsp salted butter
4 links chicken sausages, sliced
3 cups broccoli florets
4 garlic cloves, minced
½ cup tomato sauce
¼ cup red wine
½ tsp red pepper flakes
3 cups chopped kale
Salt and black pepper to taste

Directions and Total Time: approx. 30 minutes

Melt half of the butter in a wok and fry the sausages until brown, 5 minutes; set aside. Melt the remaining butter in the wok and sauté broccoli for 5 minutes. Mix in garlic and cook for 3 minutes, then pour in tomato sauce, red wine, red pepper flakes, and season with salt and pepper. Cover the lid and cook for 10 minutes or until the tomato sauce reduces by one-third. Return the sausages to the pan and heat for 1 minute. Stir in kale to wilt. Spoon onto a platter and sprinkle with Pecorino Romano cheese. Cool.

Storage: Place in airtight containers in the refrigerator for up to 5 days (or in the freezer for up to 2 months).

Per serving: Cal 363; Carbs 11g; Fat 21g; Protein 25g

Mediterranean Chicken Drumsticks

Ingredients for 4 servings

5 kaffir lime leaves
1 tbsp cumin powder
1 tbsp ginger powder
1 cup Greek yogurt
1 tbsp olive oil
2 lb chicken drumsticks
Salt and black pepper to taste
2 limes, juiced

Directions and Total Time: approx. 3 hours 45 minutes

In a bowl, combine kaffir leaves, cumin, ginger, and Greek yogurt. Add in chicken, salt, and pepper, and mix to coat. Cover the bowl with plastic wrap and marinate in the fridge for 3 hours. Preheat oven to 350 F. Arrange chicken on a greased baking sheet. Drizzle with olive oil and lime juice, cover with aluminum foil, and bake for 20-25 minutes. Remove foil, turn the broiler on, and brown the chicken for 10 minutes. Let cool completely.

Storage: Place in airtight containers in the refrigerator for up to 5 days (or in the freezer for up to 2 months).

Per serving: Cal 463; Carbs 10g; Fat 27g; Protein 44g

Chicken Cheeseburgers with Mushrooms

Ingredients for 4 servings

4 slices Gruyere cheese
1 tbsp olive oil
4 Portobello caps, destemmed
1 ½ lb ground chicken
Salt and black pepper to taste
1 tbsp tomato sauce
4 lettuce leaves
4 large tomato slices
¼ cup mayonnaise

Directions and Total Time: approx. 20 minutes

In a bowl, combine chicken, salt, pepper, and tomato sauce. Mold into 4 patties and set aside. Heat olive oil in a skillet; place in Portobello caps and cook for 3 minutes; set aside.

Put the patties in the skillet and fry until brown and compacted, 8 minutes. Place Gruyere cheese slices on the patties, allow them to melt for 1 minute and lift each patty onto each mushroom cap. Divide the lettuce on top, then tomato slices, and top with some mayonnaise. Let cool.

Storage: Place in airtight containers in the refrigerator for up to 5 days.

Per serving: Cal 512; Carbs 5g; Fat 34g; Protein 45g

Tex-Mex Chicken Bowls

Ingredients for 4 servings

½ cup shredded Mexican cheese blend
1 lb boneless chicken breasts, cut into strips
1 cup crème fraiche
2 tbsp olive oil
Salt and black pepper to taste
2 tbsp Tex-Mex seasoning
1 iceberg lettuce, chopped
2 tomatoes, and chopped
2 avocados, chopped
1 green bell pepper, sliced
1 yellow onion, thinly sliced
4 tbsp fresh cilantro leaves

Directions and Total Time: approx. 20 minutes

Heat olive oil in a skillet, season the chicken with salt, pepper, and Tex-Mex seasoning, and fry until golden, 10 minutes; transfer to a plate. Let cool. Divide the lettuce between airtight containers and top with chicken.

Storage: Keep in the refrigerator for up to 5 days. Before serving, add tomatoes, avocados, bell pepper, onion, cilantro, and Mexican cheese. Top with dollops of crème fraiche.

Per serving: Cal 491; Carbs 10g; Fat 25g; Protein 38g

Spicy Pulled Chicken with Avocado

Ingredients for 64 servings

1 white onion, chopped
¼ cup chicken stock
3 tbsp tamari sauce
3 tbsp chili pepper
1 tbsp red wine vinegar
Salt and black pepper to taste
1 ½ tbsp coconut oil
1 lb boneless chicken thighs
1 avocado, halved and pitted
½ lemon, juiced

Directions and Total Time: approx. 2 hours 30 minutes

In a pot, combine onion, stock, coconut oil, tamari sauce, chili, vinegar, salt, and pepper. Add in thighs, close the lid, and cook over low heat for 2 hours.

Scoop avocado pulp into a bowl, add lemon juice, and mash the avocado into a puree; set aside. When the chicken is ready, open the lid and use two forks to shred it. Cook further for 15 minutes. Let cool completely. Place in airtight containers.

Storage: Keep in the refrigerator for up to 5 days (or in the freezer for up to 2 months). To serve, reheat the chicken in the microwave for 1-2 minutes and top with avocado. Enjoy!

Per serving: Cal 390; Carbs 15g; Fat 28g; Protein 23g

Lime Chicken in Spicy Coconut Sauce

Ingredients for 6 servings

2 oz coconut cream	2 sweet onions, sliced
3 tbsp coconut oil	1 lime, juiced
3 chicken breasts, halved	1 tsp red pepper flakes
1 cup vegetable stock	1 tbsp fresh cilantro, chopped

Directions and Total Time: approx. 35 minutes

Cook the chicken in hot coconut oil in a pan over medium heat for about 4-5 minutes; set aside. Place the sweet onions in the pan and cook for 4 minutes. Stir in vegetable stock, red pepper flakes, coconut cream, and lime juice. Return the chicken to the pan and cook covered for 15 minutes. Sprinkle with fresh cilantro. Let cool completely.

Storage: Place in airtight containers in the refrigerator for up to 5 days (or in the freezer for up to 2 months).

Per serving: Cal 481; Carbs 11g; Fat 27g; Protein 39g

Saffron Chicken Fettuccine

Ingredients for 8 servings

1 cup heavy cream	2 garlic cloves, minced
1 cup grated mozzarella	1 tbsp almond flour
3 tbsp butter	1 pinch cardamom powder
1 egg yolk	1 pinch cinnamon powder
½ tsp ground saffron threads	1 cup chicken stock
1 yellow onion, chopped	¼ cup chopped scallions
4 chicken breasts, cut into strips	

Directions and Total Time: approx. 2 hours 25 minutes

Microwave mozzarella cheese for 2 minutes. Take out the bowl and allow cooling for 1 minute. Mix in egg yolk until well combined. Lay a parchment paper on a flat surface, pour the cheese mixture on top and cover with another parchment paper. Flatten the dough into 1/8-inch thickness. Take off the parchment paper and cut the dough into thick fettuccine strands. Place in a bowl and refrigerate for 2 hours. Bring 2 cups of water to a boil and add the fettuccine. Cook for 1 minute and drain; set aside. Melt butter in a skillet and cook the chicken for 5 minutes. Stir in saffron, onion, and garlic and cook until the onion softens, 3 minutes. Stir in almond flour, cardamom and cinnamon powders and cook for 1 minute. Add in heavy cream and chicken stock and cook for 2-3 minutes. Mix in fettuccine and scallions. Let cool completely.

Storage: Place in airtight containers in the refrigerator for up to 5 days (or in the freezer for up to 2 months).

Per serving: Cal 386; Carbs 5g; Fats 23g; Protein 36g

Chicken Alfredo Zoodles

Ingredients for 8 servings

1 cup grated Pecorino Romano cheese	
¾ cup heavy cream	4 large turnips, spiralized
4 tbsp butter	3 garlic cloves, minced
4 chicken breasts, cubed	2 tbsp chopped fresh parsley

Directions and Total Time: approx. 30 minutes

Melt butter in a skillet over medium heat and cook chicken until golden brown, 10 minutes. Transfer to a plate. In the same skillet, add and sauté turnips and garlic until softened, 6 minutes. Stir in the heavy cream and Pecorino Romano cheese until melted, about 2-3 minutes. Stir in the chicken for 3 minutes. Garnish with parsley. Let cool.

Storage: Place in airtight containers in the refrigerator for up to 5 days (or in the freezer for up to 2 months).

Per serving: Cal 375; Carbs 12g; Fats 23g; Protein 33g

Kale & Feta Chicken Bake

Ingredients for 8 servings

¼ cup shredded Monterey Jack cheese	
4 chicken breasts, cut into strips	
¼ cup crumbled feta cheese	½ tbsp red wine vinegar
½ cup grated Parmesan	1 ½ cups crushed tomatoes
2 tbsp olive oil	2 tbsp tomato paste
Salt and black pepper to taste	1 tsp Italian mixed herbs
1 small onion, chopped	2 zucchinis, chopped
2 garlic cloves, minced	1 cup baby kale

Directions and Total Time: approx. 45 minutes

Preheat oven to 400 F. Heat olive oil in a skillet, season the chicken with salt and pepper, and cook for 8 minutes; set aside. Add in and sauté onion and garlic for 3 minutes. Mix in vinegar, tomatoes, and tomato paste. Cook for 8 minutes. Season with salt, pepper, and mixed herbs. Stir in chicken, zucchini, kale, and feta cheese. Pour the mixture into a baking dish and top with Monterey Jack cheese. Bake for 15 minutes or until the cheese melts and is golden. Garnish with Parmesan cheese. Let cool.

Storage: Place in airtight containers in the refrigerator for up to 5 days (or in the freezer for up to 2 months).

Per serving: Cal 355; Carbs 11g; Fat 21g; Protein 32g

Chicken & Eggplant Gratin

Ingredients for 6 servings

2 tbsp Swiss cheese, grated	Salt and black pepper, to taste
3 tbsp butter	2 garlic cloves, minced
1 eggplant, chopped	6 chicken thighs

Directions and Total Time: approx. 55 minutes

Warm the butter in a pan over medium heat and cook chicken for 3 minutes per side. Transfer to a baking dish and season with salt and pepper. In the same pan, cook garlic and eggplant for 8 minutes; season. Spoon the mixture over the chicken, sprinkle with cheese, and bake in the oven at 350 F for 30 minutes. Let cool completely.

Storage: Place in airtight containers in the refrigerator for up to 5 days (or in the freezer for up to 2 months). To serve, reheat the gratin in the microwave for 1-2 minutes, then turn on the broiler and broil for 2 minutes. Enjoy!

Per serving: Cal 521, Carbs 7g, Fat 37g, Protein 33g

Chicken Cordon Bleu Casserole

Ingredients for 8 servings

6 oz shredded Gruyere
6 oz cream cheese
1 rotisserie chicken, shredded
4 oz smoked deli ham, chopped
1 tbsp Dijon mustard
1 tbsp plain vinegar

Directions and Total Time: approx. 30 minutes

Preheat oven to 350 F. Spread the chicken and ham on a greased baking dish. In a bowl, mix cream cheese, mustard, vinegar, and two-thirds of Gruyere cheese. Spread the mixture on top of chicken and ham and cover with the remaining cheese. Bake for 20 minutes or until the cheese melts and is golden brown. Let cool completely.

Storage: Place in airtight containers in the refrigerator for up to 5 days (or in the freezer for up to 2 months).

Per serving: Cal 476; Carbs 3g; Fat 23g; Protein 55g

Lightened Chicken Lasagna

Ingredients for 8 servings

1 ½ cups grated mozzarella
1/3 cup Parmesan cheese
2 cups crumbled ricotta
2 tbsp butter
1 ½ lb ground chicken
1 tsp garlic powder
1 tsp onion powder
2 tbsp flour
1 large egg, beaten
2 cups marinara sauce
1 tbsp Italian mixed herbs
¼ tsp red chili flakes
4 large yellow squash, sliced
¼ cup fresh basil leaves

Directions and Total Time: approx. 55 minutes

Preheat oven to 375 F. Melt butter in a skillet and cook chicken for 10 minutes; set aside. In a bowl, mix garlic and onion powders, flour, mozzarella, half of Parmesan and ricotta cheeses, and egg. In another bowl, combine marinara sauce, mixed herbs, and red chili flakes; set aside. Make a single layer of the squash slices in a greased baking dish; spread a quarter of the egg mixture on top, a layer of the chicken, then a quarter of the marinara sauce. Repeat the layering process in the same proportions and sprinkle with the remaining Parmesan cheese. Bake for 30 minutes. Top with basil. Let cool completely. Slice.

Storage: Place in airtight containers in the refrigerator for up to 5 days (or in the freezer for up to 2 months).

Per serving: Cal 343; Carbs 10g; Fat 23g; Protein 28g

Chicken & Vegetable Pot Pie

Ingredients for 8 servings

1/3 cup cremini mushrooms, sliced
4 oz cream cheese
½ cup coconut cream
½ cup shredded cheddar
3 tbsp butter
1 lb ground chicken
Salt and black pepper to taste
1 large yellow onion, chopped
2 baby zucchinis, chopped
1 cup green beans, chopped
½ cup chopped broccoli rabe
2 celery stalks, chopped
¼ tsp poultry seasoning
10 egg whites
4 tbsp coconut flour
2 ½ cups fine almond flour
2 tsp baking powder

Directions and Total Time: approx. 60 minutes

Preheat oven to 350 F. Melt 1 tbsp of butter in a skillet, add chicken, season with salt and pepper, and cook for 8 minutes or until the chicken is no longer pink; set aside. Melt the remaining butter in the same skillet and sauté onion, zucchini, green beans, broccoli rabe, celery, and mushrooms. Cook until the vegetables soften, 5 minutes. Stir in chicken, cream cheese, and coconut cream. Simmer until the sauce thickens, 5 minutes. Season with poultry seasoning and cook for 2 minutes. Turn the heat off and pour the mixture into a baking dish. Pour the egg whites into a bowl, and using a hand mixer, beat the whites until frothy, but not stiff. Mix in coconut flour, almond flour, baking powder, cheddar cheese, and salt until evenly combined. Beat the batter until smooth. Spoon the content over the vegetables. Bake for 30 minutes or until the top browns. Let cool completely.

Storage: Place in airtight containers in the refrigerator for up to 5 days (or in the freezer for up to 2 months).

Per serving: Cal 383; Carbs 8g; Fat 31g; Protein 21g

Baked Taco Chicken with Cheese

Ingredients for 8 servings

½ cup shredded cheddar
8 oz cream cheese
1 rotisserie chicken, shredded
1/3 cup mayonnaise
1 yellow onion, sliced
1 yellow bell pepper, chopped
2 tbsp taco seasoning

Directions and Total Time: approx. 30 minutes

Preheat oven to 400 F. Into a greased baking dish, add chicken, mayonnaise, cream cheese, onion, bell pepper, taco seasoning, and two-thirds of the cheese. Mix and top with the remaining cheese. Bake for 20 minutes. Let cool.

Storage: Place in airtight containers in the refrigerator for up to 5 days (or in the freezer for up to 2 months).

Per serving: Cal 276; Carbs 6g; Fat 21g; Protein 15g

Chicken Egg Muffins

Ingredients for 12 servings

¼ cup grated Monterey Jack
2 tbsp butter
1 chicken breast
2 tbsp chopped green onions
½ tsp red chili flakes
12 eggs

Directions and Total Time: approx. 35 minutes

Preheat oven to 400 F. Line a 12-hole muffin tin with cupcake liners. Melt butter in a skillet over medium heat and cook the chicken until brown on each side, 10 minutes. Transfer to a plate and shred with 2 forks. Divide between muffin holes along with green onions and red chili flakes. Crack an egg into each muffin hole and scatter the cheese on top. Bake for 15 minutes until eggs are set. Cool.

Storage: Place in airtight containers in the refrigerator for up to 5 days (or in the freezer for up to 2 months).

Per serving: Cal 165; Carbs 2g; Fat 11g; Protein 11g

Effortless Chicken Meatloaf

Ingredients for 8 servings

2 lb ground chicken	1 lemon, juiced
2 tbsp olive oil	¼ cup chopped parsley
3 tbsp corn flour	¼ cup chopped oregano
2 large eggs	4 garlic cloves, minced

Directions and Total Time: approx. 50 minutes

Preheat oven to 400 F. In a bowl, combine ground chicken and corn flour; set aside. In a small bowl, whisk the eggs with olive oil, lemon juice, parsley, oregano, and garlic. Pour the mixture onto the chicken mixture and mix well. Spoon into a greased loaf pan and press to fit. Bake for 40 minutes. Remove the pan, drain the liquid, and let cool completely. Cut into slices.

Storage: Place in airtight containers in the refrigerator for up to 5 days (or in the freezer for up to 2 months).

Per serving: Cal 362; Carbs 3g; Fat 24g; Protein 35g

Saucy Chicken Breasts

Ingredients for 4 servings

½ cup sliced Pecorino Romano cheese
½ lb sliced mozzarella cheese   4 tbsp butter
1 ½ lb chicken breasts, halved lengthwise
Salt and black pepper to taste   ¼ cup fresh parsley, chopped
2 eggs   2 garlic cloves, minced
2 tbsp Italian seasoning   2 cups crushed tomatoes
1 pinch red chili flakes   1 tbsp dried basil

Directions and Total Time: approx. 45 minutes

Preheat oven to 400 F. Season chicken with salt and pepper; set aside. In a bowl, whisk eggs with Italian seasoning and red chili flakes. On a plate, combine Pecorino cheese with parsley. Melt butter in a skillet. Dip the chicken in the egg mixture and then dredge in the cheese mixture. Place in the butter and fry on both sides until the cheese melts and is golden brown, 10 minutes; set aside. Sauté garlic in the same pan and mix in tomatoes. Top with basil, salt, and pepper, and cook for 10 minutes. Pour the sauce into a greased baking dish. Lay the chicken pieces in the sauce and top with mozzarella. Bake for 15 minutes or until the cheese melts. Let cool completely.

Storage: Place in airtight containers in the refrigerator for up to 5 days (or in the freezer for up to 2 months).

Per serving: Cal 523; Carbs 5g; Fat 31g; Protein 47g

Mustardy Chicken Shirataki

Ingredients for 8 servings

4 chicken breasts, cut into strips
2 (8 oz) packs angel hair shirataki
5 tbsp heavy cream   1 yellow onion, finely sliced
1 tbsp olive oil   1 garlic clove, minced
1 cup chopped mustard greens 1 tbsp wholegrain mustard
1 yellow bell pepper, sliced Salt and black pepper to taste

Directions and Total Time: approx. 25 minutes

Boil 2 cups of water in a medium pot. Strain the shirataki pasta and rinse well under hot running water. Allow proper draining and pour the shirataki pasta into the boiling water. Cook for 3 minutes and strain again. Place a dry skillet and stir-fry the shirataki pasta until visibly dry, 1-2 minutes; set aside. Heat olive oil in a skillet, season the chicken with salt and pepper, and cook for 8-10 minutes; set aside. Stir in onion, bell pepper, and garlic and cook until softened, 5 minutes. Mix in mustard and heavy cream; simmer for 2 minutes and mix in the chicken and mustard greens for 2 minutes. Stir in shirataki pasta. Cool.

Storage: Place in airtight containers in the refrigerator for up to 5 days (or in the freezer for up to 2 months).

Per serving: Cal 336; Carbs 11g; Fats 18g; Protein 33g

Chicken Burgers with Cheddar & Spinach

Ingredients for 4 servings

4 low carb hamburger buns, halved
1 lb chicken thighs, boneless and skinless
4 slices cheddar cheese   2 tbsp ranch dressing mix
¼ cup melted butter   ¼ cup white vinegar
1 tsp onion powder   2 tbsp hot sauce
2 tsp garlic powder   ½ cup chicken broth
Salt and black pepper to taste ¼ cup baby spinach

Directions and Total Time: approx. 1 hour 10 minutes

In a bowl, combine onion and garlic powders, salt, pepper, and ranch dressing mix. Rub the mixture onto the chicken and place it into a pot. In another bowl, mix vinegar, hot sauce, broth, and butter. Pour the mixture all over the chicken and cook on low heat for 1 hour. Using two forks, shred the chicken into small strands. Mix and adjust the taste. Divide the spinach on the bottom half of each zero-carb bun, spoon the chicken on top, and add a cheddar cheese slice. Cover with the bun tops. Let cool completely.

Storage: Place in airtight containers in the refrigerator for up to 5 days (or in the freezer for up to 2 months).

Per serving: Cal 581; Carbs 17g; Fat 45g; Protein 32g

Cajun Chicken Fettuccine

Ingredients for 8 servings

2 cups grated mozzarella   4 garlic cloves, minced
½ cup grated Parmesan   4 tsp Cajun seasoning
1 cup shredded mozzarella   1 cup Alfredo sauce
2 tbsp olive oil   ½ cup marinara sauce
1 egg yolk   2 tbsp chopped fresh parsley
4 chicken breasts, cubed   1 green bell pepper, deseeded
1 yellow onion, thinly sliced   and thinly sliced
1 red bell pepper, deseeded and thinly sliced

Directions and Total Time: approx. 2 hours 40 minutes

Microwave mozzarella cheese for 2 minutes. Take out the bowl and let cool for a minute.

Mix in egg yolk until well combined. Lay a parchment paper on a flat surface, pour the cheese mixture on top and cover with another parchment paper. Flatten the dough into 1/8-inch thickness. Take off the parchment paper and cut the dough into thick fettuccine strands. Place in a bowl and refrigerate for 2 hours. Bring 2 cups of water to a boil and add fettuccine. Cook for 1 minute and drain; set aside.

Preheat oven to 350 F. Heat olive oil in a skillet and cook chicken for 6 minutes. Transfer to a plate. Add onion, garlic, and bell peppers to the skillet and cook for 5 minutes. Return the chicken to the pot and stir in Cajun seasoning, Alfredo sauce, and marinara sauce. Cook for 3 minutes. Stir in fettuccine and transfer to a greased baking dish. Cover with the mozzarella and Parmesan cheeses and bake for 15 minutes. Garnish with parsley. Let cool.

Storage: Place in airtight containers in the refrigerator for up to 5 days (or in the freezer for up to 2 months).

Per serving: Cal 383; Carbs 4g; Fats 19g; Protein 42g

Balsamic Root Veggies & Chicken Bake

Ingredients for 4 servings

¾ lb Brussels sprouts, halved	1 tbsp balsamic vinegar
2 large zucchinis, chopped	1 tsp chopped thyme leaves
2 red bell peppers, quartered	1 tsp chopped rosemary
2 chicken breasts, cubed	½ cup toasted walnuts
¼ cup olive oil	Salt and black pepper to taste

Directions and Total Time: approx. 35 minutes

Preheat oven to 400 F. Place Brussels sprouts, zucchini, bell peppers, and chicken on a baking sheet. Season with salt and pepper, and drizzle with olive oil. Add balsamic vinegar and toss. Scatter thyme and rosemary on top. Bake for 25 minutes. Top with walnuts. Let cool completely.

Storage: Place in airtight containers in the refrigerator for up to 5 days (or in the freezer for up to 2 months).

Per serving: Cal 485; Carbs 23g; Fat 26g; Protein 35g

Winter Chicken Bake

Ingredients for 6 servings

2 tbsp olive oil	2 lb chicken breasts
3 parsnips, sliced	½ cup chicken broth
1 onion, sliced	¼ cup white wine
4 garlic cloves, crushed	

Directions and Total Time: approx. 35 minutes

Preheat oven to 360 F. Warm oil in a skillet over medium heat and brown chicken for a couple of minutes, and transfer to a baking dish. Arrange the vegetables around the chicken and add in wine and chicken broth. Bake for 25 minutes, stirring once. Let cool completely.

Storage: Place in airtight containers in the refrigerator for up to 5 days (or in the freezer for up to 2 months).

Per serving: Cal 278; Carbs 12g; Fat 11g; Protein 28g

Chicken Wings in Cranberry Sauce

Ingredients for 6 servings

2 tbsp olive oil	
4 green onions, chopped diagonally	
4 tbsp unsweetened cranberry puree	
2 lb chicken wings	Juice from 1 lime
1 tbsp chili sauce	

Directions and Total Time: approx. 40 minutes

Preheat oven to 400 F. In a bowl, mix the cranberry puree, olive oil, chili sauce, green onions, and lime juice. Add in the wings and toss to coat. Transfer to a baking dish and bake for 25-30 minutes, turning once halfway. Let cool.

Storage: Place in airtight containers in the refrigerator for up to 5 days (or in the freezer for up to 2 months).

Per serving: Cal 242, Carbs 4g, Fat 13g, Protein 21g

Chicken Traybake with Acorn Squash

Ingredients for 4 servings

2 lb chicken thighs	½ cup black olives, pitted
¼ cup olive oil	5 garlic cloves, sliced
1 lb acorn squash, cubed	1 tbsp dried oregano

Directions and Total Time: approx. 55 minutes

Set the oven to 400 F. Place the chicken skin-down in a greased baking dish. Arrange the garlic, olives, and acorn squash around the chicken, then drizzle with olive oil. Sprinkle with oregano and bake for 45 minutes. Cool.

Storage: Place in airtight containers in the refrigerator for up to 5 days (or in the freezer for up to 2 months).

Per serving: Cal: 411, Carbs: 15g, Fat: 15g, Protein: 31g

Melt-In-The-Middle Chicken with Prosciutto

Ingredients for 8 servings

1 head broccoli, cut into florets	
¼ cup shredded Parmesan	4 chicken breasts, cubed
1 ½ cups heavy cream	4 garlic cloves, minced
2 tbsp butter	1 cup baby kale, chopped
6 slices prosciutto, chopped	

Directions and Total Time: approx. 25 minutes

Put prosciutto in a skillet and fry it until crispy and brown, 5 minutes; set aside. Melt butter in the same skillet and cook chicken until no longer pink. Add garlic and sauté for 1 minute. Mix in heavy cream, prosciutto, and kale and let simmer for 5 minutes until the sauce thickens. Pour broccoli into a safe-microwave bowl, sprinkle with some water, and microwave for 2 minutes until broccoli softens. Spoon into the sauce, top with Parmesan cheese, stir, and cook until the cheese melts. Let cool completely.

Storage: Place in airtight containers in the refrigerator for up to 5 days (or in the freezer for up to 2 months).

Per serving: Cal 393; Carbs 4g; Fat 26g; Protein 34g

Chicken & Parsnip Bake with Bacon

Ingredients for 6 servings

1 cup heavy cream
2 oz cream cheese, softened
1 ¼ cups grated Pepper Jack
2 tbsp butter
2 tbsp olive oil
6 bacon slices, chopped
½ lb parsnips, diced
1 lb ground chicken
¼ cup chopped scallions

Directions and Total Time: approx. 60 minutes

Preheat oven to 300 F. Put the bacon in a pot and fry it until brown and crispy, 6 minutes; set aside. Melt butter in a skillet and sauté parsnips until softened and lightly browned. Transfer to a greased baking sheet. Heat olive oil in the same pan and cook the chicken until no longer pink, 8 minutes. Spoon onto a plate and set aside too.

Add heavy cream, cream cheese, and two-thirds of the Pepper Jack cheese to the pot. Melt the ingredients over medium heat, frequently stirring, 7 minutes. Spread the parsnips on the baking dish, top with chicken, pour the heavy cream mixture over, and scatter bacon and scallions. Sprinkle the remaining cheese on top and bake until the cheese melts and is golden, 30 minutes. Let cool.

Storage: Place in airtight containers in the refrigerator for up to 5 days (or in the freezer for up to 2 months).

Per serving: Cal 516; Carbs 3g; Fat 41g; Protein 35g

Chicken Wings with Chimichurri

Ingredients for 8 servings

16 chicken wings, halved
½ cup butter, melted
½ cup olive oil
Salt and black pepper to taste
3 garlic cloves, peeled
1 cup fresh parsley leaves
¼ cup fresh cilantro leaves
2 tbsp red wine vinegar

Directions and Total Time: approx. 55 minutes

Preheat oven to 350 F. Put the chicken in a bowl, season with salt and pepper, and pour butter all over. Toss to coat and transfer to a greased baking sheet. Bake for 40-45 minutes or until light brown and cooked within. Let cool. In a food processor, blend garlic, parsley, cilantro, salt, and pepper until smooth. Add in vinegar and gradually pour in olive oil while mixing further. Place the chicken in airtight containers and the chimichurri in a glass jar.

Storage: Keep in the refrigerator for up to 5 days. To serve, reheat the chicken in the microwave for 1-2 minutes and top with chimichurri. Enjoy!

Per serving: Cal 311; Carbs 1g; Fat 24g; Protein 17g

Bacon-Wrapped Chicken with Spinach

Ingredients for 8 servings

4 chicken breasts
8 bacon slices
2 tbsp olive oil
2 tbsp butter
Salt and black pepper to taste
1 lb spinach
4 garlic cloves, minced

Directions and Total Time: approx. 30 minutes

Preheat oven to 450 F. Wrap each chicken breast with 2 bacon slices, season with salt and pepper, and place on a baking sheet. Drizzle with olive oil and bake for 15 minutes until the bacon browns and chicken cooks within. Melt butter in a skillet and sauté spinach and garlic until the leaves wilt, 5 minutes. Season with salt and pepper. Let cool completely.

Storage: Place in airtight containers in the refrigerator for up to 5 days (or in the freezer for up to 2 months).

Per serving: Cal 420; Carbs 4g; Fat 28g; Protein 35g

Chicken Strips with Zoodles & Pine Nuts

Ingredients for 6 servings

1 ½ lb chicken breasts, cut into strips
5 garlic cloves, minced
2 tbsp avocado oil
¼ tsp pureed onion
Salt and black pepper to taste
3 large eggs, lightly beaten
¼ cup chicken broth
2 tbsp coconut aminos
1 tbsp white vinegar
½ cup chopped scallions
1 tsp red chili flakes
4 zucchinis, spiralized
½ cup toasted pine nuts

Directions and Total Time: approx. 25 minutes

In a bowl, combine half of the garlic, onion, salt, and pepper. Add chicken and mix well. Heat avocado oil in a deep skillet over medium heat and add the chicken. Cook for 8 minutes until no longer pink with a slight brown crust. Transfer to a plate. Pour the eggs into the pan and scramble for 1 minute. Spoon the eggs to the side of the chicken and set aside. Reduce the heat to low, and in a bowl, mix broth, coconut aminos, vinegar, scallions, remaining garlic, and chili flakes; simmer for 3 minutes. Stir in chicken, zucchini, and eggs. Cook for 1 minute and turn the heat off. Top with pine nuts. Let cool completely.

Storage: Place in airtight containers in the refrigerator for up to 5 days (or in the freezer for up to 2 months).

Per serving: Cal 455; Carbs 8g; Fat 37g; Protein 32g

Basil-Tomato Chicken Thighs

Ingredients for 4 servings

2 tbsp ghee
1 lb chicken thighs
2 cloves garlic, minced
1 (14-oz) can whole tomatoes
1 zucchini, diced
10 fresh basil leaves, chopped

Directions and Total Time: approx. 40 minutes

Melt ghee in a saucepan and fry the chicken for 4 minutes on each side. Remove to a plate. Sauté garlic in the same saucepan for 2 minutes, pour in tomatoes, and cook for 8 minutes. Add in zucchini and cook for 4 minutes. Stir and add the chicken. Coat with sauce and simmer for 3 minutes. Top with basil. Let cool completely.

Storage: Place in airtight containers in the refrigerator for up to 5 days (or in the freezer for up to 2 months).

Per serving: Cal 438, Carbs 10g, Fat 34g, Protein 23g

Spinach & Chicken Stew

Ingredients for 5 servings

2 oz sun-dried tomatoes, chopped
5 oz chicken thighs, skinless, boneless
½ cup heavy cream | 1 leek, chopped
2 tbsp olive oil | 3 garlic cloves, minced
1 carrot, chopped | 1 cup spinach
2 celery stalks, chopped | Salt and black pepper to taste
3 cups chicken stock | A pinch of xanthan gum

Directions and Total Time: approx. 55 minutes

In a pot over medium heat, heat olive oil and add garlic, carrot, celery, and leek; season with salt and pepper and sauté for 5-6 minutes. Stir in chicken and cook for 5 minutes. Pour in stock and sun-dried tomatoes and cook for 30 minutes. Add in xanthan gum, heavy cream, and spinach and cook for 5 minutes. Let cool completely.

Storage: Place in airtight containers in the refrigerator for up to 5 days (or in the freezer for up to 2 months).

Per serving: Cal 260, Carbs 16g, Fat 19g, Protein 10g

Pickle Chicken Breasts

Ingredients for 4 servings

3 tbsp olive oil | 16 ounces jarred pickle juice
4 oz breadcrumbs, crushed | 2 eggs, whisked
2 chicken breasts, cut into strips

Directions and Total Time: approx. 2 hours 15 minutes

In a bowl, combine chicken and pickle juice; refrigerate for 2 hours. Place the eggs in one bowl and the breadcrumbs in a separate one. Dip the chicken pieces in the eggs and then in crumbs until well coated. Set a pan over medium heat and warm olive oil. Fry chicken for 3 minutes per side; remove to paper towels to drain the excess grease. Cool.

Storage: Place in airtight containers in the refrigerator for up to 5 days (or in the freezer for up to 2 months).

Per serving: Cal 342, Carbs 20g, Fat 18g, Protein 28g

Turkish Chicken Kebabs

Ingredients for 4 servings

1 tbsp olive oil | Salt and black pepper to taste
½ cup Greek yogurt | 2 tbsp curry powder
1 lb boneless chicken thighs, cut into 1-inch pieces

Directions and Total Time: approx. 35minutes

Preheat oven to 380 F. In a bowl, combine Greek yogurt, salt, pepper, curry, and olive oil. Mix in chicken, cover the bowl with plastic wrap and marinate for 20 minutes. Remove the wrap and thread the chicken onto skewers. Grill in the middle rack of the oven for 4 minutes on each side or until fully cooked. Let cool completely.

Storage: Place in airtight containers in the refrigerator for up to 5 days (or in the freezer for up to 2 months).

Per serving: Cal 373; Carbs 4g; Fat 23g; Protein 34g

Chicken and Spinach Gratin

Ingredients for 8 servings

1 ¼ cups provolone cheese, shredded
4 oz cream cheese, cubed | 1 tsp mixed spice seasoning
3 tsp olive oil | Salt and black pepper to taste
4 chicken breasts | 2 loose cups baby spinach

Directions and Total Time: approx. 45 minutes

Preheat oven to 370 F. Season chicken with spice mix, salt, and pepper. Put it in a greased casserole dish and layer spinach all over. Mix olive oil with cream cheese and provolone cheese, and stir in 4 tbsp of water, one tbsp at a time. Pour the mixture over the chicken and cover the pot with aluminum foil. Bake for 20 minutes, remove foil and cook for 15 minutes. Let cool completely.

Storage: Place in airtight containers in the refrigerator for up to 5 days (or in the freezer for up to 2 months).

Per serving: Cal 363, Carbs 1g, Fat 21g, Protein 35g

Cheese Faux Chicken Pizza

Ingredients for 4 servings

1 lb ground chicken | 1 cup tomato sauce
1 tsp Italian seasoning | ½ cup fresh basil leaves
1 ½ cups grated mozzarella

Directions and Total Time: approx. 45 minutes

Preheat oven to 390 F. Line a round pizza pan with parchment paper. In a bowl, mix ground chicken, Italian seasoning, and 1 cup of mozzarella cheese.

Spread the pizza "dough" on the pizza pan and bake for 18 minutes. Spread the tomato sauce on top. Scatter the remaining mozzarella cheese and basil all over and bake for 15 minutes. Let cool completely. Slice.

Storage: Place in airtight containers in the refrigerator for up to 5 days (or in the freezer for up to 2 months).

Per serving: Cal 316; Carbs 1g; Fats 17g; Protein 35g

Kids' Lunch Chicken Nuggets

Ingredients for 4 servings

Salt and black pepper to taste | 2 tsp butter
½ tsp garlic powder | 1 egg
½ cup flour | 2 chicken breasts, cubed

Directions and Total Time: approx. 20 minutes

In a bowl, combine salt, garlic powder, flour, and pepper and stir. In a separate bowl, beat the egg. Add the chicken to the egg mixture, then in the flour mixture. Set a pan over medium heat and warm butter. Add in chicken nuggets, and cook for 6 minutes on each side. Remove to paper towels, drain the excess grease, and let cool completely.

Storage: Place in airtight containers in the refrigerator for up to 5 days (or in the freezer for up to 2 months).

Per serving: Cal 237, Carbs 3g, Fat 17g, Protein 21g

Jalapeño Cucumber-Turkey Canapes

Ingredients for 4 servings

2 cucumbers, sliced
2 cups leftover turkey, diced
¼ jalapeño pepper, minced
1 tbsp Dijon mustard
¼ cup mayonnaise
Salt and black pepper to taste

Directions and Total Time: approx. 10 minutes

Cut mid-level holes in cucumber slices with a knife and set aside. Mix turkey, jalapeno pepper, mustard, mayonnaise, salt, and black pepper in a bowl. Carefully fill cucumber holes with turkey mixture. Place in airtight containers.

Storage: Keep in the refrigerator for up to 5 days.

Per serving: Cal 253; Carbs 3g; Fat 14g; Protein 21g

Turkey Patties with Brussels Sprouts

Ingredients for 4 servings

For the fried Brussels sprouts

1 ½ lb Brussels sprouts
4 tbsp olive oil
2 tbsp balsamic vinegar
Salt to taste

For the burgers

4 tbsp olive oil
1 lb ground turkey
1 egg
1 onion, chopped
1 garlic clove, minced
1 tsp fresh rosemary, chopped

Directions and Total Time: approx. 35 minutes

Preheat oven to 320 F. Arrange Brussels sprouts in a baking dish. Toss to coat with olive oil and season with salt. Bake for 20 minutes, stirring once. Pour balsamic vinegar over and cook for 5 minutes. Let cool completely. Combine burger ingredients in a bowl. Form patties out of the mixture. Set a pan, warm olive oil, and fry patties until cooked through. Let cool completely.

Storage: Place in airtight containers in the refrigerator for up to 5 days (or in the freezer for up to 2 months).

Per serving: Cal 461; Carbs 12g; Fat 27g; Protein 31g

Saucy Chipotle Turkey Stew

Ingredients for 6 servings

¼ cup sour cream
4 cups leftover turkey meat, chopped
2 cups green beans
4 cups chicken stock
Salt and black pepper to taste
1 chipotle pepper, chopped
½ cup tomatillo salsa
2 tsp cumin
1 tbsp fresh cilantro, chopped

Directions and Total Time: approx. 30 minutes

Set a pan over medium heat. Add in stock and stir in green beans; cook for 10 minutes. Place in turkey, salt, tomatillo salsa, chipotle pepper, cumin, and pepper and cook for 10 minutes. Stir in sour cream. Top with cilantro and let cool.

Storage: Place in airtight containers in the refrigerator for up to 5 days (or in the freezer for up to 2 months).

Per serving: Cal 234, Carbs 2g, Fat 11g, Protein 27g

Cheesy Pepperoncini Turkey Pastrami Rolls

Ingredients for 4 servings

8 oz softened cream cheese
10 canned pepperoncini peppers, sliced and drained
10 oz turkey pastrami, sliced

Directions and Total Time: approx. 2 hours 15 minutes

Lay a plastic wrap on a flat surface and arrange the pastrami all over, slightly overlapping each other. Spread the cheese on top of the pastrami and arrange the pepperoncini on top. Hold 2 opposite ends of the plastic wrap and roll the pastrami. Twist both ends to tighten.

Storage: Place in an airtight container in the refrigerator for up to 5 days. Slice into 2-inch pinwheels before serving.

Per serving: Cal 266; Carbs 1g; Fat 24g; Protein 13g

Broccoli & Turkey Cheese Bake

Ingredients for 4 servings

1 cup cheddar cheese, grated
½ cup heavy cream
½ cup buttermilk
2 tbsp butter, melted
1 lb turkey breasts, cooked
10 oz broccoli florets
1 carrot, sliced
4 tbsp breadcrumbs, crushed
Salt and black pepper, to taste
1 tsp oregano

Directions and Total Time: approx. 40 minutes

Cook broccoli in salted water for 4 minutes. Shred the turkey and place into a bowl with buttermilk, butter, oregano, carrot, and broccoli; mix well to combine.

Season with salt and black pepper and transfer the mixture to a greased baking pan. Mix in heavy cream and top with cheddar cheese. Cover with breadcrumbs. Bake for 25 minutes at 360 F. Let cool completely.

Storage: Place in airtight containers in the refrigerator for up to 5 days (or in the freezer for up to 2 months).

Per serving: Cal 412; Carbs 11g; Fat 17g; Protein 33g

Duck Stew with Yellow Squash

Ingredients for 4 servings

1 tbsp coconut oil
1 pound duck breast, skin on and sliced
2 yellow squash, sliced
2 green onions, chopped
1 carrot, chopped
1 green bell pepper, chopped
Salt and black pepper to taste

Directions and Total Time: approx. 40 minutes

Set a saucepan over medium heat and warm coconut oil. Sauté the duck for 3 minutes per side; reserve. Stir green onions in the saucepan for 2 minutes. Place in the yellow squash, bell pepper, carrot, salt, and pepper and cook for 10 minutes. Return the duck and cook for 10-15 minutes. Let cool completely. Place in airtight containers.

Storage: Keep in the refrigerator for up to 5 days (or in the freezer for up to 2 months). Microwave for 2 minutes to serve.

Per serving: Cal 373; Carbs 8g; Fat 21g, Protein 33g

BEEF

Jalapeño Beef Lettuce Wraps

Ingredients for 4 servings

3 tbsp ghee, divided
1 large white onion, chopped
2 garlic cloves, minced
1 jalapeño pepper, chopped
1 lb chuck steak, sliced thinly against the grain
2 tsp red curry powder
1 cup cauliflower rice
8 small lettuce leaves
Salt and black pepper to taste

Directions and Total Time: approx. 30 minutes

Melt 2 tbsp of ghee in a large deep skillet; season the beef and cook until brown and cooked within, 10 minutes; set aside. Sauté the onion for 3 minutes. Pour in garlic, salt, pepper, and jalapeño and cook for 1 minute.

Add the remaining ghee, curry powder, and beef. Cook for 5 minutes and stir in the cauliflower rice. Sauté until adequately mixed and the cauliflower is slightly softened, 2 to 3 minutes. Adjust the taste with salt and black pepper.

Lay out the lettuce leaves on a lean flat surface and spoon the beef mixture onto the middle part of them, 3 tbsp per leaf. Wrap the leaves and let cool completely.

Storage: Place in airtight containers in the refrigerator for up to 5 days (or in the freezer for up to 3 months).

Per serving: Cal 318; Carbs 10g; Fat 18g; Protein 27g

Meat Lovers's Pizza

Ingredients for 4 servings

4 ½ oz shredded mozzarella
6 oz shredded cheese
2 tbsp cream cheese, softened
2 tbsp butter
¾ cup almond flour
½ tsp dried basil
1 egg
1 tsp plain vinegar
8 oz ground beef sausage
¼ cup tomato sauce

Directions and Total Time: approx. 40 minutes

Preheat oven to 400 F. Line a pizza pan with parchment paper. Melt cream and mozzarella cheeses in a skillet while stirring until evenly combined. Turn the heat off and mix in almond flour, egg, and vinegar. Let cool slightly.

Flatten the mixture onto the pizza pan. Cover with another parchment paper, and using a rolling pin, smoothen the dough into a circle. Take off the parchment paper on top, prick the dough all over with a fork and bake it for 10 to 15 minutes until golden brown.

While the crust bakes, melt butter in a skillet over medium heat and fry sausage until brown, 8 minutes. Turn the heat off. Spread the tomato sauce on the crust, top with basil, meat, and mozzarella cheese, and return to the oven. Bake for 12 minutes. Let cool completely. Slice.

Storage: Place in airtight containers in the refrigerator for up to 5 days (or in the freezer for up to 3 months).

Per serving: Cal 361; Carbs 3g; Fat 21g; Protein 37g

Enchilada Beef Stuffed Peppers

Ingredients for 6 servings

¼ cup grated cheddar cheese
Sour cream for serving
3 tbsp butter, softened
Salt and black pepper to taste
6 bell peppers, deseeded
1 white onion, chopped
3 cloves garlic, minced
2 lb ground beef
2 tsp enchilada seasoning
1 cup cauliflower rice

Directions and Total Time: approx. 60 minutes

Preheat oven to 400 F. Melt butter in a skillet over medium heat and sauté onion and garlic for 3 minutes. Stir in beef, enchilada seasoning, salt, and pepper. Cook for 10 minutes. Mix in the cauli rice until well incorporated. Spoon the mixture into the peppers, top with the cheddar cheese, and put the stuffed peppers in a greased baking dish. Bake for 40 minutes. Drop generous dollops of sour cream on the peppers and let cool completely.

Storage: Place in airtight containers in the refrigerator for up to 5 days (or in the freezer for up to 3 months).

Per serving: Cal 409; Carbs 11g; Fat 27g; Protein 37g

Hot Beef & Cauliflower Curry

Ingredients for 4 servings

2 tbsp olive oil
10 oz cauliflower florets
1 lb ground beef
1 tbsp ginger-garlic paste
6 oz canned whole tomatoes
Salt and chili pepper to taste

Directions and Total Time: approx. 30 minutes

Sauté ground beef in hot olive oil over medium heat for 5 minutes while breaking any lumps. Stir in ginger-garlic paste, salt, and chili pepper. Pour in tomatoes and cauliflower and cook for 6 minutes. Add in 1 cup of water and bring to a boil; cook for 10 minutes. Let cool.

Storage: Place in airtight containers in the refrigerator for up to 5 days (or in the freezer for up to 2 months).

Per serving: Cal 380; Carbs 10g; Fat 28g; Protein 24g

Scottish Beef Stew

Ingredients for 4 servings

2 tbsp lard
1 parsnip, chopped
1 onion, chopped
1 ¼ lb beef chuck roast, cubed
12 oz sweet potatoes, cut into quarters
Salt and black pepper to taste
1 ½ cups beef stock
2 tsp rosemary, chopped

Directions and Total Time: approx. 40 minutes

Melt lard in a skillet over medium heat and cook the onion for 4 minutes. Add in the beef, season with salt and pepper, and brown on all sides for about 7-8 minutes. Add in sweet potatoes, parsnip, rosemary, and beef stock. Stir and cook on low heat for 15-20 minutes. Let cool completely.

Storage: Place in airtight containers in the refrigerator for up to 5 days (or in the freezer for up to 2 months).

Per serving: Cal 475; Carbs 23g; Fat 26g; Protein 42g

Beef Sausage Frittata with Cheese

Ingredients for 4 servings

2 tbsp shredded cheddar	8 whole eggs
2 tbsp sour cream	1 red bell pepper, chopped
2 tbsp butter	½ lb ground beef sausage

Directions and Total Time: approx. 55 minutes

Preheat the oven to 350 F. Crack the eggs into a bowl. Add the sour cream and whisk to mix the ingredients; set aside. Melt butter in a large skillet over medium heat. Add bell peppers and sauté until soft, 6 minutes; set aside. Add the beef sausage and cook until brown, continuously stirring and breaking the lumps into small bits, 10 minutes. Flatten the beef on the bottom of skillet, scatter bell peppers on top, pour the egg mixture all over, and scatter the top with cheddar cheese. Put the skillet in the oven and bake for 30 minutes or until the eggs set and the cheddar cheese melts. Let cool completely.

Storage: Place in airtight containers in the refrigerator for up to 5 days (or in the freezer for up to 3 months).

Per serving: Cal 255; Carbs 5g; Fat 16g; Protein 20g

Beef & Zucchini Lasagna

Ingredients for 4 servings

½ cup Pecorino Romano cheese

1 ½ cups grated mozzarella	1 tsp onion powder
2 cups crumbled goat cheese	2 tbsp flour
2 tbsp lard	1 large egg
4 yellow zucchini, sliced	2 cups marinara sauce
Salt and black pepper to taste	1 tbsp Italian herb seasoning
½ lb ground beef	¼ tsp red chili flakes
1 tsp garlic powder	¼ cup fresh basil leaves

Directions and Total Time: approx. 40 minutes

Preheat oven to 375 F. Melt the lard in a skillet and cook beef for 10 minutes; set aside. In a bowl, combine garlic powder, onion powder, flour, salt, pepper, mozzarella cheese, half of Pecorino cheese, goat cheese, and egg. Mix Italian herb seasoning and chili flakes with marinara sauce. Make a single layer of the zucchini in a greased baking dish, spread ¼ of the egg mixture on top, and ¼ of the marinara sauce. Repeat the process and top with the remaining Pecorino cheese. Bake in the oven for 20 minutes. Garnish with basil, slice, and let cool.

Storage: Place in airtight containers in the refrigerator for up to 5 days (or in the freezer for up to 3 months).

Per serving: Cal 570; Carbs 17g; Fat 33g; Protein 43g

Classic Beef Meatloaf

Ingredients for 4 servings

2 tbsp olive oil	1 lemon, zested
1 ½ lb ground beef	¼ cup chopped tarragon
3 tbsp corn flour	Salt and black pepper to taste
2 large eggs	4 garlic cloves, minced

Directions and Total Time: approx. 75 minutes

Preheat the oven to 400 F. Grease a loaf pan with cooking spray. In a bowl, combine beef, salt, pepper, and corn flour; set aside. In another bowl, whisk the eggs with olive oil, lemon zest, tarragon, oregano, and garlic. Pour the mixture onto the beef mix and evenly combine. Spoon the meat mixture into the pan and press to fit in. Bake in oven for 1 hour. Remove the pan, tilt to drain the meat's liquid, and let cool for 5 minutes. Let cool completely. Slice.

Storage: Place in airtight containers in the refrigerator for up to 5 days (or in the freezer for up to 3 months).

Per serving: Cal 371; Carbs 4g; Fat 23g; Protein 28g

Beef & Broccoli Bake with Pancetta

Ingredients for 6 servings

1 ¼ cups grated cheddar	2 oz cream cheese, softened
1 cup coconut cream	2 tbsp olive oil
1 large broccoli head, cut into florets	
Salt and black pepper to taste	1 lb ground beef
6 slices pancetta, chopped	¼ cup chopped scallions

Directions and Total Time: approx. 60 minutes

Preheat the oven to 300 F. Fill a pot with water and bring to a boil. Pour in broccoli and blanch for 2 minutes. Drain and set aside. Place pancetta in the pot and fry for 5 minutes. Remove to a plate. Heat oil in the pot and cook the beef until brown for 5-6 minutes. Add in coconut cream, cream cheese, two-thirds of cheddar cheese, salt, and pepper and stir for 7 minutes. Arrange the broccoli florets in a baking dish, pour the beef mixture over, and scatter the top with pancetta and scallions. Bake in the oven until the cheese is bubbly and golden, 20 minutes. Top with the remaining cheddar and bake for 10 more minutes. Let cool completely.

Storage: Place in airtight containers in the refrigerator for up to 5 days (or in the freezer for up to 3 months).

Per serving: Cal 543; Carbs 27g; Fat 31g; Protein 34g

Slow-cooker BBQ Beef Sliders with Spinach

Ingredients for 6 servings

4 cheddar cheese slices	¼ cup melted butter
4 hamburger buns, halved	
2 lb chuck roast, boneless	¼ cup white vinegar
1 tsp onion powder	2 tbsp tamari sauce
2 tsp garlic powder	½ cup bone broth
1 tbsp smoked paprika	Salt and black pepper to taste
2 tbsp tomato paste	¼ cup baby spinach

Directions and Total Time: approx. 4 hours 15 minutes

Cut the beef into 2 pieces. In a bowl, combine salt, pepper, onion and garlic powders, and paprika. Rub the mixture onto beef and place it in a slow cooker. In another bowl, mix tomato paste, vinegar, tamari sauce, broth, and melted butter. Pour over the beef and cook for 4 hours on High.

When the beef cooks, shred it using 2 forks. Divide the spinach between buns, spoon the meat on top, and add a cheddar slice. Put in resealable plastic bags.

Storage: Keep in the refrigerator for up to 3 days.

Per serving: Cal 512; Carbs 14g; Fat 27g; Protein 42g

Hot Beef Burgers with Coleslaw

Ingredients for 4 servings

2 tbsp ghee	4 burger buns
1 pound ground beef	¼ cup mayonnaise
½ tsp onion powder	1 tsp Sriracha sauce
½ tsp garlic powder	4 tbsp coleslaw
1 tsp Dijon mustard	Salt and black pepper to taste

Directions and Total Time: approx. 15 minutes

Mix together beef, onion powder, garlic powder, salt, pepper, and mustard in a bowl. Create 4 burgers. Melt ghee in a skillet and cook the burgers for 3 minutes per side. Let cool completely. Place on buns topped with mayonnaise, sriracha sauce, and coleslaw.

Storage: Place in airtight containers in the refrigerator for up to 2 days.

Per serving: Cal 573; Carbs 25g; Fat 39g; Protein 32g

Cabbage & Beef Stacks

Ingredients for 4 servings

1 lb chuck steak, sliced thinly across the grain

¼ cup olive oil	1 tsp Italian mixed herb blend
1 headcanon cabbage, grated	½ cup bone broth
3 tbsp coconut flour	Salt and black pepper to taste

Directions and Total Time: approx. 55 minutes

Preheat the oven to 400 F. In a zipper bag, add coconut flour, salt, and pepper. Mix and add the beef slices. Seal the bag and shake to coat. Make little mounds of cabbage in a greased baking dish. Drizzle with some olive oil. Remove the beef strips from the coconut flour mixture, shake off the excess flour, and place 2-3 beef strips on each cabbage mound. Sprinkle the Italian herb blend and drizzle again with the remaining olive oil. Roast for 30 minutes. Remove the pan and carefully pour in the broth. Return to the oven and roast further for 10 minutes, until beef cooks through. Let cool completely.

Storage: Place in airtight containers in the refrigerator for up to 5 days (or in the freezer for up to 3 months).

Per serving: Cal 463; Carbs 15g; Fat 31g; Protein 28g

Beef Pad Thai with Zucchini

Ingredients for 8 servings

2 lb chuck steak, sliced thinly against the grain

2 tbsp peanut oil	1 tsp freshly pureed garlic
3 ¼ tbsp peanut butter	¼ tsp freshly ground ginger
1 tsp red pepper flakes	Salt and black pepper to taste

3 large eggs, lightly beaten	2 garlic cloves, minced
1/3 cup beef broth	4 zucchinis, spiralized
2 tbsp tamari sauce	½ cup bean sprouts
1 tbsp white vinegar	½ cup crushed peanuts
½ cup chopped green onions	

Directions and Total Time: approx. 25 minutes

In a bowl, combine garlic puree, ginger, salt, and pepper. Add in beef and toss to coat. Heat peanut oil in a deep skillet and cook the beef for 12 minutes; transfer to a plate. Pour the eggs into the skillet and scramble for 1 minute; set aside. Reduce the heat and combine broth, peanut butter, tamari sauce, vinegar, green onions, minced garlic, and red pepper flakes. Mix until adequately combined and simmer for 3 minutes. Stir in beef, zucchini, bean sprouts, and eggs. Cook for 1 minute. Top with peanuts. Let cool.

Storage: Place in airtight containers in the refrigerator for up to 5 days (or in the freezer for up to 3 months).

Per serving: Cal 565; Carbs 13g; Fat 42g; Protein 40g

Beef and Veggie Skillet

Ingredients for 4 servings

4 cups mixed vegetables (broccoli, bell peppers, snap peas)

1 lb lean beef, thinly sliced	1 tsp red pepper flakes
3 cloves garlic, minced	1 tsp garlic powder
2 tbsp soy sauce	Salt and black pepper to taste

Directions and Total Time: approx. 20 minutes

Warm olive oil in a large skillet over medium heat. Add minced garlic and sliced beef. Cook until beef is browned. Stir-fry in mixed vegetables until they are tender-crisp. Drizzle soy sauce over the beef and vegetables. Add salt, pepper, and red pepper flakes. Let cool.

Storage: Place in 8 airtight containers in the refrigerator for up to 5 days (or in the freezer for up to 3 months).

Per serving: Cal 312; Carbs 15g; Fat 15g; Protein 29g

Sticky BBQ Rib Steak

Ingredients for 6 servings

2 lb rib steak, membrane removed

2 tbsp avocado oil	3 tbsp barbecue dry rub
3 tbsp maple syrup	

Directions and Total Time: approx. 2 hours 40 minutes

Preheat the oven to 300 F. Line a baking sheet with aluminum foil. In a bowl, mix avocado oil and maple syrup and brush the mixture onto the meat. Sprinkle BBQ rub all over the ribs. Put them on the baking sheet and bake until the meat is tender and crispy on the top, 2 ½ hours. Let cool completely.

Storage: Place in airtight containers in the refrigerator for up to 5 days (or in the freezer for up to 3 months).

Per serving: Cal 494; Carbs 12g; Fat 36g; Protein 49g

Beef Portobello Cheeseburgers

Ingredients for 4 servings

4 large Portobello caps, destemmed and rinsed
4 slices Monterey Jack
1 tbsp coconut oil
1 lb ground beef
Salt and black pepper to taste
1 tbsp Worcestershire sauce
4 lettuce leaves
4 large tomato slices
¼ cup mayonnaise

Directions and Total Time: approx. 25 minutes

In a bowl, combine beef, salt, pepper, and Worcestershire sauce. Using your hands, mold the meat into 4 patties, and set aside. Heat the coconut oil in a skillet over medium heat. Place in the Portobello caps and cook until softened, 4 minutes. Remove to serving plates. Cook the beef patties in the skillet until brown, 10 minutes in total. Place the cheese slices on the beef, allow to melt for 1 minute and lift each beef patty onto each mushroom cap. Let cool completely. Cover with lettuce, tomato slices, and mayo.

Storage: Place in airtight containers in the refrigerator for up to 5 days (or in the freezer for up to 3 months).

Per serving: Cal 362; Carbs 7g; Fat 22g; Protein 29g

Tex-Mex Cheeseburgers

Ingredients for 4 servings

¼ cup Mexican cheese blend, grated
1 large tomato, sliced into 4 pieces and deseeded
4 tbsp avocado oil mayonnaise
1 lb ground beef
½ cup chopped cilantro
1 lemon, zested and juiced
Salt and black pepper to taste
1 tsp ground cumin
2 tbsp hot chili sauce
1 lb spinach leaves
1 medium red onion, sliced
1 avocado, halved, sliced

Directions and Total Time: approx. 15 minutes

Preheat the grill on high heat. In a bowl, add ground beef, cilantro, lemon zest, juice, salt, pepper, cumin, and chili sauce. Mix the ingredients until evenly combined. Make 4 patties from the mixture. Grill for 3 minutes on each side. Let cool completely. Lay 2 spinach leaves side to side in 4 portions on a clean flat surface. Place a beef patty on each and spread 1 tbsp of mayo on top. Add a slice of tomato and onion, sprinkle with some cheese, and place avocado on top. Cover with 2 pieces of spinach leaves each.

Storage: Place in airtight containers in the refrigerator for up to 2 days.

Per serving: Cal 345; Carbs 11g; Fat 23g; Protein 21g

Tangy Beef Meatballs

Ingredients for 4 servings

1 tbsp olive oil
2 tbsp melted butter
1 lb ground beef
1 red onion, finely chopped
2 red bell peppers, chopped
2 garlic cloves, minced
1 tsp dried basil
2 tbsp tamari sauce
Salt and black pepper to taste
1 tbsp dried rosemary

Directions and Total Time: approx. 30 minutes

Preheat the oven to 400 F. In a bowl, mix beef, onion, bell peppers, garlic, butter, basil, tamari sauce, salt, pepper, and rosemary. Form meatballs from the mixture and place them on a greased baking sheet. Drizzle olive oil over the beef and bake in the oven for 20 minutes or until browned on the outside. Let cool completely.

Storage: Place in airtight containers in the refrigerator for up to 5 days (or in the freezer for up to 3 months).

Per serving: Cal 420; Carbs 15g; Fat 31g; Protein 24g

Taco Beef Pizza

Ingredients for 8 servings

1 cup shredded mozzarella
2 tbsp cream cheese, softened
1 cup grated cheddar cheese
1 cup sour cream
½ cup cheese sauce
1 egg
¾ cup almond flour
1 lb ground beef
2 tsp taco seasoning
1 cup chopped lettuce
1 tomato, diced
¼ cup sliced black olives

Directions and Total Time: approx. 35 minutes

Preheat oven to 390 F. Line a pizza pan with parchment paper. Microwave the mozzarella and cream cheeses for 1 minute. Remove and mix in egg and almond flour. Spread the mixture on the pan and bake for 15 minutes. Put the beef in a pot and cook for 5 minutes. Stir in taco seasoning. Spread the cheese sauce on the crust and top with the meat. Add cheddar cheese, lettuce, tomato, and black olives. Bake until the cheese melts, 5 minutes. Cool.

Storage: Place in airtight containers in the refrigerator for up to 5 days (or in the freezer for up to 3 months). Before serving, reheat the pizza in the microwave for 1-2 minutes. Top with sour cream. Enjoy!

Per serving: Cal 477; Carbs 7g; Fat 32g; Protein 26g

Beef & Brussels Sprout Stir-Fry

Ingredients for 4 servings

2 tbsp olive oil
¼ cup toasted walnuts, chopped
1 ½ cups Brussels sprouts, halved
1 garlic clove, minced
½ white onion, chopped
Salt and black pepper to taste
1 lb ground beef
1 bok choy, quartered
2 tbsp chopped scallions
1 tbsp black sesame seeds

Directions and Total Time: approx. 25 minutes

Heat 1 tbsp of olive oil in a skillet over medium heat and sauté garlic and onion for 3 minutes. Stir in ground beef and cook until brown while breaking the lumps, 7 minutes. Pour in Brussels sprouts, bok choy, walnuts, scallions, and season with salt and black pepper. Sauté for 5 minutes. Top with sesame seeds Let cool completely.

Storage: Place in airtight containers in the refrigerator for up to 5 days (or in the freezer for up to 3 months).

Per serving: Cal 432; Carbs 13g; Fat 27g; Protein 32g

One-Pan Beef with Cauli Rice

Ingredients for 6 servings

3 tbsp olive oil	½ cup green beans, chopped
1 tbsp avocado oil	3 garlic cloves, minced
1 lb chuck steak, cubed	4 cups cauliflower rice
2 large eggs, beaten	¼ cup coconut aminos
1 red onion, finely chopped	1 cup toasted cashew nuts
½ cup chopped bell peppers	

Directions and Total Time: approx. 25 minutes

Heat 2 tbsp olive oil in a wok over medium heat and cook the beef until tender, 7-8 minutes; set aside. Pour the eggs in the wok and scramble for 2-3 minutes; set aside. Add the remaining olive oil and avocado oil to heat. Stir in onion, bell peppers, green beans, and garlic. Sauté until soft, 3 minutes. Pour in cauli rice and coconut aminos, and stir until evenly combined. Mix in the beef, eggs, and cashew nuts and cook for 3 minutes. Let cool completely.

Storage: Place in airtight containers in the refrigerator for up to 5 days (or in the freezer for up to 3 months).

Per serving: Cal 468; Carbs 32g; Fat 27; Protein 29g

Cheesy Beef Stew with Walnuts

Ingredients for 8 servings

1 cup shredded cheddar	2 large tomatoes, diced
1 cup half and half	Salt and black pepper to taste
2 tbsp olive oil	1 tbsp smoked paprika
2 tbsp butter	2 tsp chili powder
1 lb chuck roast, cubed	2 cups beef broth
1 large yellow onion, chopped	½ cup walnuts, chopped
3 garlic cloves, minced	2 cups cauliflower rice

Directions and Total Time: approx. 55 minutes

Heat olive oil in a pot over medium heat. Season the beef with salt and pepper and cook for 3 minutes. Stir in onion, garlic, and tomatoes for 5 minutes. Mix in paprika and chili and cook for 2 minutes. Pour in beef broth and bring to a boil; simmer for 25 minutes. Pour in cauli rice and ½ cup water and cook for 5 minutes. Stir in the half and half and cheddar cheese for 3-4 minutes. Melt butter in a skillet and cook walnuts for 3 minutes. Transfer to a cutting board, chop and sprinkle over the stew. Let cool.

Storage: Place in airtight containers in the refrigerator for up to 5 days (or in the freezer for up to 2 months).

Per serving: Cal 347; Carbs 10g; Fat 26g, Protein 23g

Beef Sirloin with Thai Sauce

Ingredients for 4 servings

3 tbsp ghee	2 long red chilies, sliced
1 lb sirloin, cut into rounds	1 cup beef stock
2 garlic cloves, minced	1 cup coconut milk
½ cup brown onions, chopped	1 tbsp Thai green curry paste
1 green bell pepper, sliced	1 lime, juiced
1 red bell pepper, sliced	

Directions and Total Time: approx. 40 minutes

Melt the half of ghee in a pan over medium heat and cook the beef for 3 minutes on each side. Remove to a plate. Add the remaining ghee to the skillet and sauté garlic and onion for 3 minutes. Stir-fry in bell peppers and red chili until softened, 5 minutes.

Pour in beef stock, coconut milk, curry paste, and lime juice. Let simmer for 4 minutes. Put the beef back into the sauce, cook for 10 minutes, and transfer the pan to the oven. Cook further under the broiler for 5 minutes. Cool.

Storage: Place in airtight containers in the refrigerator for up to 5 days (or in the freezer for up to 3 months).

Per serving: Cal 492; Carbs 14g; Fat 35g; Protein 30g

Bell Pepper & Mushroom Beef Skewers

Ingredients for 4 servings

2 tbsp coconut oil	1 lime, juiced
1 lb beef tri-tip steak, cubed	1 tbsp ginger powder
1 tbsp tamari sauce	½ tsp ground cumin
2 cups cremini mushrooms, halved	
2 yellow bell peppers, deseeded and cut into squares	

Directions and Total Time: approx. 1 hour 15 minutes

In a bowl, mix coconut oil, tamari sauce, lime juice, ginger, and cumin powder. Add in the beef, mushrooms, and bell peppers; toss to coat. Cover the bowl with plastic wrap and marinate for 1 hour. Preheat the grill to high heat. Take off the plastic wrap and thread the mushrooms, beef, and bell peppers in this order on skewers until the ingredients are exhausted. Grill the skewers for 5 minutes per side. Let cool completely.

Storage: Place in airtight containers in the refrigerator for up to 5 days (or in the freezer for up to 3 months).

Per serving: Cal 383; Carbs 8g; Fat 23g; Protein 41g

Beef Meatloaf Wrapped in Bacon

Ingredients for 6 servings

½ cup shredded Parmesan	1 egg, lightly beaten
½ cup coconut cream	1 tbsp dried sage
2 tbsp olive oil	4 tbsp toasted pecans, chopped
1 white onion, finely chopped	Salt and black pepper to taste
1 lb ground beef	6 bacon slices

Directions and Total Time: approx. 40 minutes

Preheat oven to 400 F. Heat olive oil in a skillet and sauté the onion for 3 minutes. In a bowl, mix ground beef, onion, coconut cream, Parmesan cheese, egg, sage, pecans, salt, and pepper. Form into a loaf, wrap it with bacon slices, secure with toothpicks, and place it on a greased baking sheet. Bake for 30 minutes. Let cool completely. Slice.

Storage: Place in airtight containers in the refrigerator for up to 5 days (or in the freezer for up to 3 months).

Per serving: Cal 472; Carbs 6g; Fat 39g; Protein 26g

Pressure Cooked Chuck Steak with Cabbage

Ingredients for 8 servings

3 tbsp coconut oil	1 tsp dried Italian herb blend
1 large white onion, chopped	1 ½ tbsp balsamic vinegar
3 garlic cloves, minced	½ cup beef broth
2 cups shredded red cabbage	2 lb chuck steak
1 lemon, zested and juiced	Salt and black pepper to taste

Directions and Total Time: approx. 40 minutes

Select Sauté mode on your pressure cooker. Heat coconut oil and sauté onion, garlic, and red cabbage for 3 minutes. Stir in lemon zest, lemon juice, Italian herb blend, balsamic vinegar, salt, and pepper for 2 minutes; mix in the broth. Place the beef in the cooker. Close the lid, secure the pressure valve, and select Manual/Pressure Cook mode on High for 25 minutes. Once the timer is done, perform a natural pressure release, then a quick pressure release to let out any remaining steam, and open the lid. Remove the beef, and using two forks, shred it. Select Sauté and reduce the sauce, 5 minutes. Spoon the pulled beef with sauce over on a bed of zucchini noodles. Let cool completely.

Storage: Place in airtight containers in the refrigerator for up to 5 days (or in the freezer for up to 3 months).

Per serving: Cal 393; Carbs 11g; Fat 22g; Protein 34g

Shiitake Beef Stir-Fry

Ingredients for 6 servings

4 cups shiitake mushrooms, halved
2 sprigs rosemary, leaves extracted

1 tbsp coconut oil	6 slices prosciutto, chopped
2 green bell peppers, chopped	1 tbsp freshly pureed garlic
1 ½ lb chuck steak	

Directions and Total Time: approx. 30 minutes

Using a sharp knife, slice the chuck steak thinly against the grain and cut into smaller pieces. Heat a skillet over medium heat and cook prosciutto until brown and crispy; set aside. Melt coconut oil in the skillet and cook the beef until brown, 6-8 minutes. Remove to the prosciutto plate. Add mushrooms and bell pepper to the skillet and sauté until softened, 5 minutes. Stir in prosciutto, beef, rosemary, and garlic. Season to taste and cook for 4 minutes. Let cool completely.

Storage: Place in airtight containers in the refrigerator for up to 5 days (or in the freezer for up to 3 months).

Per serving: Cal 587; Carbs 21g; Fat 32g; Protein 57g

Mediterranean Beef Casserole

Ingredients for 8 servings

4 oz goat cheese, crumbled	Salt and black pepper to taste
1 cup heavy cream	2 oz pitted green olives
2 tbsp butter	1 garlic clove, minced
1 lb ground beef	2 oz basil pesto

Directions and Total Time: approx. 40 minutes

Preheat oven to 400 F. Grease a casserole dish with cooking spray. Melt butter in a deep skillet and cook the beef until brown, stirring frequently. Season with salt and pepper. Spoon and spread the beef at the bottom of the casserole dish. Top with olives, goat cheese, and garlic. In a bowl, mix pesto and heavy cream and pour the mixture all over the beef. Bake until lightly brown around the edges and bubbly, 25 minutes. Let cool completely.

Storage: Place in airtight containers in the refrigerator for up to 5 days (or in the freezer for up to 3 months).

Per serving: Cal 263; Carbs 2g; Fat 19g; Protein 21g

Beef with Mushrooms in Coconut Sauce

Ingredients for 8 servings

2 tbsp coconut cream	1/3 cup coconut milk
3 tbsp unsalted butter	1/2 tsp dried thyme
1 yellow onion, chopped	2 tbsp chopped parsley
2 rib-eye steaks	3 tbsp black olives, sliced
¼ cup button mushrooms, sliced	

Directions and Total Time: approx. 25 minutes

Melt 2 tbsp butter in a deep skillet over medium heat. Add and sauté the mushrooms for 4 minutes until tender. Stir in onion and cook further for 3 minutes; set aside. Melt the remaining butter in the skillet and cook the beef for 10 minutes on both sides. Pour mushrooms and onion back to the skillet and add milk, coconut cream, thyme, and parsley. Stir and simmer for 2 minutes. Mix in black olives and turn the heat off. Let cool completely.

Storage: Place in airtight containers in the refrigerator for up to 5 days (or in the freezer for up to 3 months).

Per serving: Cal 412; Carbs 5g; Fat 33g; Protein 20g

Hot Beef Cauliflower "Pilaf"

Ingredients for 4 servings

2 tbsp olive oil	½ tsp Italian seasoning
½ lb ground beef	2 ½ cups cauliflower rice
Salt and black pepper to taste	2 tbsp tomato paste
1 yellow onion, chopped	½ cup beef broth
2 garlic cloves, minced	¼ cup chopped parsley
1 habanero pepper, minced	

Directions and Total Time: approx. 30 minutes

Warm olive oil in a skillet over medium heat and cook the beef for 8 minutes until browned. Season with salt and pepper and spoon into a plate. In the same skillet, sauté onion, garlic, and habanero pepper for 2 minutes. Mix in Italian seasoning, cauli rice, tomato paste, and broth. Season to taste and cook for 10 minutes. Mix in beef for 3 minutes. Top with parsley. Let cool.

Storage: Place in airtight containers in the refrigerator for up to 5 days (or in the freezer for up to 3 months).

Per serving: Cal 266; Carbs 8g; Fat 14g; Protein 15g

New York Steak with Shirataki Fettucine

Ingredients for 4 servings

1 cup freshly grated Pecorino Romano cheese
1 lb thick-cut New York strip steaks, cut into 1-inch cubes
2 (8 oz) packs shirataki fettuccine
Salt and black pepper to taste   4 tbsp butter
4 garlic cloves, minced   2 tbsp chopped fresh parsley

Directions and Total Time: approx. 25 minutes

Boil 2 cups of water in a pot. Strain the shirataki pasta and rinse well under hot running water. Allow proper draining and pour into the boiling water. Cook for 3 minutes and strain again. Place a dry skillet and stir-fry the shirataki pasta until visibly dry, 1-2 minutes; set aside. Melt butter in a skillet over medium heat, season the steaks with salt and pepper, and cook for 10 minutes. Stir in garlic and cook for 1 minute. Mix in parsley and shirataki; toss to coat. Top with the Pecorino Romano cheese. Let cool.

Storage: Place in airtight containers in the refrigerator for up to 5 days (or in the freezer for up to 3 months).

Per serving: Cal 522; Carbs 12g; Fats 32g; Protein 36g

Favorite Beef Fajitas

Ingredients for 4 servings

2 tbsp olive oil   2 large white onion, chopped
1 lb flank steak, cut in halves   1 cup sliced bell peppers
2 tbsp Adobo seasoning   12 low-carb tortillas

Directions and Total Time: approx. 35 minutes

Rub the steak with adobo seasoning and marinate in the fridge for 1 hour. Preheat grill and cook steak for 6 minutes on each side, flipping once. Remove from heat and wrap in foil and let sit for 10 minutes. Heat olive oil in a skillet and sauté onion and bell peppers for 5 minutes. Cut steak against the grain into strips and share on the tortillas. Top with vegetables. Let cool completely.

Storage: Place in airtight containers in the refrigerator for up to 5 days (or in the freezer for up to 3 months).

Per serving: Cal 430, Carbs 25g, Fat 21g, Protein 40g

Italian Beef Tart with Ricotta Cheese

Ingredients for 8 servings

¼ cup ricotta, crumbled   1 tbsp Italian mixed herbs
¼ cup cheddar, shredded   4 tbsp tomato paste
2 tbsp olive oil   4 tbsp coconut flour
3 tbsp coconut oil, melted   ¾ cup almond flour
1 small brown onion, chopped 4 tbsp flaxseeds
1 garlic clove, finely chopped 1 tsp baking powder
1 lb ground beef   1 egg

Directions and Total Time: approx. 1 hour 30 minutes

Preheat oven to 350 F. Line a pie dish with parchment paper. Heat olive oil in a large skillet over medium heat and sauté onion and garlic until softened, 3 minutes.

Add in beef and cook until brown. Season with herbs and stir in tomato paste and ½ cup water; reduce the heat to low. Simmer for 20 minutes; set aside.

In a food processor, add the flours, flaxseeds, baking powder, coconut oil, egg, and 4 tbsp water. Mix starting on low speed to medium until evenly combined, and a dough is formed. Spread the dough in the pie pan and bake for 12 minutes. Remove and spread the meat filling on top. Scatter with ricotta and cheddar cheeses. Bake until the cheeses melt and are golden brown on top, 35 minutes. Let cool completely. Slice.

Storage: Place in airtight containers in the refrigerator for up to 5 days (or in the freezer for up to 3 months).

Per serving: Cal 505; Carbs 13g; Fat 42g; Protein 37g

Blue Cheese and Ground Beef Bowls

Ingredients for 8 servings

¼ cup blue cheese   1 tsp garlic powder
1 cup coconut cream   Salt and black pepper to taste
2 tbsp butter   1 tbsp red wine vinegar
1 canon cabbage, shredded   1 ½ lb ground beef
1 tsp onion powder   ½ cup fresh parsley, chopped

Directions and Total Time: approx. 30 minutes

Melt butter in a deep skillet and sauté cabbage, onion and garlic powders, salt, pepper, and vinegar for 5 minutes; set aside. Add the beef to the skillet and cook until browned, frequently stirring and breaking the lumps, 10 minutes. Stir in coconut cream and blue cheese until the cheese melts, 3 minutes. Return the cabbage mixture and add parsley. Stir-fry for 2 minutes. Let cool completely.

Storage: Place in airtight containers in the refrigerator for up to 5 days (or in the freezer for up to 3 months).

Per serving: Cal 343; Carbs 4g; Fat 29g; Protein 24g

Stir-fried Chili Beef with Mixed Vegetables

Ingredients for 4 servings

1 ½ tbsp ghee   Salt and chili pepper to taste
4 tbsp peanut butter   2 tsp ginger-garlic paste
2 cups mixed vegetables   ¼ cup chicken broth
1 lb beef loin, cut into strips

Directions and Total Time: approx. 20 minutes

Melt ghee in a wok over medium heat. Rub the beef with salt, chili pepper, and ginger-garlic paste. Pour the beef into the wok and cook for 6 minutes until no longer pink. In a small bowl, mix the peanut butter with some broth, add to the beef and stir; cook for 2 minutes. Pour in the remaining broth, cook for 4 minutes and add the mixed veggies. Simmer for 5 minutes. Adjust the taste. Let cool.

Storage: Place in airtight containers in the refrigerator for up to 5 days (or in the freezer for up to 3 months).

Per serving: Cal 392, Carbs 9g, Fat 28g, Protein 33g

Philly Cheesesteak Omelet

Ingredients for 2 servings

2 oz provolone cheese, sliced	2 tbsp almond milk
2 tbsp olive oil	1 yellow onion, sliced
½ lb beef rib-eye shaved steak	½ green bell pepper, sliced
4 large eggs	Salt and black pepper to taste

Directions and Total Time: approx. 15 minutes

In a bowl, beat the eggs with milk. Heat half of the oil in a skillet and pour in half of the eggs. Fry until cooked on one side, flip, and cook until well done. Slide into a plate and fry the remaining eggs. Place them into another plate. Heat the remaining olive oil in the same skillet and sauté the onion and bell pepper for 5 minutes; set aside. Season beef with salt and pepper and cook it in the skillet until brown with no crust. Add onion and pepper back to the skillet and cook for 1 minute. Lay provolone cheese in the omelet and top with the hot meat mixture. Roll the eggs and place them back to the skillet to melt the cheese. Cool.

Storage: Place in airtight containers in the refrigerator for up to 5 days (or in the freezer for up to 3 months).

Per serving: Cal 443; Carbs 6g; Fat 31g; Protein 37g

Easy Beef Meatloaf with Balsamic Glaze

Ingredients for 6 servings

2 tbsp grated Parmesan	¼ cup mushrooms, sliced
1 lb ground beef	1 egg
1 onion, chopped	2 tbsp parsley, chopped
¼ cup almond flour	¼ cup chopped bell peppers
2 garlic cloves, minced	½ tsp balsamic vinegar

Glaze

1 cup balsamic vinegar	1 tbsp sugar-free ketchup
1 tbsp brown sugar	

Directions and Total Time: approx. 55 minutes

Combine all meatloaf ingredients in a large bowl. Press the mixture into a greased loaf pan. Bake in the preheated oven at 370 F for about 30 minutes. Combine all glaze ingredients in a saucepan over medium heat. Simmer for 10 minutes or until the glaze thickens. Spread some glaze over the meatloaf. Save the extra for future use. Put the meatloaf back in the oven and cook for 5 minutes. Cool.

Storage: Place in airtight containers in the refrigerator for up to 5 days (or in the freezer for up to 3 months).

Per serving: Cal 264; Carbs 11g; Fat 10g; Protein 23g

Beef Alfredo Spaghetti Squash

Ingredients for 6 servings

2 medium spaghetti squashes, halved

1/3 cup grated Parmesan	½ tsp garlic powder
1/3 cup grated mozzarella	Salt and black pepper to taste
2 tbsp olive oil	1 tsp cornstarch
2 tbsp butter	1 ½ cups heavy cream
1 lb ground beef	½ tsp nutmeg

Directions and Total Time: approx. 1 hour 10 minutes

Preheat oven to 375 F. Drizzle the squash with olive oil and season with salt and pepper. Place on a lined with foil baking dish and roast for 45 minutes. Let cool and shred the inner part of the noodles; set aside.

Melt butter in a pot over medium heat; add in beef, garlic powder, salt, and pepper, and cook for 10 minutes, stirring often. Stir in arrowroot starch, heavy cream, and nutmeg. Cook until the sauce thickens, 2-3 minutes. Spoon the sauce into the squashes and cover with Parmesan and mozzarella cheeses. Cook under the broiler for 3 minutes. Let cool completely.

Storage: Place in airtight containers in the refrigerator for up to 5 days (or in the freezer for up to 3 months).

Per serving: Cal 390; Carbs 4g; Fats 28g; Protein 26g

Cheesy Beef-Asparagus Shirataki Mix

Ingredients for 6 servings

2 (8 oz) packs angel hair shirataki

3 tbsp olive oil	2 shallots, finely chopped
1 lb fresh asparagus, cut into	3 garlic cloves, minced
1-inch pieces	Salt and black pepper to taste
1 lb ground beef	1 cup grated Parmesan cheese

Directions and Total Time: approx. 35 minutes

Bring 2 cups of water to a boil. Strain the shirataki pasta and rinse well under hot running water. Drain and transfer to the boiling water. Cook for 3 minutes and strain again. Place a dry skillet and stir-fry the shirataki pasta until visibly dry, 1 to 2 minutes; set aside.

Heat olive oil in a skillet and add the beef. Cook for 10 minutes. Transfer to a plate. In the same skillet, sauté asparagus for 7 minutes. Stir in shallots and garlic and cook until fragrant, 2 minutes. Season with salt and pepper. Stir in beef and shirataki and toss until combined. Let cool completely. Top with Parmesan cheese.

Storage: Place in airtight containers in the refrigerator for up to 5 days (or in the freezer for up to 3 months).

Per serving: Cal 354; Carbs 10g; Fat 19g; Protein 28g

Beef Steaks with Assorted Grilled Veggies

Ingredients for 4 servings

1 cup red and 1 cup green bell peppers, cut into strips	
4 tbsp olive oil	½ lb asparagus, trimmed
1 lb sirloin steaks	1 eggplant, sliced
Salt and black pepper to taste	2 zucchinis, sliced
3 tbsp balsamic vinegar	1 red onion, sliced

Directions and Total Time: approx. 25 minutes

Place all the vegetables in a bowl. Mix salt, pepper, olive oil, and balsamic vinegar in a separate bowl. Rub the beef all over with half of the mixture. Pour the remaining mixture over the vegetables. Let cool completely.

Heat a grill pan over medium heat. Drain the steaks and reserve the marinade. Sear the steaks in the pan on both sides for 10 minutes, flipping once halfway through; reserve. Pour the vegetables and marinade in the pan and cook for 5 minutes, turning once. Let cool completely.

Storage: Place in airtight containers in the refrigerator for up to 5 days (or in the freezer for up to 3 months).

Per serving: Cal 429; Carbs 4g; Fat 25g; Protein 32g

Country-Style Beef Ribs

Ingredients for 6 servings

4 tbsp olive oil	A pinch of mustard powder
2 lb beef ribs	1 tbsp brown sugar
3 heads garlic, cut in half	Salt and black pepper to taste
3 onions, halved	2 tbsp fresh sage, chopped
2 lemons, zested	¼ cup red wine

Directions and Total Time: approx. 50 minutes

Score shallow crisscross patterns on the meat. Mix brown sugar, mustard powder, sage, salt, pepper, and lemon zest to make a rub; apply it all over the beef, particularly into the cuts. Place garlic heads and onion halves in a baking dish, toss with olive oil and bake in the oven for 15 minutes at 410 F. Place beef on top of the onion and garlic. Pour in ¼ cup water and red wine, cover with foil and bake for 15 minutes. Remove the foil and bake for 10 minutes. Let cool completely slice the beef.

Storage: Place in airtight containers in the refrigerator for up to 5 days (or in the freezer for up to 3 months).

Per serving: Cal 570; Carbs 10g; Fat 49g; Protein 27g

Coconut Swedish Meatballs

Ingredients for 4 servings

½ cup coconut cream	Salt and black pepper to taste
2 tbsp olive oil	2 tbsp almond flour
2 tbsp butter	1 cup beef broth
1 lb ground beef	¼ freshly chopped dill
1 tsp garlic powder	¼ cup chopped parsley
1 tsp onion powder	

Directions and Total Time: approx. 30 minutes

Preheat oven to 400 F. In a bowl, combine beef, garlic powder, onion powder, salt, and pepper. Form meatballs from the mixture and place them on a greased baking sheet. Drizzle with olive oil and bake until the meat cooks, 10-15 minutes. Remove the baking sheet. Melt butter in a saucepan and stir in almond flour until smooth. Gradually mix in broth, while stirring until thickened, 2 minutes. Stir in coconut cream and dill, simmer for 1 minute and stir in meatballs. Spoon the meatballs with sauce onto airtight containers and top with parsley. Let cool completely.

Storage: Keep in the refrigerator for up to 5 days (or in the freezer for up to 3 months).

Per serving: Cal 459; Carbs 2g; Fat 32g; Protein 33g

Thai Beef Shirataki

Ingredients for 4 servings

2 (8 oz) packs angel hair shirataki
1 cup sliced shiitake mushrooms

2 tbsp olive oil	2 tbsp toasted sesame seeds
1 lb flank steak, sliced	1 tbsp chopped peanuts
1 white onion, thinly sliced	1 tbsp chopped scallions
1 red bell pepper, sliced	3 tbsp coconut aminos
2 garlic cloves, minced	2 tbsp fish sauce
2 tbsp Thai basil, chopped	1 tbsp hot sauce

Directions and Total Time: approx. 30 minutes

Boil 2 cups of water. Strain the shirataki pasta and rinse very well under hot running water. Allow proper draining and pour the shirataki pasta into the boiling water. Cook for 3 minutes and strain again. Place a dry skillet and stir-fry the shirataki until visibly dry, 1-2 minutes; set aside.

Heat olive oil in a skillet and sear the beef on both sides until brown, 10 minutes; set aside. Add onion, bell pepper, garlic, and mushrooms to the skillet and sauté for 5 minutes. Return the beef to the skillet and add the pasta. Combine aminos, fish sauce, and hot sauce in a bowl.

Pour the mixture over the beef. Top with Thai basil and toss to coat. Cook for 1-2 minutes. Let cool completely. Top with sesame seeds, peanuts, and scallions.

Storage: Place in airtight containers in the refrigerator for up to 5 days (or in the freezer for up to 3 months).

Per serving: Cal 358; Carbs 7g; Fats 18g; Protein 27g

Taco-Seasoned Beef Pizza

Ingredients for 6 servings

2 cups shredded mozzarella	2 eggs, beaten
2 cups Mexican 4 cheese blend	1 lb ground beef
2 tbsp cream cheese, softened	2 tsp taco seasoning
2 tbsp olive oil	½ cup chicken broth
¾ cup almond flour	1 ½ cups salsa

Directions and Total Time: approx. 50 minutes

Preheat oven to 390 F. Line a pizza pan with parchment paper. Microwave 2 cups of mozzarella cheese and cream cheese for 30 seconds. Remove and mix in almond flour and eggs. Spread the mixture on the pizza pan and bake for 15 minutes.

Warm olive oil in a pan over medium heat and cook the ground beef for 5 minutes. Stir in taco seasoning and chicken broth. Cook for 3 minutes. Mix in salsa. Spread the beef mixture onto the crust and scatter the Mexican cheese blend on top. Bake until the cheese melts, 15 minutes. Slice and let cool completely.

Storage: Place in airtight containers in the refrigerator for up to 5 days (or in the freezer for up to 3 months).

Per serving: Cal 432; Carbs 8g; Fats 31g; Protein 27g

New York-Style Beef Steaks

Ingredients for 4 servings

½ cup half-and-half	1 red onion, chopped
1 tbsp olive oil	½ cup beef stock
1 tbsp butter	1 tbsp yellow mustard
2 tbsp rosemary, chopped	2 tsp lemon juice
1 tbsp garlic powder	A sprig of sage
4 beef steaks	Salt and black pepper to taste

Directions and Total Time: approx. 25 minutes

Rub olive oil and garlic powder all over the steaks and season with salt and pepper. Heat butter in a pan, place in beef steaks, and cook for 6 minutes, flipping once; set aside. In the same pan, add red onion and cook for 3 minutes until tender. Stir in beef stock, half-and-half, yellow mustard, and sage sprig and cook for 8 minutes. Stir in lemon juice, salt, and pepper. Remove and discard the sage sprig. Sprinkle with rosemary. Let cool completely.

Storage: Place in airtight containers in the refrigerator for up to 5 days (or in the freezer for up to 3 months).

Per serving: Cal 481; Carbs 10g; Fat 32g; Protein 43g

Sirloin Tacos with Guacamole

Ingredients for 8 servings

2 tbsp olive oil	Salt to taste
2 lb sirloin steak, cut into strips	2 shallots, sliced
2 tbsp Cajun seasoning	1 red bell pepper, sliced
4 oz guacamole	8 zero-carb tortillas

Directions and Total Time: approx. 90 minutes

Rub the steaks all over with Cajun seasoning and place in the fridge for 1 hour. Preheat grill to high. Remove the steaks and grill them for 6 minutes per side. Wrap in foil and let sit for 10 minutes. Heat olive oil in a skillet and sauté shallots and bell pepper for 5 minutes. Let cool.

Storage: Place in airtight containers in the refrigerator for up to 5 days (or in the freezer for up to 3 months). Before serving, reheat in the microwave for 1-2 minutes. Share the strips in the tortillas and top with veggies and guacamole.

Per serving: Cal 381; Carbs 5g; Fat 21g; Protein 24g

Beef & Cauli Rice Gratin with Cabbage

Ingredients for 4 servings

1 cup shredded Gouda cheese	1 cup cauliflower rice
2 tbsp olive oil	2 cups shredded cabbage
1 lb ground beef	14 oz canned diced tomatoes

Directions and Total Time: approx. 30 minutes

Preheat oven to 370 F. Warm olive oil in a saucepan over medium heat and sauté the beef for 6 minutes. Add in cauli rice, cabbage, tomatoes, and ¼ cup water. Stir and bring to a boil for 5 minutes to thicken the sauce. Spoon the beef mixture onto a greased baking dish. Sprinkle with cheese and bake for 15 minutes. Let cool completely.

Storage: Place in airtight containers in the refrigerator for up to 5 days (or in the freezer for up to 3 months).

Per serving: Cal 385, Carbs 5g, Fat 30g, Protein 25g

Simple Bolognese Sauce

Ingredients for 4 servings

1 tbsp olive oil	½ tsp oregano
1 lb ground beef	½ tsp marjoram
2 garlic cloves, minced	½ tsp rosemary
1 onion, chopped	7 oz canned tomatoes, diced

Directions and Total Time: approx. 30 minutes

Heat olive oil in a saucepan over medium heat. Sauté onion and garlic for 3 minutes until softened. Add beef and cook until browned, about 5 minutes. Stir in herbs and tomatoes. Cook for 15 minutes. Let cool completely.

Storage: Place in airtight containers in the refrigerator for up to 5 days (or in the freezer for up to 3 months).

Per serving: Cal 358; Carbs 13g; Fat 27g; Protein 20g

Cuban Picadillo

Ingredients for 4 servings

2 tbsp olive oil	1 tbsp dried sage
1 lb ground beef	Salt and black pepper to taste
1 onion, chopped	2 carrots, sliced
2 garlic cloves, minced	2 celery stalks, chopped
14 oz canned diced tomatoes	1 cup vegetable broth

Directions and Total Time: approx. 35 minutes

Warm olive oil in a pan over medium heat. Sauté onion, celery, and garlic for 5 minutes. Add in ground beef and cook for 6 minutes. Pour in tomatoes, carrots, broth, salt, pepper, and sage. Simmer for 15 minutes. Let cool.

Storage: Place in airtight containers in the refrigerator for up to 5 days (or in the freezer for up to 2 months).

Per serving: Cal 353, Carbs 11g, Fat 25g, Protein 23g

Beef & Zucchini Mugs

Ingredients for 4 servings

8 oz roast beef deli slices, torn apart	
6 oz shredded cheddar cheese	2 small zucchini, sliced
5 tbsp sour cream	2 tbsp chopped green chilies

Directions and Total Time: approx. 10 minutes

Place the beef slices on the bottom of 4 wide mugs and spread 1 tbsp of sour cream. Top with 2 zucchini slices and green chilies. Pour the remaining sour cream over and sprinkle with cheddar cheese. Place the mugs in the microwave for 1-2 minutes until the cheese melts. Remove the mugs and let cool completely.

Storage: Place in airtight containers in the refrigerator for up to 5 days (or in the freezer for up to 3 months).

Per serving: Cal 238; Carbs 10g; Fat 19g; Protein 24g

Beef Burger Bake

Ingredients for 6 servings

¼ cup shredded Monterey Jack cheese

1 cup coconut cream	2 tomatoes, chopped
1 tbsp butter	1 tbsp dried basil
1 lb ground beef	Salt and black pepper to taste
1 garlic clove, minced	2 eggs
1 red onion, chopped	2 tbsp tomato paste

Directions and Total Time: approx. 35 minutes

Preheat oven to 400 F. Melt the butter in a large skillet over medium heat and add the beef. Cook for 6 minutes. Stir in garlic and onion and cook for another 3 minutes. Mix in tomatoes, basil, salt, and pepper until the tomatoes soften. Add 2/3 of Monterey Jack cheese and stir to melt. In a bowl, crack the eggs and whisk with tomato paste, salt, and coconut cream. Spoon the beef mixture into a greased baking sheet and spread the egg mixture on top. Sprinkle with the remaining cheese and bake for 20 minutes. Cool.

Storage: Place in airtight containers in the refrigerator for up to 5 days (or in the freezer for up to 3 months).

Per serving: Cal 361; Carbs 8g; Fat 26g; Protein 27g

Beef Zucchini Boats

Ingredients for 4 servings

1 ¼ cups shredded cheddar	1 red bell pepper, chopped
2 tbsp butter	2 garlic cloves, minced
1 tbsp olive oil	1 shallot, finely chopped
2 zucchinis	2 tbsp taco seasoning
1 lb ground beef	½ cup finely chopped parsley

Directions and Total Time: approx. 45 minutes

Preheat oven to 400 F. Grease a baking sheet with cooking spray. Using a knife, cut zucchini into halves and scoop out the pulp; set aside. Chop the flesh. Melt the butter in a skillet over medium heat and cook the beef until brown, frequently stirring and breaking the lumps, 10 minutes. Stir in bell pepper, zucchini pulp, garlic, shallot, and taco seasoning and cook until softened, 5 minutes. Place the boats on the baking sheet with the open side up. Spoon in the beef mixture, divide the parsley on top, drizzle with olive oil, and top with cheddar cheese. Bake for 20 minutes until the cheese melts and is golden brown on top.

Storage: Place in airtight containers in the refrigerator for up to 5 days (or in the freezer for up to 3 months).

Per serving: Cal 495; Carbs 8g; Fat 33g; Protein 43g

Beef Spaghetti with Veggies

Ingredients for 8 servings

1 ½ lb ground beef	4 cloves garlic, minced
1 lb whole wheat spaghetti	1 (14-oz) can diced tomatoes
2 cups cherry tomatoes, halved	2 tbsp olive oil
2 cups spinach, chopped	1 tsp dried oregano
1 onion, chopped	Salt and black pepper to taste

Directions and Total Time: approx. 25 minutes

Cook the whole wheat spaghetti according to package instructions. In a large skillet, heat olive oil over medium heat. Add diced onion and minced garlic. Cook until softened. Stir in ground beef and cook until browned, 4-6 minutes. Add in cherry tomatoes, chopped spinach, dried oregano, and dried basil. Cook until the spinach wilts. Pour in crushed tomatoes and mix well. Simmer for 10-15 minutes. Season with salt and pepper. Add the cooked whole wheat spaghetti to the skillet. Toss until well combined. Allow the dish to cool.

Storage:

Divide into airtight 8 containers for up to 5 days (or in the freezer for up to 3 months). Top with Parmesan cheese when serving if desired.

Per serving: Cal 472; Carbs 45g; Fats 17g; Protein 33g

Authentic Salisbury Steak

Ingredients for 6 servings

1 lb ground beef	¼ cup beef broth
1 tbsp onion flakes	1 tbsp chopped parsley
¾ cup almond flour	1 tbsp Worcestershire sauce

Directions and Total Time: approx. 35 minutes

Combine all ingredients in a bowl. Mix well and make 6 patties out of the mixture. Arrange them on a lined baking sheet. Bake in the oven at 375 F for 25-30 minutes. Cool.

Storage: Place in airtight containers in the refrigerator for up to 5 days (or in the freezer for up to 3 months).

Per serving: Cal 255; Carbs 13g; Fat 10g; Protein 23g

Beef & Cheese Avocado Boats

Ingredients for 4 servings

4 tbsp grated Monterey Jack	2 tsp taco seasoning
4 tbsp sour cream	2 tsp smoked paprika
2 tbsp avocado oil	½ cup raw pecans, chopped
1 lb ground beef	1 tbsp hemp seeds, hulled
Salt and black pepper to taste	2 avocados, halved and pitted
1 tsp onion powder	1 medium tomato, sliced
1 tsp cumin powder	¼ iceberg lettuce, shredded
1 tsp garlic powder	

Directions and Total Time: approx. 30 minutes

Heat half of avocado oil in a skillet and cook beef for 10 minutes. Season with salt, pepper, onion powder, cumin, garlic, taco seasoning, and smoked paprika. Add the pecans and hemp seeds and stir-fry for 10 minutes. Fold in 2 tbsp Monterey Jack cheese to melt. Let cool completely.

Spoon the filling into avocado holes, top with 1-2 slices of tomatoes, some lettuce, 1 tbsp each of sour cream, and the remaining Monterey Jack cheese.

Storage: Place in airtight containers in the refrigerator for up to 3 days.

Per serving: Cal 523; Carbs 14g; Fat 34g; Protein 42g

Korean-Style Rib-Eye Steak

Ingredients for 4 servings

1 lb rib-eye steak, sliced into ¼-inch strips
2 tbsp olive oil
1 tbsp coconut oil
1 tsp sesame oil
2 tsp maple syrup
Salt and black pepper to taste
1 tbsp coconut flour
½ tsp xanthan gum
1 tsp freshly pureed ginger
1 clove garlic, minced

1 red chili, minced
4 tbsp tamari sauce
1 tsp fish sauce
2 tbsp white wine vinegar
1 tsp hot sauce
1 small bok choy, quartered
½ jalapeño, sliced into rings
1 tbsp toasted sesame seeds
1 scallion, chopped

Directions and Total Time: approx. 20 minutes

Season the beef with salt and pepper and rub with coconut flour and xanthan gum; set aside. Heat olive oil in a skillet and fry the beef until brown on all sides. Heat coconut oil in a wok and sauté ginger, garlic, red chili, and bok choy for 5 minutes. Mix in tamari sauce, sesame oil, fish sauce, vinegar, hot sauce, and maple syrup; cook for 2 minutes. Add the beef and cook for 2 minutes. Let cool completely. Top with jalapeño pepper, scallion, and sesame seeds.

Storage: Place in airtight containers in the refrigerator for up to 5 days (or in the freezer for up to 3 months).

Per serving: Cal 442; Carbs 6g; Fat 26g; Protein 33g

Sunday Beef Ragu with Vegetable Pasta

Ingredients for 4 servings

1 cup grated Parmesan cheese
2 tbsp butter
1 lb ground beef
8 mixed bell peppers, spiralized

Salt and black pepper to taste
¼ cup tomato sauce
1 small red onion, spiralized

Directions and Total Time: approx. 30 minutes

Heat the butter in a skillet and cook the beef until brown, 10 minutes. Season with salt and pepper. Stir in tomato sauce and cook for 10 minutes, until the sauce reduces by a quarter. Add in bell pepper and onion noodles and cook for 1 minute. Top with Parmesan cheese. Let cool.

Storage: Place in airtight containers in the refrigerator for up to 5 days (or in the freezer for up to 3 months).

Per serving: Cal 431; Carbs 12g; Fats 25g; Protein 38g

Cowboy Steaks with Shiitake Mushrooms

Ingredients for 6 servings

2 cups shiitake mushrooms, sliced
2 tbsp butter
2 tsp olive oil

2 rib-eye steaks
Salt and black pepper to taste

Directions and Total Time: approx. 20 minutes

Heat olive oil in a pan over medium heat. Rub the steaks with salt and pepper and cook for 4 minutes per side; reserve. Melt butter in the pan and sauté shiitakes for 6 minutes. Pour the mushrooms over the steaks. Let cool.

Storage: Place in airtight containers in the refrigerator for up to 5 days (or in the freezer for up to 3 months).

Per serving: Cal 435; Carbs 1g; Fat 33g; Protein 30g

Beef Pinwheels

Ingredients for 4 servings

1 cup cotija cheese, crumbled
1 lb flank steak
1 cup kale

1 habanero pepper, chopped
2 tbsp cilantro, chopped

Directions and Total Time: approx. 40 minutes

Cover the meat with plastic wrap on a flat surface and flatten with a mallet. Take off the wraps. Sprinkle with half of the cheese, top with kale, habanero pepper, cilantro, and the remaining cheese. Roll the steak over on the stuffing and secure with toothpicks. Place on a greased baking sheet and cook in the oven for 30 minutes at 400 F, flipping once. Cool completely and slice into pinwheels.

Storage: Place in airtight containers in the refrigerator for up to 5 days.

Per serving: Cal 349; Carbs 2g; Fat 22g; Protein 33g

Italian Stuffed Mushrooms

Ingredients for 6 servings

½ cup shredded Pecorino Romano cheese
2 tbsp shredded Parmesan
2 tbsp olive oil
½ celery stalk, chopped
1 shallot, finely chopped
1 lb ground beef
2 tbsp mayonnaise
1 tsp Old Bay seasoning

½ tsp garlic powder
2 large eggs
6 Portobello mushroom caps
1 tbsp corn flour
1 tbsp chopped parsley

Directions and Total Time: approx. 50 minutes

Preheat oven to 350 F. Heat olive oil in a skillet and sauté celery and shallot for 3 minutes; set aside. Add beef to the skillet and cook for 10 minutes; add to the shallot mixture. Pour in mayonnaise, Old Bay seasoning, garlic powder, and Pecorino cheese and crack in the eggs. Combine the mix evenly. Arrange the mushrooms on a greased baking sheet and fill with the meat mixture. Combine corn flour and Parmesan cheese in a bowl and sprinkle over the mushroom filling. Bake until the cheese melts, 30 minutes. Top with parsley. Let cool completely.

Storage: Place in airtight containers in the refrigerator for up to 5 days (or in the freezer for up to 3 months).

Per serving: Cal 310; Carbs 6g; Fat 28g; Protein 18g

Asian-Style Braised Beef with Kelp Noodles

Ingredients for 4 servings

1 ½ lb sirloin steak, cut into strips
2 (16- oz) packs kelp noodles, thoroughly rinsed
1 tbsp coconut oil
2 pieces star anise

1 cinnamon stick
1 garlic clove, minced

1-inch ginger, grated
3 tbsp coconut aminos
2 tbsp brown sugar
¼ cup red wine

4 cups beef broth
1 head napa cabbage, steamed
2 tbsp scallions, thinly sliced

Directions and Total Time: approx. 2 hours

Heat oil in a pot over and sauté anise, cinnamon, garlic, and ginger until fragrant, 5 minutes. Add in beef and sear it on both sides, 10 minutes. In a bowl, combine aminos, brown sugar, red wine, and ¼ cup water. Pour the mixture into the pot, close the lid, and bring to a boil. Reduce the heat and simmer for 1 to 1 ½ hours or until the meat is tender. Strain the pot's content through a colander into a bowl and pour the braising liquid back into the pot. Discard cinnamon and anise and set aside. Add beef broth and simmer for 10 minutes. Put kelp noodles in the broth and cook until softened and separated, 6 minutes. Let cool completely. Spoon the noodles and some broth into airtight containers, add beef strips, cabbage, and scallions.

Storage: Place in the refrigerator for up to 5 days (or in the freezer for up to 3 months).

Per serving: Cal 528; Carbs 38g; Fat 25g; Protein 44g

Beef Stuffed Collard Wraps

Ingredients for 6 servings

1 tbsp butter
2 lb corned beef
Salt and black pepper to taste
2 tsp Worcestershire sauce
1 tsp Dijon mustard
1 tsp whole peppercorns
¼ tsp cloves
¼ tsp allspice

½ tsp red pepper flakes
1 large bay leaf
1 lemon, zested and juiced
¼ cup white wine
¼ cup freshly brewed coffee
2/3 tbsp brown sugar
8 large Swiss collard leaves
1 medium red onion, sliced

Directions and Total Time: approx. 80 minutes

In a pot, add beef, butter, salt, pepper, Worcestershire sauce, mustard, peppercorns, cloves, allspice, red pepper flakes, bay leaf, lemon zest, lemon juice, white wine, coffee, and brown sugar. Close the lid and cook over low heat for 1 hour. Ten minutes before the end, bring a pot of water to a boil, add collards with one slice of onion for 30 seconds and transfer them to an ice bath; let them sit for 2-3 minutes. Remove, pat dry, and lay on a flat surface. Remove the meat from the pot, place it on a cutting board, and slice. Divide the meat between the collards, top with onion slices, and roll the leaves. Let cool completely.

Storage: Place in airtight containers in the refrigerator for up to 5 days (or in the freezer for up to 3 months).

Per serving: Cal 359; Carbs 12g; Fat 23g; Protein 41g

Hot Meatballs Over Homemade Pasta

Ingredients for 6 servings

1 cup crumbled feta cheese
1 cup shredded mozzarella
½ cup olive oil

1 egg yolk
1 yellow onion, chopped
6 garlic cloves, minced

2 tbsp tomato paste
2 large tomatoes, chopped
¼ tsp saffron powder
2 cinnamon sticks
1 cup chicken broth
Salt and black pepper to taste
1 cup breadcrumbs
1 lb ground beef
1 egg
¼ cup almond milk

¼ tsp nutmeg powder
1 tbsp smoked paprika
1 ½ tsp fresh ginger paste
1 tsp cumin powder
½ tsp cayenne pepper
½ tsp clove powder
4 tbsp chopped cilantro
4 tbsp chopped scallions
4 tbsp chopped parsley
¼ cup almond flour

Directions and Total Time: approx. 2 hours 50 minutes

Microwave mozzarella cheese for 2 minutes. Mix in egg yolk until combined. Lay parchment paper on a flat surface, pour the cheese mixture on top, and cover with another parchment paper piece. Flatten the dough into 1/8-inch thickness. Take off the parchment paper.

Cut the dough into spaghetti strands; refrigerate for 2 hours. When ready, bring 2 cups of water to a boil in a saucepan and add the "pasta". Cook for 1 minute, drain and let cool. In a pot, heat 2 tbsp of olive oil and sauté onion and half of the garlic for 3 minutes. Stir in tomato paste, tomatoes, saffron, and cinnamon; cook for 2 minutes. Mix in chicken broth, salt, and pepper. Simmer for 10 minutes.

In a bowl, mix crumbs, beef, egg, almond milk, remaining garlic, salt, pepper, nutmeg, paprika, ginger, cumin, cayenne, clove powder, cilantro, parsley, 3 tbsp of scallions, and almond flour. Form balls out of the mixture. Heat the remaining olive oil in a skillet and fry the meatballs for 10 minutes. Place them into the sauce and continue cooking for 5-10 minutes. Divide the pasta into airtight containers and spoon the meatballs with sauce on top. Let cool completely.

Storage: Keep in the refrigerator for up to 5 days (or in the freezer for up to 3 months). To serve, reheat in the microwave for 1-2 minutes. Garnish with feta cheese and scallions.

Per serving: Cal 506; Carbs 13g; Fat 35g; Protein 38g

Greek-Style Beef Salad

Ingredients for 4 servings

½ cup feta cheese, crumbled
1 taste olive oil
1 lb skirt steak, sliced
Salt and black pepper to taste

4 radishes, sliced
1 ½ cups mixed salad greens
3 chopped pickled peppers
2 tbsp red wine vinaigrette

Directions and Total Time: approx. 15 minutes

Brush steaks with olive oil and season with salt and pepper. Heat a pan over medium heat and cook steaks for about 5-6 minutes in total. Remove and let cool completely.

Storage: Place in airtight containers in the refrigerator for up to 5 days (or in the freezer for up to 3 months). Before serving, reheat in the microwave for 1-2 minutes. Mix the salad greens, radishes, pickled peppers, and vinaigrette in a salad bowl. Top with the beef slices and sprinkle with feta.

Per serving: Cal 464, Carbs 11g, Fat 24g, Protein 32g

Chili Beef with Spiralized Parsnips

Ingredients for 6 servings

1 cup grated Parmesan cheese   3 tbsp butter
1 ¼ cups heavy cream
1 lb beef stew meat, cut into strips
1 cup sun-dried tomatoes in oil, chopped
Salt and black pepper to taste   ¼ tsp dried basil
4 large parsnips, spiralized   ¼ tsp red chili flakes
4 garlic cloves, minced   2 tbsp chopped parsley

Directions and Total Time: approx. 30 minutes

Melt butter in a skillet over medium heat and sauté the parsnips until softened, 5-7 minutes; set aside. Season the beef with salt and pepper and add to the same skillet; cook until brown, 8-10 minutes. Stir in sun-dried tomatoes and garlic and cook until fragrant, 1 minute. Reduce the heat to low and stir in heavy cream and Parmesan cheese. Simmer until the cheese melts. Sprinkle with basil and red chili flakes. Fold in the parsnips until well coated and cook for 2 more minutes. Top with parsley. Let cool completely.

Storage: Place in airtight containers in the refrigerator for up to 5 days (or in the freezer for up to 3 months).

Per serving: Cal 387; Carbs 26g; Fats 23g; Protein 25g

BBQ Swiss-Style Pizza

Ingredients for 6 servings

1 cup grated mozzarella   ¼ cup BBQ sauce
1 ½ cups grated Gruyere   ¼ cup sliced red onion
1 lb ground beef   2 bacon slices, chopped
2 eggs, beaten

Directions and Total Time: approx. 45 minutes

Preheat oven to 390 F. Line a round pizza pan with parchment paper. In a bowl, mix beef, mozzarella cheese, and eggs. Spread the pizza "dough" on the pan and bake for 20 minutes. Spread BBQ sauce on top, scatter Gruyere cheese all over, followed by the red onion and bacon slices. Bake for 15 minutes or until the cheese has melted and the back is crispy. Let cool completely.

Storage: Place in airtight containers in the refrigerator for up to 5 days (or in the freezer for up to 3 months).

Per serving: Cal 538; Carbs 6g; Fats 32g; Protein 46g

Cheesy Beef Zucchini Canapés

Ingredients for 4 servings

1 cup Colby cheese, grated   1 lb ground beef
2 tbsp olive oil   1 red onion, chopped
4 zucchinis   2 tbsp chopped pimiento

Directions and Total Time: approx. 30 minutes

Preheat oven to 350 F. Slice the zucchini into rounds; set aside. Heat oil in a skillet and sauté the ground beef, red onion, and red pepper for 6 minutes. Arrange the zucchini rounds on a greased baking dish.

Spoon the beef over the zucchini and sprinkle with Colby cheese. Bake in the oven for 15 minutes. Let cool completely.

Storage: Place in airtight containers in the refrigerator for up to 5 days (or in the freezer for up to 3 months).

Per serving: Cal 435, Carbs 4g, Fat 28g, Protein 41g

Mom's Beef Meatza

Ingredients for 6 servings

¼ cup shredded Parmesan   1 tsp rosemary
1 cup shredded Pepper Jack   1 tsp thyme
1 cup shredded mozzarella   3 garlic cloves, minced
1 ½ lb ground beef   1 tsp basil
Salt and black pepper to taste   ½ tbsp oregano
1 large egg   ¾ cup tomato sauce

Directions and Total Time: approx. 30 minutes

Preheat oven to 350 F. In a bowl, combine beef, salt, pepper, egg, rosemary, thyme, garlic, basil, and oregano. Transfer the mixture to a greased baking pan, and using your hands, flatten to a two-inch thickness. Bake for 15 minutes until the beef has a light brown crust. Remove and spread tomato sauce on top. Sprinkle with Parmesan, Pepper Jack, and mozzarella cheeses. Return to oven to bake until the cheeses melt, 5 minutes. Let cool completely.

Storage: Place in airtight containers in the refrigerator for up to 5 days (or in the freezer for up to 3 months).

Per serving: Cal 453; Carbs 9g; Fat 28g; Protein 44g

Breakfast Beef Bowls

Ingredients for 4 servings

1 lb beef sirloin, cut into strips
2 tbsp coconut oil
2 tbsp olive oil   1 tbsp brown sugar
¼ cup tamari sauce   6 garlic cloves, minced
2 tbsp lemon juice   1 lb cauliflower rice
3 tsp garlic powder   4 large eggs
   2 tbsp chopped scallions

Directions and Total Time: approx. 2 hours 30 minutes

In a bowl, mix tamari sauce, lemon juice, garlic powder, and brown sugar. Pour beef into a zipper bag and add in the mixture. Massage the meat to coat well. Refrigerate for 2 hours. Heat coconut oil in a wok and fry the beef until the liquid evaporates and the meat cooks through, 12 minutes; set aside. Sauté garlic for 1 minute in the same wok. Mix in cauli rice until softened, 5 minutes. Spoon into airtight containers and set aside. Wipe the wok clean and heat the olive oil. Crack in the eggs and fry sunshine-style, 1 minute. Place an egg on each cauliflower rice container. Top with scallions. Let cool completely.

Storage: Keep in the refrigerator for up to 5 days.

Per serving: Cal 466; Carbs 12g; Fat 32g; Protein 34g

PORK

Pork Chops with Lemony Asparagus

Ingredients for 4 servings

4 tbsp butter	1 lb asparagus, trimmed
4 pork chops	1 tbsp dried cilantro
Salt and black pepper to taste	1 small lemon, juiced
2 garlic cloves, minced	

Directions and Total Time: approx. 25 minutes

Melt 2 tbsp of butter in a skillet over medium heat. Season pork chops with salt and pepper and fry on both sides until brown, 10 minutes in total; set aside. Melt the remaining butter in the skillet and sauté garlic until fragrant, 1 minute. Add in asparagus and cook until slightly softened with some crunch, 4 minutes. Add cilantro and lemon juice and toss to coat well. Let cool completely.

Storage: Place in airtight containers in the refrigerator for up to 5 days (or in the freezer for up to 2 months).

Per serving: Cal 443; Carbs 7g; Fat 28g; Protein 42g

Green Pork Stir-Fry with Avocado

Ingredients for 4 servings

2 tbsp avocado oil	Salt and black pepper to taste
4 pork shoulder chops	6 green onions, chopped
1 ½ cups green beans	1 tbsp chopped parsley
2 large avocados, chopped	

Directions and Total Time: approx. 30 minutes

Heat avocado oil in a skillet, season pork with salt and pepper, and fry until brown, 12 minutes; set aside. To the same skillet, sauté green beans until sweating and slightly softened, 10 minutes. Mix in avocados and green onions and cook for 2 minutes. Top with parsley. Let cool.

Storage: Place in airtight containers in the refrigerator for up to 5 days (or in the freezer for up to 2 months).

Per serving: Cal 557; Carbs 14g; Fat 36g; Protein 43g

Spare Ribs with Béarnaise Sauce

Ingredients for 8 servings

3 tbsp butter, melted	2 tsp white wine vinegar
4 tbsp olive oil	½ tsp onion powder
4 egg yolks, beaten	Salt and black pepper to taste
2 tbsp chopped tarragon	2 lb spare ribs, divided into 8

Directions and Total Time: approx. 20 minutes

In a bowl, whisk butter gradually into the egg yolks until evenly mixed. In another bowl, combine tarragon, white wine vinegar, and onion powder. Mix into the egg mixture and season with salt and black pepper; reserve the sauce.

Warm the olive oil in a skillet over medium heat. Season the spare ribs on both sides with salt and pepper.

Cook in the oil on both sides until brown, 12 minutes. Divide the spareribs between airtight containers and pour the béarnaise sauce all over. Let cool completely.

Storage: Keep in the refrigerator for up to 5 days (or in the freezer for up to 2 months).

Per serving: Cal 481; Carbs 2g; Fat 36g; Protein 23g

Slow-Cooked Pork Stew

Ingredients for 6 servings

½ lb snow peas, halved crosswise	
2 tbsp olive oil	2 ½ cups chicken broth
½ lb sweet potatoes, diced	1 tbsp tomato paste
1 ½ lb pork stew meat	1 tbsp Worcestershire sauce
1 parsnip, chopped	1 tsp dried thyme
1 yellow onion, chopped	1 tsp paprika
1 celery stalk, chopped	Salt and black pepper to taste
2 garlic cloves, minced	

Directions and Total Time: approx. 4 hours 10 minutes

Combine the olive oil, sweet potatoes, pork, parsnip, snow peas, onion, celery, and garlic in your slow cooker. In a bowl, mix the broth, tomato paste, Worcestershire sauce, thyme, paprika, salt, and black pepper. Pour the mixture into the slow cooker and stir to combine. Cover and cook for 4 hours on High. Let cool completely.

Storage: Place in airtight containers in the refrigerator for up to 7 days (or in the freezer for up to 2 months).

Per serving: Cal 388; Carbs 17g; Fat 23g, Protein 35g

Pork Roast with Brussels Sprouts

Ingredients for 6 servings

1 ½ cups coconut cream	5 black peppercorns
1 tbsp coconut oil	2 ½ cups beef broth
2 lb pork roast	2 garlic cloves, minced
Salt and black pepper to taste	1 ½ oz fresh ginger, grated
2 tsp dried thyme	1 tbsp smoked paprika
1 bay leaf	½ lb Brussel sprouts, halved

Directions and Total Time: approx. 2 hours

Preheat oven to 360 F. Place the pork in a baking dish and season with salt, pepper, and thyme. Pour the broth over, add in bay leaf and peppercorns, and cover with aluminum foil. Bake for 90 minutes. Remove the foil and discard the cooking juices into a bowl; reserve. In a bowl, combine garlic, ginger, coconut oil, and paprika. Rub the mixture onto the meat and roast for 8 more minutes or until golden brown. Remove, slice thinly, and let cool completely. Strain the juices through a colander into a pot and simmer until reduced to about 1 ½ cups. Pour in Brussels sprouts and cook for 10 minutes. Stir in coconut cream and cook for 5 minutes. Leave to cool completely.

Storage: Place in airtight containers in the refrigerator for up to 5 days (or in the freezer for up to 2 months).

Per serving: Cal 523; Carbs 11g; Fat 43g; Protein 47g

Pork and Mushroom Meatballs

Ingredients for 12 servings

1 cup cremini mushrooms, chopped
1 cup grated Parmesan
½ cup coconut cream
2 tbsp olive oil
2 tbsp butter
1 ½ lb ground pork
2 garlic cloves, minced
2 small red onions, chopped

1 tsp dried basil
Salt and black pepper to taste
½ almond milk
2 cups tomato sauce
6 fresh basil leaves to garnish
1 lb parsnips, chopped
1 cup water

Directions and Total Time: approx. 70 minutes

Preheat oven to 350 F. Line a baking tray with parchment paper. In a bowl, add pork, half of the garlic, half of the onion, mushrooms, basil, salt, and pepper and mix until evenly combined. Mold 12 bite-size balls out of the mixture. Pour ½ cup Parmesan cheese and almond milk each in 2 separate bowls. Dip the balls in the milk and then in the cheese. Place on the tray and bake for 20 minutes.

Heat olive oil in a saucepan and sauté the remaining onion and garlic; sauté until fragrant and soft. Pour in tomato sauce and cook for 20 minutes. Add in the meatballs and simmer for 7 minutes. In a pot, add parsnips, 1 cup water, and salt. Bring to a boil and cook for 10 minutes until the parsnips soften. Drain and pour into a bowl. Add butter, salt, and pepper; mash into a puree using a potato mash. Stir in coconut cream and remaining Parmesan cheese until combined. Spoon mashed parsnip into airtight containers, top with meatballs and sauce, and garnish with basil leaves. Let cool completely.

Storage: Keep in the refrigerator for up to 5 days (or in the freezer for up to 2 months).

Per serving: Cal 213; Carbs 7g; Fat 11g; Protein 17g

Pork Camembert Fondu

Ingredients for 4 servings

10 oz whole Camembert cheese
½ lb boneless pork chops, cut into small cubes
2 tbsp olive oil
2 oz pecans
1 garlic clove, minced
1 tbsp chopped parsley

Directions and Total Time: approx. 40 minutes

Preheat oven to 400 F. While the cheese is in its box, using a knife, score around the top and side of about a ¼-inch and take off the top layer of the skin. Place the cheese on a baking tray and melt in the oven for 10 minutes.

Meanwhile, heat olive oil in a skillet and fry the pork until brown on all sides, 12 minutes. Transfer to a bowl and add pecans, garlic, and parsley. Spoon the pork mixture onto the melted cheese and bake in the oven for 10 minutes until the cheese softens and the nuts toast. Let cool completely.

Storage: Place in airtight containers in the refrigerator for up to 5 days (or in the freezer for up to 2 months).

Per serving: Cal 452; Carbs 2g; Fat 27g; Protein 25g

Lemony Pork Chops with Capers

Ingredients for 4 servings

1 tbsp avocado oil
3 tbsp butter
1 lb cut pork chops, boneless
½ lemon, juiced
2 tbsp capers
1 cup beef broth
2 tbsp chopped parsley

Directions and Total Time: approx. 30 minutes

Heat avocado oil in a skillet and cook pork chops on both sides until brown, 14 minutes. Set aside. Melt butter in the skillet and cook capers until sizzling; keep stirring to avoid burning, 3 minutes. Pour in broth and lemon juice, use a spatula to scrape any bits stuck at the bottom, and boil until the sauce reduces by half. Add back the pork and sprinkle with parsley. Simmer for 3 minutes. Let cool.

Storage: Place in airtight containers in the refrigerator for up to 5 days (or in the freezer for up to 2 months).

Per serving: Cal 341; Carbs 2g; Fat 23g; Protein 31g

Sheet Pan Pork with Cheese & Olives

Ingredients for 6 servings

½ cup cottage cheese, crumbled
1 ¼ cups heavy cream
2 tbsp avocado oil
1 ½ lb ground pork
¼ cup sliced Kalamata olives
2 garlic cloves, minced
½ cup marinara sauce

Directions and Total Time: approx. 40 minutes

Preheat oven to 400 F. Grease a casserole dish with cooking spray. Heat avocado oil in a deep skillet, add the ground pork and cook until brown, 10 minutes. Stir frequently and break any lumps that form. Spread the pork on the bottom of the casserole. Scatter olives, cottage cheese, and garlic on top. In a bowl, mix marinara sauce and heavy cream and pour all over the meat. Bake until the top is bubbly and lightly brown, 20-25 minutes. Cool.

Storage: Place in airtight containers in the refrigerator for up to 5 days (or in the freezer for up to 2 months).

Per serving: Cal 451; Carbs 2g; Fat 35g; Protein 33g

Slow-Cooked Pulled Pork

Ingredients for 6 servings

2 tbsp olive oil
2 tbsp butter
½ cup sliced yellow onion
2 lb pork shoulder
4 tbsp taco seasoning
Salt to taste
3 ½ cups chicken broth
5 tbsp potato starch
1 ¼ cups almond flour
2 eggs, cracked into a bowl

Directions and Total Time: approx. 8 hours 20 minutes

In a skillet, heat olive oil and sauté onion for 3 minutes or until softened. Transfer to the slow cooker. Season pork shoulder with taco seasoning, salt, and place it in the skillet. Sear on each side for 3 minutes and place in the slow cooker. Pour the chicken broth on top. Cover the lid and cook for 7 hours on Low. Shred the pork with 2 forks.

Cook further over low heat for 1 hour; set aside. In a bowl, combine potato starch, almond flour, and salt. Mix in eggs until a thick dough forms and add 1 cup of water. Separate the dough into 8 pieces.

Lay a parchment paper on a flat surface, grease with cooking spray, and put a dough piece on top. Cover with another parchment paper and, using a rolling pin, flatten the dough into a circle. Repeat the same process for the remaining dough balls. Melt a quarter of the butter in a skillet and cook the flattened dough one after another on both sides until light brown. Transfer the tortillas to airtight containers and spoon the shredded meat over. Cool.

Storage: Keep in the refrigerator for up to 5 days.

Per serving: Cal 346; Carbs 3g; Fat 23g; Protein 38g

Greek-Style Pork Tenderloin

Ingredients for 4 servings

¼ cup olive oil   2 tbsp Greek seasoning
2 tbsp lard   2 tbsp red wine vinegar
2 lemon, juiced   1 ½ lb pork tenderloin

Directions and Total Time: approx. 1 hour 60 minutes

Preheat oven to 425 F. In a bowl, combine olive oil, lemon juice, Greek seasoning, and red wine vinegar.

Place the pork on a clean flat surface, cut a few incisions, and brush the marinade all over. Cover with plastic wrap and refrigerate for 1 hour. Melt lard in a skillet, remove and unwrap the pork, and sear until brown on the outside. Place in a greased baking dish, brush with any reserved marinade and bake for 45 minutes. Let cool completely.

Storage: Place in airtight containers in the refrigerator for up to 5 days (or in the freezer for up to 2 months).

Per serving: Cal 383; Carbs 2g; Fat 21g; Protein 38g

Curried Pork Medallions with Cabbage

Ingredients for 4 servings

1 cup coconut cream   6 tbsp butter
1 lb pork tenderloin, sliced into ½-inch medallions
1 Canon cabbage, shredded   1 celery, chopped
Salt and black pepper to taste 1 tbsp red curry powder

Directions and Total Time: approx. 45 minutes

Melt half of the butter in a skillet over medium heat and sauté cabbage for 10-15 minutes or until soft and slightly golden; reserve. Melt remaining butter in the skillet, add in celery and sauté for 2 minutes. Add in the pork and fry until brown on the outside, and cooked within 10 minutes. Season with salt and pepper; mix in curry and heat for 30 seconds. Stir in coconut cream and simmer for 5 minutes. Let cool completely.

Storage: Place in airtight containers in the refrigerator for up to 5 days (or in the freezer for up to 2 months).

Per serving: Cal 505; Carbs 8g; Fat 39g; Protein 33g

Seasoned Pork Meatballs

Ingredients for 4 servings

2 tbsp sesame oil   4 garlic cloves, minced
3 tbsp coconut oil   1 tsp freshly pureed ginger
1 lb ground pork   1 tsp red chili flakes
2 scallions, chopped   2 tbsp tamari sauce
1 zucchini, grated   Salt and black pepper to taste

Directions and Total Time: approx. 20 minutes

In a bowl, combine ground pork, scallions, zucchini, garlic, ginger, chili flakes, salt, pepper, tamari sauce, and sesame oil. Form 1-inch oval shapes and place them on a plate. Heat coconut oil in a skillet over medium heat and brown the balls for 12 minutes. Transfer to a paper towel-lined plate to drain the excess fat. Let cool completely.

Storage: Place in airtight containers in the refrigerator for up to 5 days (or in the freezer for up to 2 months).

Per serving: Cal 326; Carbs 7g; Fat 27g; Protein 24g

Pork & Parmesan Meatballs

Ingredients for 6 servings

4 oz grated Parmesan cheese   1 tsp paprika powder
3 tbsp softened cream cheese   1 pinch cayenne pepper
2 tbsp olive oil   1 tbsp Dijon mustard
¼ cup chopped pimientos   1 lb ground pork
1/3 cup mayonnaise   1 large egg

Directions and Total Time: approx. 30 minutes

In a bowl, mix well pimientos, mayonnaise, cream cheese, paprika, cayenne pepper, mustard, Parmesan cheese, ground pork, and egg. Mix and form large meatballs. Heat olive oil in a non-stick skillet and fry the meatballs in batches on both sides until brown, 10 minutes. Let cool.

Storage: Place in airtight containers in the refrigerator for up to 5 days (or in the freezer for up to 2 months).

Per serving: Cal 375; Carbs 10g; Fat 31g; Protein 23g

Chipotle-Coffee Pork Chops

Ingredients for 4 servings

2 tbsp lard   Salt and black pepper to taste
1 tbsp finely ground coffee   ½ tsp cumin powder
½ tsp chipotle powder   1 ½ tsp brown sugar
½ tsp garlic powder   4 bone-in pork chops

Directions and Total Time: approx. 1 hour 20 minutes

In a bowl, mix coffee, chipotle powder, garlic powder, cumin, salt, pepper, and brown sugar. Rub spices all over the pork. Cover with plastic wraps and refrigerate for 1 hour. Preheat oven to 350 F. Melt lard in a skillet and sear pork on both sides for 3 minutes. Transfer the skillet to the oven and bake for 10 minutes. Let cool completely.

Storage: Place in airtight containers in the refrigerator for up to 5 days (or in the freezer for up to 2 months).

Per serving: Cal 391; Carbs 1g; Fat 21g; Protein 43g

Pork-Filled Portobello Mushrooms

Ingredients for 4 servings

12 portobello mushroom caps
¼ cup shredded Parmesan
7 oz cream cheese
2 tbsp butter
½ lb ground pork

1 tsp paprika
Salt and black pepper to taste
3 tbsp chives, finely chopped

Directions and Total Time: approx. 30 minutes

Preheat oven to 400 F. Melt butter in a skillet, add the ground pork, season with paprika, salt, and pepper, and stir-fry until brown, 10 minutes. Mix in chives and cream cheese until evenly combined. Spoon the mixture into the mushrooms and transfer them to a greased baking sheet. Top with the Parmesan cheese and bake until mushrooms turn golden and the cheese melts, 10 minutes. Let cool.

Storage: Place in airtight containers in the refrigerator for up to 5 days (or in the freezer for up to 2 months).

Per serving: Cal 295; Carbs 5g; Fat 23g; Protein 19g

Herby Pork & Zucchini Omelet

Ingredients for 4 servings

4 tbsp olive oil
3 zucchinis, halved lengthwise
1 garlic clove, crushed
1 small plum tomato, diced
2 tbsp chopped scallions
1 tsp dried basil

1 tsp cumin powder
1 tsp smoked paprika
1 lb ground pork
3 large eggs, beaten
3 tsp crushed pork rinds
1/3 cup chopped cilantro

Directions and Total Time: approx. 30 minutes

Preheat a grill to medium. Drizzle the zucchini with some olive oil. Place them on the grill and broil until brown, 5 minutes. Heat remaining olive oil in a skillet and sauté garlic, tomato, and scallions for 8 minutes. Mix in basil, cumin, and paprika. Add and brown the ground pork for 10 minutes; reserve. Spread the pork mixture onto the grilled zucchini slices; flatten the mixture. Transfer to a greased baking dish. Divide the eggs between the zucchini and place in a preheated to 380 F oven. Cook until set, 8 minutes. Sprinkle pork rinds and cilantro on top. Let cool.

Storage: Place in airtight containers in the refrigerator for up to 5 days (or in the freezer for up to 2 months).

Per serving: Cal 432; Carbs 14g; Fat 32g; Protein 25g

Jamaican Pork Roast

Ingredients for 8 servings

1 tbsp olive oil
4-pound pork roast

¼ cup jerk spice blend
2 cups vegetable stock

Directions and Total Time: approx. 4 hours 10 minutes

Rub the pork with olive oil and jerk spice blend. Heat a Dutch oven over medium heat and sear the meat well on all sides. Add the vegetable broth. Cover the pot, reduce the heat, and let cook for 4 hours. Let cool completely.

Storage: Place in airtight containers in the refrigerator for up to 5 days (or in the freezer for up to 2 months).

Per serving: Cal 467; Carbs 2g; Fat 21g; Protein 26g

Pork Sausage Stew

Ingredients for 6 servings

3 tbsp avocado oil
1 lb pork sausages, sliced
1 red bell pepper, chopped
1 onion, chopped
Salt and black pepper to taste
1 cup fresh parsley, chopped
6 green onions, chopped

1 cup chicken stock
2 garlic cloves, minced
24 oz canned tomatoes
16 oz okra, sliced
6 oz tomato sauce
2 tbsp coconut aminos
1 tbsp hot sauce

Directions and Total Time: approx. 30 minutes

Set a pot over medium heat and warm avocado oil. Place in sausages and cook for 2 minutes. Stir in onion, green onions, garlic, bell pepper, parsley, salt, and pepper and cook for 5 minutes. Add in hot sauce, chicken stock, tomatoes, coconut aminos, okra, and tomato sauce and bring to a boil. Cook for 15 minutes. Let cool completely.

Storage: Place in airtight containers in the refrigerator for up to 5 days (or in the freezer for up to 2 months).

Per serving: Cal 314, Carbs 7g, Fat 25g, Protein 16g

Pork Chops with Cauliflower Steaks

Ingredients for 4 servings

2 heads cauliflower, cut into 4 steaks
½ cup Parmesan cheese
2 tbsp butter
2 tbsp olive oil

4 pork chops
1 tbsp mesquite seasoning

Directions and Total Time: approx. 20 minutes

Season pork with mesquite flavoring. Melt butter in a skillet and fry pork on both sides for 10 minutes; set aside. Heat olive oil in a grill pan and cook cauli steaks on all sides for 4 minutes. Sprinkle with Parmesan cheese. Cool.

Storage: Place in airtight containers in the refrigerator for up to 5 days (or in the freezer for up to 2 months).

Per serving: Cal 429; Carbs 6g; Fat 27g; Protein 47g

Saucy Pork Spareribs

Ingredients for 4 servings

1 tbsp olive oil
4 tbsp sugar-free BBQ sauce
2 tbsp brown sugar

3 tsp cayenne powder
1 tsp garlic powder
1 lb pork spareribs

Directions and Total Time: approx. 90 minutes

Mix brown sugar, olive oil, cayenne, and garlic in a bowl. Brush on the meaty sides of the ribs and wrap in foil. Sit for 30 minutes in the fridge. Preheat oven to 400 F, place wrapped ribs on a baking sheet, and cook for 40 minutes. Remove foil, brush it with BBQ sauce, and brown under the broiler for 10 minutes on both sides. Let cool completely.

Storage: Place in airtight containers in the refrigerator for up to 5 days (or in the freezer for up to 2 months).

Per serving: Cal 445, Carbs 3g, Fat 33g, Protein 25g

Crispy Pork Belly with Creamy Kale

Ingredients for 8 servings

1 cup coconut cream	6 cloves garlic, minced
2 tbsp coconut oil	¼ cup ginger thinly sliced
2 lb pork belly, chopped	4 long red chilies, halved
Salt and black pepper to taste	1 cup coconut milk
1 white onion, chopped	2 cups chopped kale

Directions and Total Time: approx. 80 minutes

Season pork belly with salt and pepper and refrigerate for 30 minutes. Bring to a boil 2 cups water in a pot, add in pork and cook for 15 minutes. Drain and transfer to a skillet. Warm in half of the coconut oil and fry in the pork for 15 minutes until the skin browns and crackles. Turn a few times to prevent burning. Spoon onto a plate and discard the fat. Heat the remaining coconut oil in the same skillet and sauté onion, garlic, ginger, and chilies for 5 minutes. Pour in coconut milk and coconut cream and cook for 1 minute. Add kale and cook until wilted, stirring occasionally. Stir in the pork. Cook for 2 minutes. Let cool.

Storage: Place in airtight containers in the refrigerator for up to 5 days (or in the freezer for up to 2 months).

Per serving: Cal 312; Carbs 6g; Fat 23g; Protein 21g

Basil Pork Chops with Beetroot Greens

Ingredients for 4 servings

2 cups chopped beetroot greens

1 tbsp olive oil	2 tbsp freshly chopped basil
2 tbsp butter	4 pork chops
2 tbsp balsamic vinegar	Salt and black pepper to taste
2 tsp freshly pureed garlic	

Directions and Total Time: approx. 30 minutes

Preheat oven to 400 F. In a saucepan over low heat, add vinegar, garlic, salt, pepper, and basil. Cook until the mixture is syrupy. Heat olive oil in a skillet and sear pork on both sides for 8 minutes. Brush the vinegar glaze on the pork and bake for 8 minutes. Melt butter in another skillet and sauté beetroot greens for 5 minutes. Let cool.

Storage: Place in airtight containers in the refrigerator for up to 5 days (or in the freezer for up to 2 months).

Per serving: Cal 391; Carbs 3g; Fat 26g; Protein 42g

Mushroom & Bacon Pizza

Ingredients for 4 servings

1 cup shredded provolone cheese
1 (7 oz) can sliced mushrooms, drained

½ cup grated mozzarella	6 bacon slices
10 eggs	2/3 cup tomato sauce
1 tsp Italian seasoning	2 cups chopped kale, wilted

Directions and Total Time: approx. 35 minutes

Preheat oven to 400 F. Line a pizza-baking pan with parchment paper. Whisk 6 eggs into a bowl and mix in the provolone cheese and Italian seasoning. Spread the mixture on a pizza-baking pan and bake until golden, 15 minutes. Remove from oven and let cool for 2 minutes.

Fry bacon in a skillet over medium heat until brown and crispy, 5 minutes. Transfer to a plate. Spread tomato sauce on the crust, and top with kale, mozzarella cheese, and mushrooms. Bake in the oven for 8 minutes. Crack the remaining 4 eggs on top, cover with bacon, and continue baking until the eggs set, 2-3 minutes. Let cool completely.

Storage: Place in airtight containers in the refrigerator for up to 5 days (or in the freezer for up to 2 months).

Per serving: Cal 434; Carbs 14g; Fat 27g; Protein 31g

Mexican-Style Pork Bowl

Ingredients for 4 servings

½ cup sharp cheddar, shredded	¼ cup sliced black olives
1 tbsp butter	1 avocado, cubed
1 lb ground pork	¼ cup tomatoes, diced
½ cup beef broth	1 green onion, sliced
4 tbsp taco seasoning	1 tbsp fresh cilantro, chopped
Salt and black pepper to taste	

Directions and Total Time: approx. 25 minutes

Melt butter in a skillet over medium heat. Cook the ground pork until brown while breaking any lumps, 10 minutes. Mix in broth, taco seasoning, salt, and pepper; cook until most of the liquid evaporates, 5 minutes. Mix in cheddar cheese to melt. Let cool completely.

Storage: Place in airtight containers in the refrigerator for up to 5 days (or in the freezer for up to 2 months). Before serving, reheat in the microwave for 1-2 minutes. Top with olives, avocado, tomatoes, green onion, and cilantro.

Per serving: Cal 416; Carbs 13g; Fat 28g; Protein 33g

Picadillo with Spiralized Red Bell Peppers

Ingredients for 4 servings

2 lb red and yellow bell peppers, spiralized

2 tbsp butter	1 tsp garlic powder
1 lb ground pork	2 avocados, pitted, mashed
Salt and black pepper to taste	2 tbsp chopped pecans

Directions and Total Time: approx. 15 minutes

Melt butter in a skillet and cook the pork until brown, 5 minutes. Season with salt and pepper. Stir in bell peppers and garlic powder and cook until the peppers are slightly tender, 2 minutes. Mix in mashed avocados and cook for 1 minute. Top with the pecans. Let cool completely.

Storage: Place in airtight containers in the refrigerator for up to 5 days (or in the freezer for up to 2 months).

Per serving: Cal 456; Carbs 29g; Fat 26g; Protein 27g

Tomato-Mozzarella Pork Bake

Ingredients for 4 servings

1 cup shredded mozzarella	1 cup corn flour
4 boneless pork chops	1 large egg, beaten
Salt and black pepper to taste	1 cup tomato sauce

Directions and Total Time: approx. 25 minutes

Preheat oven to 400 F. Season the pork with salt and pepper and coat the meat in the egg first, then in flaxseed. Place on a greased baking sheet. Pour tomato sauce over and sprinkle with mozzarella cheese. Bake for 15 minutes or until the cheese melts and pork cooks through. Let cool.

Storage: Place in airtight containers in the refrigerator for up to 5 days (or in the freezer for up to 2 months).

Per serving: Cal 512; Carbs 27g; Fat 15g; Protein 52g

Habanero Pork & Egg Sutée

Ingredients for 4 servings

2 tbsp sesame oil	1 habanero pepper, chopped
2 large eggs	1 lb Brussels sprouts, halved
2 garlic cloves, minced	3 tbsp coconut aminos
½ tsp ginger puree	1 tbsp white wine vinegar
1 medium white onion, diced	2 tbsp sesame seeds
1 lb ground pork	Salt and black pepper to taste

Directions and Total Time: approx. 25 minutes

Heat 1 tbsp of sesame oil in a skillet and scramble the eggs until set, 1 minute; set aside. Heat remaining sesame oil in the same skillet and sauté garlic, ginger, and onion until soft and fragrant, 4 minutes. Add in ground pork and habanero pepper and season with salt and pepper. Cook for 10 minutes. Mix in Brussels sprouts, aminos, and wine vinegar and cook until the sprouts are tender. Stir in the eggs. Top with sesame seeds. Let cool completely.

Storage: Place in airtight containers in the refrigerator for up to 5 days (or in the freezer for up to 2 months).

Per serving: Cal 475; Carbs 16g; Fat 32g; Protein 29g

Mustard-Garlic Pork Loin Roast

Ingredients for 4 servings

2 tsp olive oil	Salt and black pepper to taste
2 lb boneless pork loin roast	1 tbsp Dijon mustard
5 cloves garlic, minced	1 tsp dried basil

Directions and Total Time: approx. 30 min

Preheat oven to 400 F. Place the pork loin in a greased baking dish. In a bowl, mix garlic, salt, pepper, Dijon mustard, and basil. Rub the mixture onto the pork. Drizzle with olive oil and bake for 15 minutes or until cooked within and brown outside. Let cool completely. Slice.

Storage: Place in airtight containers in the refrigerator for up to 5 days (or in the freezer for up to 2 months).

Per serving: Cal 311; Carbs 2g; Fat 12g; Protein 38g

Lettuce Rolls with Mushrooms & Bacon

Ingredients for 8 servings

1 cup shredded cheddar	8 bacon slices, chopped
2 tbsp olive oil	1 ½ lb ground pork
½ cup sliced cremini mushrooms	
1 iceberg lettuce, leaves separated	

Directions and Total Time: approx. 30 minutes

In a skillet over medium heat, cook bacon until brown and crispy, about 5 minutes. Transfer to a paper-towel-lined plate. Heat the olive oil in the skillet and sauté the mushrooms for 5 minutes or until softened. Add in the ground pork and cook it until brown, 10 minutes, while breaking the lumps that form. Divide the pork between lettuce leaves, and sprinkle with cheddar cheese, and top with bacon. Wrap and let cool. Place in airtight containers.

Storage: Keep in the refrigerator for up to 3 days.

Per serving: Cal 463; Carbs 2g; Fat 34g; Protein 32g

Mediterranean Pork Tenderloin

Ingredients for 6 servings

1 cup loosely packed fresh baby spinach	
3/4 cup crumbled feta cheese	½ tsp cumin powder
2 tbsp olive oil	2 cups cauliflower rice
1 ½ lb pork tenderloin, cubed	½ cup water
Salt and black pepper to taste	1 cup grape tomatoes, halved

Directions and Total Time: approx. 20 minutes

Heat olive oil in a skillet, season the pork with salt, pepper, and cumin and sear on both sides for 5 minutes until brown. Stir in cauli rice and pour in water. Cook for 5 minutes or until cauliflower softens. Mix in spinach, cook for 3 minutes and add the tomatoes. Let cool completely. Spoon into airtight containers and sprinkle with feta.

Storage: Keep in the refrigerator for up to 3 days.

Per serving: Cal 377; Carbs 9g; Fat 23g; Protein 33g

Pork Medallions Pork in Morel Sauce

Ingredients for 6 servings

2 tbsp olive oil	2 tbsp butter
1 ½ lb pork tenderloin, cut into 8 medallions	
16 fresh morels, rinsed	½ cup red wine
4 large green onions, chopped	¾ cup chicken broth

Directions and Total Time: approx. 30 minutes

Heat olive oil in a pot and sear the pork until brown, 5 minutes; set aside. Add morels and green onions to the pot and cook until softened, 2 minutes. Mix in red wine and chicken broth. Place the pork in the sauce and simmer for 15 minutes. Swirl in butter, adjust the taste, and let cool.

Storage: Place in airtight containers in the refrigerator for up to 5 days (or in the freezer for up to 2 months).

Per serving: Cal 328; Carbs 3g; Fat 18g; Protein 31g

Layered Pork & Mushroom Bake

Ingredients for 6 servings

1 cup portobello mushrooms, chopped
1 cup ricotta, crumbled   1 ¼ pounds ground pork
1 cup Italian cheese blend   4 green onions, chopped
3 tbsp olive oil   15 oz canned tomatoes
4 carrots, thinly sliced   4 tbsp breadcrumbs, crushed
Salt to taste   ¼ cup chopped parsley
1 clove garlic, minced   ⅓ cup water

Directions and Total Time: approx. 40 minutes

Mix parsley, ricotta cheese, and Italian cheese blend in a bowl; set aside. Heat olive oil in a skillet and cook the ground pork for 3 minutes. Add in garlic, half of the green onions, mushrooms, and 2 tbsp of pork rinds. Continue cooking for 3 minutes. Stir in tomatoes and water and cook for 3 minutes. Sprinkle a baking dish with 2 tbsp of pork rinds, top with half of the carrots and salt, 2/3 of the pork mixture, and the cheese mixture. Repeat the layering process a second time to exhaust the ingredients. Cover the baking dish with foil and bake for 20 minutes at 370 F. Remove the foil and brown the top of the casserole with the broiler side of the oven for 2 minutes. Let cool.

Storage: Place in airtight containers in the refrigerator for up to 5 days (or in the freezer for up to 2 months).

Per serving: Cal 525; Carbs 11g; Fat 33g; Protein 38g

Spicy BBQ Pork Chops

Ingredients for 4 servings

1 tbsp melted butter   1 ½ tsp garlic powder
½ cup corn flour   1 tbsp dried parsley
1 tsp dried thyme   1/2 tsp onion powder
1 tsp paprika   1/8 tsp basil
Salt and black pepper to taste   4 pork chops
¼ tsp chili powder   ½ cup BBQ sauce

Directions and Total Time: approx. 70 minutes

Preheat oven to 400 F. In a bowl, mix corn flour, thyme, paprika, salt, pepper, chili, garlic powder, parsley, onion powder, and basil. Rub the pork chops with the mixture. Melt butter in a skillet and sear pork on both sides, 8 minutes. Transfer to a greased baking sheet, brush with BBQ sauce and bake for 50 minutes. Let cool.

Storage: Place in airtight containers in the refrigerator for up to 5 days (or in the freezer for up to 2 months).

Per serving: Cal 435; Carbs 1.6g; Fat 23g; Protein 44g

Pork Sausages with Cheese Sauce

Ingredients for 4 servings

8 oz cream cheese, softened   1 egg, beaten
1 tbsp olive oil   3 tbsp freshly chopped chives
2 tsp almond flour   3 tsp freshly pureed onion
16 oz pork sausages   3 tbsp chicken broth
6 tbsp corn flour   2 tbsp almond milk

Directions and Total Time: approx. 30 minutes

Prick the sausages with a fork all around. Roll in the almond flour, dip in the egg, and then in the corn flour. Heat olive oil in a skillet and fry sausages until brown, 15 minutes. Transfer to a plate. In a saucepan, combine cream cheese, chives, onion, chicken broth, and almond milk. Cook and stir over medium heat until smooth and evenly mixed, 5 minutes. Place the sausages in airtight containers and spoon the sauce on top. Let cool completely.

Storage: Keep in the refrigerator for up to 5 days (or in the freezer for up to 2 months).

Per serving: Cal 461; Carbs 5g; Fat 32g; Protein 34g

Braised Pork Shanks with Wine Sauce

Ingredients for 6 servings

3 tbsp olive oil   1 ½ cups crushed tomatoes
3 lb pork shanks   ½ cup red wine
3 celery stalks, chopped   ¼ tsp red chili flakes
5 garlic cloves, minced   ¼ cup chopped parsley

Directions and Total Time: approx. 2 hours 10 minutes

Preheat oven to 300 F. Heat olive oil in a saucepan and brown pork on all sides for 4 minutes; set aside. Add in celery and garlic and sauté for 3 minutes. Return the pork. Top with tomatoes, red wine, and red chili flakes. Cover the lid and put the saucepan in the oven. Cook for 2 hours. In the last 15 minutes, open the lid, sprinkle with parsley, and increase the temperature to 450 F. Let cool.

Storage: Place in airtight containers in the refrigerator for up to 5 days (or in the freezer for up to 2 months).

Per serving: Cal 432; Carbs 3g; Fat 25g; Protein 42g

Saucy Pork Chops with Raspberry Sauce

Ingredients for 4 servings

1 lb pork tenderloin, cut into ½-inch medallions
2/3 cup grated Parmesan   ½ cup almond flour
3 tbsp butter, divided   2 large eggs, lightly beaten
2 cups fresh raspberries   Salt and black pepper to taste
1 tsp chicken bouillon granules   1 garlic clove, minced

Directions and Total Time: approx. 20 minutes

To a blender, add raspberries, ¼ cup of water, and chicken granules; process until smooth and set aside. In two separate bowls, pour almond flour and Parmesan cheese. Season the meat with salt and pepper. Coat in the almond flour, then in the eggs, and finally in the cheese.

Melt 2 tbsp of butter in a skillet and fry the pork for 3 minutes per side or until golden brown. Set aside. In the same skillet, melt the remaining butter and sauté garlic for 1 minute. Stir in raspberry mixture and cook for 3 minutes. Spoon sauce on top of the pork. Let cool completely.

Storage: Place in airtight containers in the refrigerator for up to 5 days (or in the freezer for up to 2 months).

Per serving: Cal 428; Carbs 6g; Fat 27g; Protein 43g

Maple-Mint Pork Chops with Brie Cheese

<u>Ingredients</u> for 4 servings

4 slices brie cheese	1 tsp maple syrup
3 tbsp olive oil	Salt and black pepper to taste
2 large red onions, sliced	4 pork chops
2 tbsp balsamic vinegar	2 tbsp chopped mint leaves

<u>Directions</u> and Total Time: approx. 40 minutes

Heat 1 tbsp olive oil in a skillet until smoky. Reduce to low and sauté onions until brown. Pour in the vinegar, maple syrup, and salt. Cook with frequent stirring to prevent burning until the onions caramelize, 15 minutes; set aside. Heat the remaining olive oil in the same skillet, season the pork with salt and black pepper, and cook for 12 minutes. Put a brie slice on each meat and top with the caramelized onions; let the cheese melt for 2 minutes. Spoon the pork with the topping onto airtight containers and garnish with mint. Let cool completely.

Storage: Keep in the refrigerator for up to 5 days (or in the freezer for up to 2 months).

Per serving: Cal 487; Carbs 10g; Fat 28g; Protein 46g

Holiday Pork Lo Mein

<u>Ingredients</u> for 4 servings

1 lb pork tenderloin, cut into ¼-inch strips	
1 cup shredded mozzarella	1 yellow bell pepper, sliced
3 tbsp sesame oil	1 garlic clove, minced
1 cup green beans, halved	4 green onions, chopped
1 egg yolk	1 tsp toasted sesame seeds
1-inch ginger knob, grated	3 tbsp coconut aminos
Salt and black pepper to taste	2 tsp maple syrup
1 red bell pepper, sliced	1 tsp fresh ginger paste

<u>Directions</u> and Total Time: approx. 2 hours 25 minutes

Microwave mozzarella cheese for 2 minutes. Let cool for 1 minute and mix in the egg yolk until well combined. Lay a parchment paper on a flat surface, pour the cheese mixture on top and cover with another parchment paper. Flatten the dough into 1/8-inch thickness. Take off the parchment paper and cut the dough into thin spaghetti strands. Place in a bowl and refrigerate for 2 hours. Bring 2 cups of water to a boil in a saucepan and add in the pasta. Cook for 1 minute and drain; set aside.

Heat sesame oil in a skillet, season pork with salt and pepper, and sear on both sides for 5 minutes. Transfer to a plate. In the same skillet, mix in bell peppers, green beans and cook for 3 minutes. Stir in garlic, ginger, and green onions and cook for 1 minute. Mix in pork and pasta. In a bowl, toss coconut aminos, maple syrup, and ginger paste. Pour the mixture over the pork mixture; cook for 1 minute. Sprinkle with sesame seeds. Let cool completely.

Storage: Place in airtight containers in the refrigerator for up to 5 days (or in the freezer for up to 2 months).

Per serving: Cal 387; Carbs 12g; Fats 19g; Protein 40g

Southern Pork Meatballs

<u>Ingredients</u> for 8 servings

4 oz cream cheese	½ tsp Italian seasoning
3 tbsp butter, melted	2 tsp cumin
3 green onions, chopped	Salt and black pepper to taste
1 tbsp garlic powder	1 tsp turmeric
1 lb ground pork	¼ tsp brown sugar
1 jalapeño pepper, chopped	½ tsp baking powder
1 tsp dried oregano	1 ½ cups flax meal
2 tsp parsley	½ cup almond flour

<u>Directions</u> and Total Time: approx. 45 minutes

Preheat oven to 350 F. In a food processor, add green onions, garlic powder, jalapeño, and ½ cup water; blend well. Set a pan over medium heat, warm in 2 tbsp butter, and cook the ground pork for 3 minutes. Stir in onion mixture and cook for 2 minutes. Add in parsley, salt, cumin, turmeric, oregano, Italian seasoning, and pepper and cook for 3 minutes. In a bowl, combine the almond flour, brown sugar, flax meal, and baking powder. In a separate bowl, combine 3 tbsp melted butter with cream cheese. Combine the 2 mixtures to obtain a dough. Form 8 balls from the mixture, set on parchment paper, and roll each into a circle. Split the pork mixture on one-half of the dough circles, cover with the other half, seal edges, and lay on a lined sheet. Bake for 25 minutes. Let cool.

Storage: Place in airtight containers in the refrigerator for up to 5 days (or in the freezer for up to 2 months).

Per serving: Cal 283; Carbs 4g; Fat 21g; Protein 17g

Spicy-Sweet Sambal Pork Noodles

<u>Ingredients</u> for 6 servings

2 (8 oz) packs Miracle noodles	
2 tbsp olive oil	1 tbsp tomato paste
1 tbsp unsalted butter	2 fresh basil leaves, chopped
1 lb ground pork	2 tbsp sambal oelek
4 garlic cloves, minced	2 tbsp plain vinegar
1-inch ginger, grated	2 tbsp coconut aminos
1 tsp brown sugar	Salt to taste

<u>Directions</u> and Total Time: approx. 50 minutes

Bring 2 cups water to a boil. Strain the Miracle noodles and rinse well under hot running water. Allow proper draining and pour them into the boiling water. Cook for 3 minutes and strain again. Place a dry skillet and stir-fry the shirataki noodles until visibly dry, 1-2 minutes; set aside. Heat olive oil in a pot and cook the ground pork for 5 minutes. Stir in garlic, ginger, and sugar and cook for 1 minute. Add in tomato paste and mix in sambal oelek, vinegar, 1 cup water, aminos, and salt. Continue cooking over low heat for 20 minutes. Add in noodles and butter, and mix well into the sauce. Garnish with basil. Let cool.

Storage: Place in airtight containers in the refrigerator for up to 5 days (or in the freezer for up to 2 months).

Per serving: Cal 376; Carbs 11g; Fats 27g; Protein 23g

Creamy Pork with Basil-Lemon Fettuccine

Ingredients for 4 servings

1 cup shaved Parmesan cheese
4 pork loin medallions, cut into thin strips
1 cup shredded mozzarella   ½ cup green beans, chopped
1 cup crème fraiche   1 lemon, zested and juiced
1 tbsp olive oil   ¼ cup chicken broth
1 egg yolk   6 basil leaves, chopped
Salt and black pepper to taste

Directions and Total Time: approx. 2 hours 35 minutes

Microwave mozzarella cheese for 2 minutes. Allow cooling for 1 minute. Mix in egg yolk until well combined. Lay a parchment paper on a flat surface, pour the cheese mixture on top and cover with another parchment paper.

Flatten the dough into 1/8-inch thickness. Take off the parchment paper and cut the dough into thick fettuccine strands. Place in a bowl and refrigerate for 2 hours. Bring 2 cups of water to a boil in a saucepan and add the fettuccine. Cook for 1 minute and drain; set aside.

Heat oil in a skillet, season the pork with salt and pepper, and cook for 10 minutes. Mix in green beans and cook for 5 minutes. Stir in lemon zest, lemon juice, and broth. Cook for 5 more minutes. Add crème fraiche, fettuccine, and basil, and cook for 1 minute. Top with Parmesan cheese. Let cool completely.

Storage: Place in airtight containers in the refrigerator for up to 5 days (or in the freezer for up to 2 months).

Per serving: Cal 496; Carbs 7g; Fats 29g; Protein 57g

Sesame Pork Bites

Ingredients for 4 servings

1 tbsp sesame oil   ½ cup sesame seeds
½ cup + 1 tbsp red wine   1 tsp freshly pureed garlic
1 tbsp + 1/3 cup tamari sauce   ½ tsp freshly grated ginger
1 lb pork tenderloin, cubed   1 scallion, finely chopped
½ cup sugar-free maple syrup

Directions and Total Time: approx. 2 hours 45 minutes

In a zipper bag, combine ½ cup of red wine with 1 tbsp of tamari sauce. Add in pork cubes, seal the bag, and marinate the meat in the fridge for at least 2 hours.

Preheat oven to 350 F. Remove the pork from the fridge and drain. Pour maple syrup and sesame seeds into two separate bowls; roll the pork in maple syrup and then in the sesame seeds. Place on a greased baking sheet and bake for 35 minutes. In a bowl, mix the remaining red wine, tamari sauce, sesame oil, garlic, and ginger. Pour the sauce into a bowl. Transfer pork to a platter and garnish with scallions. Pour the sauce over. Let cool completely.

Storage: Place in airtight containers in the refrigerator for up to 5 days (or in the freezer for up to 2 months).

Per serving: Cal 352; Carbs 6g; Fat 18g; Protein 39g

Asian-Style Pork with Spaghetti Squash

Ingredients for 6 servings

2 lb spaghetti squashes, halved and deseeded
3 tbsp peanut oil   2 tbsp coconut aminos
1 tbsp olive oil   1 tbsp fish sauce
¼ cup peanut butter   4 boneless pork chops
2 tbsp minced lemongrass   Salt and black pepper to taste
3 tbsp fresh ginger paste   1 lb kale, chopped
2 tbsp sugar-free maple syrup   ½ cup coconut milk

Directions and Total Time: approx. 100 minutes

In a bowl, mix lemongrass, 2 tbsp of ginger paste, maple syrup, aminos, and fish sauce. Place the pork in the liquid and coat well. Refrigerate for 30 minutes. Heat 2 tbsp of peanut oil in a skillet, remove pork from the marinade and sear on both sides for 10-15 minutes. Set aside.

Preheat oven to 380 F. Place the spaghetti squashes on a baking sheet, brush with olive oil, and season with salt and pepper. Bake for 45 minutes. Remove the squash and shred with two forks into spaghetti-like strands; set aside. Heat the remaining peanut oil in the same skillet and sauté the remaining ginger paste. Add in kale and cook for 2 minutes; set aside. In a bowl, whisk coconut milk with peanut butter until well combined. Divide the pork between airtight containers, add the spaghetti squash and kale to the side, and drizzle the peanut sauce on top. Cool.

Storage: Keep in the refrigerator for up to 5 days (or in the freezer for up to 2 months).

Per serving: Cal 478; Carbs 23g; Fats 27g; Protein 46g

Blackened Pork with Minty Chimichurri

Ingredients for 4 servings

¼ cup olive oil   ¼ cup rosemary, chopped
2 tbsp butter, melted   2 cloves garlic, minced
1 lime, juiced   1 lb pork tenderloin
¼ cup chopped mint leaves   Salt and black pepper to taste

Directions and Total Time: approx. 60 minutes

In a bowl, mix mint, rosemary, garlic, lime juice, olive oil, and salt and combine well. Leave the chimichurri to sit for 5-10 minutes to release all of the flavors. Put in a glass jar.

Preheat charcoal grill to 450 F, creating a direct heat area and an indirect heat area. Rub the pork with butter and season with salt and pepper. Place the meat over direct heat and sear for 3 minutes on each side; then move to the indirect heat area. Close the lid and cook for 25 minutes on one side, then open, flip, and cook closed for 20 minutes. Remove from the grill and let sit for 5 minutes before slicing. Let cool completely. Place in airtight containers.

Storage: Keep the chimichurri and pork in the refrigerator for up to 2 days. Before serving, reheat the pork in the microwave for 1-2 minutes. Top with chimichurri.

Per serving: Cal 388, Carbs 5g, Fat 18g, Protein 28g

English Pork & Root Veggie Pie

Ingredients for 8 servings

2 tbsp butter	1 onion, chopped
1 cup turnip mash	1 tbsp sage
2 lb ground pork	

Crust

2 oz cheddar, shredded	2 cups almond flour
2 oz butter	¼ tsp xanthan gum
1 egg	A pinch of salt

Directions and Total Time: approx. 60 minutes

Stir all crust ingredients in a bowl. Make 2 balls out of the mixture and refrigerate for 10 minutes. In a pan, warm 2 tbsp of butter and sauté onion and ground pork for 8 minutes. Let cool for a few minutes ,and add in turnip mash and sage. Mix with hands. Roll out the pie crusts and place one at the bottom of a greased pie pan. Spread filling over the crust and top with the other coat. Bake in the oven for 30 minutes at 350 F. Let cool completely.

Storage: Place in airtight containers in the refrigerator for up to 5 days (or in the freezer for up to 2 months).

Per serving: Cal 340; Carbs 2g; Fat 27g; Protein 23g

Prosciutto Pizza with Basil

Ingredients for 4 servings

4 prosciutto slices, cut into thirds

2 oz sliced mozzarella	1 egg, beaten
2 cups grated mozzarella	⅓ cup tomato sauce
2 tbsp cream cheese, softened	6 fresh basil leaves
½ cup almond flour	

Directions and Total Time: approx. 40 minutes

Preheat oven to 390 F. Line a pizza pan with parchment paper. Microwave grated mozzarella and 2 tbsp of cream cheese for 1 minute. Mix in almond meal and egg. Spread the mixture on the pizza pan and bake for 15 minutes; set aside. Spread the tomato sauce on the crust. Arrange the mozzarella slices on the sauce and then the prosciutto. Bake again for 15 minutes or until the cheese melts. Remove and top with basil. Let cool completely. Slice.

Storage: Place in airtight containers in the refrigerator for up to 5 days (or in the freezer for up to 2 months).

Per serving: Cal 330; Carbs 18g; Fats 19g; Protein 23g

Baked Pasta & Cheese Pork Carnitas

Ingredients for 6 servings

1 lb pork shoulder, divided into 6 pieces

1 cup shredded mozzarella	Salt and black pepper to taste
1 cup grated Monterey Jack	1 tsp dried thyme
4 oz cream cheese, softened	1 cup chicken broth
1 cup heavy cream	2 shallots, chopped
2 tbsp olive oil	2 garlic cloves, minced
2 tbsp butter	½ tsp white pepper
1 egg yolk	½ tsp nutmeg powder

Directions and Total Time: approx. 3 hours 40 minutes

Microwave mozzarella cheese for 2 minutes. Let cool for a minute. Mix in egg yolk until well combined. Lay a parchment paper on a flat surface, pour the cheese mixture on top and cover with another parchment paper. Flatten the dough into 1/8-inch thickness. Take off the parchment paper and cut the dough into small cubes the size of macaroni. Place in a bowl and refrigerate for 2 hours. Bring 2 cups of water to a boil and add in macaroni. Cook for 1 minute and drain; set aside.

Heat olive oil in a pot, season pork with salt, pepper, and thyme, and sear on both sides until brown. Pour in chicken broth and cook over low heat for 1 hour or until softened. Remove to a plate and shred into small strands; set aside.

Preheat oven to 380 F. Melt butter in a pot and sauté shallots and garlic for 3 minutes. Pour in 1 cup of water to deglaze the pot and stir in half of Monterey Jack and cream cheeses for 4 minutes. Mix in heavy cream and season with salt, pepper, white pepper, and nutmeg powder. Mix in pasta and pork. Pour mixture into a baking dish and cover with remaining Monterey Jack cheese. Bake for 20 minutes. Let cool completely and slice.

Storage: Place in airtight containers in the refrigerator for up to 5 days (or in the freezer for up to 2 months).

Per serving: Cal 540; Carbs 3g; Fat 43g; Protein 33g

Pork Meatballs in Basil-Tomato Sauce

Ingredients for 12 servings

1 cup asiago cheese, shredded	3 cloves garlic, minced
1 cup Pecorino cheese, grated	2 eggs, beaten
½ cup buttermilk	Salt and black pepper to taste
1 lb ground pork	1 can (29-ounce) tomato sauce
1 cup pork rinds, crushed	2 tbsp chopped basil

Directions and Total Time: approx. 45 minutes

Preheat oven to 370 F. Mix buttermilk, ground pork, garlic, asiago cheese, eggs, salt, pepper, and pork rinds in a bowl, until combined. Shape the pork mixture into 12 balls and arrange them on a greased baking pan. Bake for 20 minutes. Remove and pour in tomato sauce and sprinkle with Pecorino cheese. Cover the pan with foil and put it back in the oven for 10 minutes. Remove the foil and cook for 5 more minutes. Garnish with basil. Let cool.

Storage: Place in airtight containers in the refrigerator for up to 5 days (or in the freezer for up to 2 months).

Per serving: Cal 230; Carbs 4g; Fat 15g; Protein 21g

Grilled Pork & Halloumi Parcels

Ingredients for 4 servings

4 oz halloumi cheese, cubed	2 tsp chili powder
3 tbsp olive oil	1 tsp cumin powder
1 lb turnips, cubed	4 boneless pork chops
½ cup salsa verde	Salt and black pepper to taste

Directions and Total Time: approx. 25 minutes

Preheat the grill to 400 F. Cut out four 18x12-inch sheets of heavy-duty aluminum foil. Grease the sheets with cooking spray. In a bowl, combine turnips, salsa verde, chili, and cumin. Season with salt and pepper. Place a pork chop on each foil sheet, spoon the turnip mixture on the meat, and sprinkle olive oil and halloumi cheese on top. Wrap the foil, place it on the grill grate, and cook for 10 minutes. Turn the foil packs over and cook further for 8 minutes. Let cool completely.

Storage: Place in airtight containers in the refrigerator for up to 5 days (or in the freezer for up to 2 months).

Per serving: Cal 457; Carbs 12g; Fat 26g; Protein 42g

Caribbean Pulled Pork

Ingredients for 4 servings

2 pounds pork tenderloin	½ cup jerk seasoning
1 cup chicken stock	Salt and pepper to taste

Directions and Total Time: approx. 2 hours 15 minutes

Rub the pork shoulder with jerk seasoning and set it in a greased baking dish. Pour in the chicken stock and cook for 1 hour 30 minutes in the oven at 350 F covered with aluminum foil. Discard the foil and cook for another 20 minutes. Leave to rest for 10-15 minutes and shred it with 2 forks. Let cool completely.

Storage: Place in airtight containers in the refrigerator for up to 5 days (or in the freezer for up to 2 months). Before serving, reheat the pulled pork in the microwave for 1-2 minutes. Top with avocado slices. Enjoy!

Per serving: Cal 412, Carbs 8g, Fat 7g, Protein 63g

Pork Rolls with Bacon & Cheese

Ingredients for 4 servings

⅓ cup cottage cheese	1 onion, chopped
1 tbsp olive oil	1 tbsp garlic powder
4 bacon strips	2 tomatoes, chopped
2 tbsp fresh parsley, chopped	⅓ cup chicken stock
4 pork loin chops, boneless	Salt and black pepper to taste

Directions and Total Time: approx. 40 minutes

Lay a bacon strip on top of each pork chop, then scatter the parsley and cottage cheese on top. Roll each pork piece and secure it with toothpicks. Set a pan over medium heat and warm oil. Cook the pork parcels until browned and remove to a plate. Add the onion to the pan and cook for 5 minutes. Pour in the chicken stock and garlic powder and cook for 3 minutes. Get rid of the toothpicks from the pork parcels and return them to the pan. Stir in black pepper, salt, parsley, and tomatoes, and bring to a boil. Set heat to low and cook for 25 minutes while covered. Cool.

Storage: Place in airtight containers in the refrigerator for up to 5 days (or in the freezer for up to 2 months).

Per serving: Cal 433; Carbs 6g; Fat 23g; Protein 44g

Pork Tenderloin in Coconut-Paprika Sauce

Ingredients for 4 servings

1 cup coconut cream	4 tsp smoked paprika
1 tbsp butter	Salt and black pepper to taste
1 lb pork tenderloin, cubed	1 tsp almond flour

Directions and Total Time: approx. 20 minutes

Season the pork with paprika, salt, and pepper and sprinkle with almond flour. Melt butter in a skillet and sauté the pork until lightly browned, 5 minutes. Stir in coconut cream; let boil. Cook until the sauce slightly thickens, 7 minutes. Let cool completely.

Storage: Place in airtight containers in the refrigerator for up to 5 days (or in the freezer for up to 2 months).

Per serving: Cal 272; Carbs 3g; Fat 16g; Protein 26g

Special Pork Masala

Ingredients for 4 servings

1 lb pork shoulder, cut into bite-size pieces	
2 tbsp ghee	2 tbsp Greek yogurt
1 tbsp freshly grated ginger	½ tsp chili powder
2 tbsp freshly pureed garlic	2 tbsp garam masala
1 medium red onion, sliced	1 bunch cilantro, chopped
1 cup crushed tomatoes	2 green chilies, sliced

Directions and Total Time: approx. 30 minutes

Bring a pot of water to a boil to blanch meat for 3 minutes; drain and set aside. Melt ghee in a skillet and sauté ginger, garlic, and onions until caramelized, 5 minutes. Mix in tomatoes, yogurt, and pork. Season with chili and garam masala. Stir and cook for 10 minutes. Mix in cilantro and green chilies. Let cool completely.

Storage: Place in airtight containers in the refrigerator for up to 5 days (or in the freezer for up to 2 months).

Per serving: Cal 332; Carbs 12g; Fat 17g; Protein 27g

Pork & Cauliflower Goulash

Ingredients for 4 servings

2 tbsp butter	14 ounces canned tomatoes
1 cup mushrooms, sliced	1 garlic clove, minced
1 lb ground pork	1 tbsp smoked paprika
Salt and black pepper to taste	1 tbsp tomato puree
2 cups cauliflower florets	1 ½ cups water
1 onion, chopped	

Directions and Total Time: approx. 40 minutes

Melt butter in a pan over medium heat, stir in pork, and brown for 5 minutes. Place in mushrooms, garlic, and onion, and cook for 4 minutes. Stir in paprika, 1 ½ of water, tomatoes, tomato puree, cauliflower, salt, and pepper. Bring to a boil and cook for 20 minutes. Let cool.

Storage: Place in airtight containers in the refrigerator for up to 5 days (or in the freezer for up to 2 months).

Per serving: Cal 473; Carbs 8g; Fat 28g; Protein 22g

Jerk Pork Roast

Ingredients for 4 servings

2 tbsp coconut oil	2 tbsp soy sauce, sugar-free
1 ½ lb pork roast	½ cup vegetable stock
¼ cup jerk seasoning	2 tbsp brown sugar

Directions and Total Time: approx. 70 minutes

Preheat oven to 350 F. Rub the pork with coconut oil, jerk seasoning, and sugar. Heat olive oil in a pan over medium heat and sear the meat on all sides, about 4-5 minutes.

Put the pork in a baking dish, add vegetable stock and soy sauce, cover with aluminum foil, and bake for 45 minutes, turning once halfway. Then, remove the foil and continue cooking until thoroughly cooked. Let cool completely.

Storage: Place in airtight containers in the refrigerator for up to 5 days (or in the freezer for up to 2 months).

Per serving: Cal 423; Carbs 9g; Fat 22g; Protein 48g

Turnip Noodles with Pesto Pork

Ingredients for 4 servings

1 cup grated Parmesan cheese	Salt and black pepper to taste
1 tbsp butter	½ cup basil pesto
4 boneless pork chops	4 large turnips, spiralized

Directions and Total Time: approx. 1 hour 10 minutes

Preheat oven to 350 F. Season pork with salt and pepper and place on a greased baking sheet. Spread pesto on the pork and bake for 45 minutes. Pull out the baking sheet and divide half of Parmesan cheese on top. Bake further for 5 minutes; set aside. Melt butter in a skillet and sauté the turnips for 7 minutes. Stir in the remaining Parmesan and top with the pork. Let cool completely.

Storage: Place in airtight containers in the refrigerator for up to 5 days (or in the freezer for up to 2 months).

Per serving: Cal 532; Carbs 14g; Fat 28g; Protein 54g

Pork Medallions with Pancetta & Onions

Ingredients for 4 servings

1 lb pork loin, cut into medallions	
2 onions, chopped	½ cup vegetable stock
6 pancetta slices, chopped	Salt and black pepper to taste

Directions and Total Time: approx. 25 minutes

Set a pan over medium heat and cook pancetta for 3 minutes. Add in onions and stir-fry for 3 minutes; set aside. Add pork medallions to the pan and season with salt and pepper. Brown for 3 minutes on each side, turn, reduce heat, and cook for 7 minutes. Stir in vegetable stock and cook for 2 minutes. Return pancetta and onions and cook for 1 minute. Let cool completely.

Storage: Place in airtight containers in the refrigerator for up to 5 days (or in the freezer for up to 2 months).

Per serving: Cal 325, Carbs 6g, Fat 18g, Protein 36g

Grilled BBQ Pork Chops

Ingredients for 4 servings

4 pork loin chops, boneless	½ tsp ginger powder
½ cup sugar-free BBQ sauce	½ tsp garlic powder
1 tbsp brown sugar	2 tsp smoked paprika

Directions and Total Time: approx. 1 hour 20 minutes

In a bowl, mix brown sugar, ginger powder, ½ tsp garlic powder, and smoked paprika and rub pork chops on all sides with the mixture. Cover the pork chops with plastic wraps and place in the refrigerator for 1 hour.

Preheat grill. Unwrap the meat, place on the grill grate, and cook for 2 minutes per side. Reduce the heat and brush with bbq sauce; grill for 5 minutes. Flip and brush again with bbq sauce. Cook for 5 minutes. Let cool.

Storage: Place in airtight containers in the refrigerator for up to 5 days (or in the freezer for up to 2 months).

Per serving: Cal 363, Carbs 1g, Fat 28g, Protein 34g

Gingery Pork Sautée with Walnuts

Ingredients for 4 servings

1 lb pork tenderloin, cut into strips	
2 tbsp coconut oil	1 oz walnuts
1 tsp olive oil	1 tbsp freshly grated ginger
Salt and black pepper to taste	3 garlic cloves, minced
1 green bell pepper, diced	1 habanero pepper, minced
1 small red onion, diced	2 tbsp tamari sauce

Directions and Total Time: approx. 25 minutes

Heat coconut oil in a wok, season pork with salt and pepper, and cook until no longer pink, 10 minutes. Set to one side of the wok and add the bell pepper, onion, walnuts, ginger, garlic, olive oil, and habanero pepper. Sauté until fragrant and onion softened, 5 minutes. Mix everything and season with tamari sauce. Stir-fry until well combined, about 1 minute. Let cool completely.

Storage: Place in airtight containers in the refrigerator for up to 5 days (or in the freezer for up to 2 months).

Per serving: Cal 325; Carbs 7g; Fat 16g; Protein 38g

Swiss Cheese Pork Quiche

Ingredients for 6 servings

¼ cup shredded Swiss cheese	4 tbsp chia seeds
1 cup coconut cream	6 eggs
1 tbsp butter	½ lb smoked pork shoulder
2 tbsp melted butter	1 yellow onion, chopped
1 ¼ cups almond flour	1 tsp dried thyme
1 tbsp potato starch	Salt and black pepper to taste

Directions and Total Time: approx. 70 minutes

Preheat oven to 350 F. Add almond flour, psyllium husk, chia seeds, salt, butter, and 1 egg to a food processor. Mix until a firm dough forms. Oil your hands and spread the dough on the bottom of a greased springform pan.

Refrigerate while you make the filling. Melt butter in a skillet and cook the pork and onion until the meat browns, 10-12 minutes. Stir in thyme, salt, and pepper. Remove the pie crust from the fridge and spoon pork and onion onto the crust. In a bowl, whisk coconut cream, half of the Swiss cheese, and the remaining eggs. Pour the mixture over the meat filling and top with the remaining cheese. Bake until the cheese melts and a toothpick inserted into the quiche comes out clean, 45 minutes. Remove the pan, release the lock, and take off the ring. Cool. Slice into wedges.

Storage: Place in airtight containers in the refrigerator for up to 5 days (or in the freezer for up to 2 months).

Per serving: Cal 374; Carbs 11g; Fat 31g; Protein 17g

Lemony Pork Steaks with Mushrooms

Ingredients for 4 servings

3 tbsp olive oil	3 tbsp butter
8 oz white button mushrooms, chopped	
4 bone-in pork steaks	6 garlic cloves, minced
2 tsp lemon pepper seasoning	1 lemon, juiced
1 cup vegetable stock	Salt and black pepper to taste

Directions and Total Time: approx. 25 minutes

Heat 2 tbsp each of olive oil and butter in a skillet over medium heat and cook the meat until brown, 10 minutes; set aside. Heat the remaining oil and butter in the skillet. Pour in the stock to deglaze the bottom of the pan, add lemon pepper seasoning, garlic, and mushrooms, and cook until softened, 5 minutes. Return the pork, add lemon juice, and cook until the liquid reduces by two-thirds. Adjust the taste with salt and pepper. Let cool completely.

Storage: Place in airtight containers in the refrigerator for up to 5 days (or in the freezer for up to 2 months).

Per serving: Cal 490; Carbs 3g; Fat 32g; Protein 46g

Cheese Pork Burgers with Fresh Salad

Ingredients for 4 servings

3 oz Swiss cheese, shredded	2 firm tomatoes, sliced
3 tbsp extra-virgin olive oil	¼ red onion, sliced
1 lb ground pork	Salt and black pepper to taste
2 hearts romaine lettuce, torn	

Directions and Total Time: approx. 20 minutes

Season pork with salt and pepper, mix and shape several medium-sized patties. Heat 2 tbsp oil in a skillet and fry the patties on both sides for 10 minutes. Transfer to a wire rack to drain oil. When cooled, cut into quarters.

Storage: Place in airtight containers in the refrigerator for up to 5 days (or in the freezer for up to 2 months). Before serving, reheat the patties in the microwave for 1-2 minutes. Mix the lettuce, tomatoes, and onion in a bowl, and season with oil, salt, and pepper. Toss and sprinkle with the Swiss cheese. Place the patties on top. Enjoy!

Per serving: Cal 454, Carbs 2g, Fat 37g, Protein 26g

Canadian Bacon Pie

Ingredients for 6 servings

1 cup steamed cauliflower florets, chopped
6 oz Canadian bacon, chopped

¼ cup shredded mozzarella	2 cups almond flour
2 tbsp olive oil	¼ tsp xanthan gum
¼ cup butter	1 lb ground pork
1 egg	⅓ cup pureed onion
½ tsp salt	¾ tsp allspice

Directions and Total Time: approx. 10 minutes

Preheat oven to 350 F. Whisk egg, butter, almond flour, mozzarella cheese, xanthan gum, and salt in a bowl. Make 2 balls out of the mixture and refrigerate for 30 minutes. Heat olive oil in a pan and cook ground pork, Canadian bacon, onion, and allspice for 5-6 minutes. Remove to a bowl and mix in cauliflower.

Roll out the pie balls and place one at the bottom of a greased pie pan. Spread the pork mixture over the crust. Top with the other coat. Bake for 50 minutes. Let cool.

Storage: Place in airtight containers in the refrigerator for up to 5 days (or in the freezer for up to 2 months).

Per serving: Cal 485; Carbs 4g; Fat 41g; Protein 29g

Classic Hawaiian Loco Moco

Ingredients for 8 servings

2 tbsp heavy cream	5 large eggs
3 tbsp coconut oil	1 shallot, finely chopped
1 tbsp salted butter	1 cup sliced oyster mushrooms
2 tbsp olive oil	1 cup vegetable stock
1 ½ lb ground pork	1 tsp Worcestershire sauce
1/3 cup corn flour	1 tsp tamari sauce
½ tsp nutmeg powder	½ tsp xanthan gum
1 tsp onion powder	

Directions and Total Time: approx. 35 minutes

In a bowl, combine ground pork, corn flour, nutmeg, and onion powder. In another bowl, whisk 1 egg with heavy cream and mix in the pork mixture. The batter will be sticky. Mold 8 patties from the mixture; set aside.

Heat coconut oil in a skillet over medium heat. Fry the patties on both sides until no longer pink, 8-10 minutes. Place in airtight containers to cool completely. Melt the butter in the same skillet and cook shallot and mushrooms until softened, 7 minutes. In a bowl, mix vegetable stock, Worcestershire and tamari sauces. Pour the mixture over the mushrooms and cook for 3 minutes. Stir in xanthan gum and allow it to thicken for about 1 minute. Let cool completely. Pour the mushroom gravy over the patties.

Storage: Keep in the refrigerator for up to 5 days (or in the freezer for up to 2 months). Before serving, reheat in the microwave for 1-2 minutes. Heat the olive oil in a skillet and fry the eggs sunshine style, 1 minute. Top the patties. Enjoy!

Per serving: Cal 323; Carbs 2g; Fat 21g; Protein 28g

Citrus Pork Chos & Broccoli Tips

Ingredients for 4 servings

1 tbsp olive oil	3 cloves garlic, pureed
1 tbsp butter	4 pork loin chops
3 tbsp lemon juice	2 tbsp white wine
1 lb fresh broccoli tips, halved	

Directions and Total Time: approx. 60 minutes

Preheat the broiler to 400 F. Mix the lemon juice, garlic, and olive oil in a bowl. Brush the pork with the mixture, place in a baking sheet, and cook for 15-20 minutes on each side until browned. Share into airtight containers.

Melt butter in a small wok or pan and cook broccoli tips for 5 minutes until tender. Drizzle with white wine and cook for another 5 minutes. Let cool completely. Ladle broccoli to the side of the chops.

Storage: Keep in the refrigerator for up to 5 days (or in the freezer for up to 2 months).

Per serving: Cal 430, Carbs 12g, Fat 24g, Protein 46g

Fried Eggs with Pancetta & Cherry Tomatoes

Ingredients for 4 servings

3 tbsp olive oil	8 eggs
1 tbsp butter, softened	¼ cup cherry tomatoes, halved
4 oz pancetta, chopped	Salt and black pepper to taste

Directions and Total Time: approx. 25 minutes

Pour pancetta in a skillet and fry until crispy, 6 minutes; set aside. Heat the olive oil in the skillet and fry the eggs until the whites set, but the yolks are still runny, 1 minute. Transfer them to airtight containers and top with pancetta; let cool. Melt butter in the skillet, fry tomatoes until brown around the edges, 8 minutes. Remove to the airtight containers. Season to taste and let cool completely.

Storage: Keep in the refrigerator for up to 3 days.

Per serving: Cal 288; Carbs 1g; Fat 23g; Protein 20g

Easy Chorizo in Cabbage Sauce

Ingredients for 6 servings

1 ¼ cups coconut cream	½ cup fresh sage, chopped
4 tbsp butter	½ lemon, zested
18 oz chorizo sausages	2 tbsp toasted pine nuts
1 head green Canon cabbage, shredded	

Directions and Total Time: approx. 20 minutes

Melt 2 tbsp of butter in a skillet over medium heat and fry the chorizo until lightly brown on the outside, 10 minutes. Remove to a plate. Melt the remaining butter and sauté cabbage, occasionally stirring, 4 minutes. Mix in coconut cream and simmer until the cream reduces by half. Sprinkle with sage and lemon zest. Divide the chorizo between airtight containers, spoon the cabbage to the chorizo side, and sprinkle the pine nuts on top. Cool.

Storage: Keep in the refrigerator for up to 5 days (or in the freezer for up to 2 months).

Per serving: Cal 530; Carbs 13g; Fat 46g; Protein 18g

Pork Sausage & Bacon in a Skillet

Ingredients for 4 servings

1 cup grated Pecorino Romano cheese

2 tbsp olive oil	6 garlic cloves, minced
1 cup sliced pork sausage	1 cup cherry tomatoes, halved
4 bacon slices, chopped	7 fresh basil leaves
4 large kohlrabi, spiralized	1 tbsp pine nuts for topping

Directions and Total Time: approx. 20 minutes

Heat olive oil in a skillet and cook sausage and bacon until brown, 5 minutes. Transfer to a plate. Stir the kohlrabi and garlic in the skillet and cook until tender, 5-7 minutes. Add in cherry tomatoes and cook for 2 minutes. Mix in the sausage, bacon, basil, and Pecorino Romano cheese. Top with pine nuts. Let cool completely.

Storage: Place in airtight containers in the refrigerator for up to 5 days (or in the freezer for up to 2 months).

Per serving: Cal 279; Carbs 6g; Fat 21g; Protein 8g

Tex-Mex Pork Bake

Ingredients for 4 servings

½ cup shredded Monterey Jack cheese

1 cup sour cream	2 tbsp chopped jalapeños
2 tbsp butter	½ cup crushed tomatoes
1 lb ground pork	2 scallions, chopped
3 tbsp Tex-Mex seasoning	

Directions and Total Time: approx. 40 minutes

Preheat oven to 330 F. Grease a baking dish with cooking spray. Melt butter in a skillet over medium heat and cook the pork until brown, 8 minutes. Stir in Tex-Mex seasoning, jalapeños, and tomatoes; simmer for 5 minutes. Transfer the mixture to the dish and use a spoon to level at the bottom of the dish. Sprinkle the Monterey Jack cheese on top and bake for 20 until the cheese is golden brown. Let cool completely.

Storage: Place in airtight containers in the refrigerator for up to 5 days (or in the freezer for up to 2 months). Before serving, reheat in the microwave for 1-2 minutes. Top with scallions and sour cream. Enjoy!

Per serving: Cal 410; Carbs 7g; Fat 24g; Protein 43g

Mexican-Style Pizza

Ingredients for 4 servings

1 cup sliced smoked mozzarella cheese
2 cups shredded mozzarella cheese

2 tbsp cream cheese, softened	3 oz chorizo, sliced
1 tbsp olive oil	¼ cup marinara sauce
¾ cup almond flour	1 jalapeño pepper, sliced
2 tbsp almond meal	¼ red onion, thinly sliced

Directions and Total Time: approx. 40 minutes

Preheat oven to 390 F. Line a pizza pan with parchment paper. Microwave the mozzarella and cream cheeses for 30 seconds. Remove, and mix in almond flour and almond meal. Spread the mixture on the pizza pan and bake for 10 minutes or until crusty. Heat olive oil and cook chorizo until brown, 5 minutes. Spread marinara sauce on the crust, and top with smoked mozzarella cheese, chorizo, jalapeño pepper, and onion. Bake until the cheese melts, 15 minutes. Let cool completely. Slice into wedges.

Storage: Place in airtight containers in the refrigerator for up to 5 days (or in the freezer for up to 2 months).

Per serving: Cal 474; Carbs 4g; Fats 37g; Protein 26g

Baked Pork Chops with Mushroom Sauce

Ingredients for 4 servings

2 (14-oz) cans mushroom soup
1 onion, chopped   ½ cup sliced mushrooms
4 pork chops   Salt and black pepper to taste

Directions and Total Time: approx. 55 minutes

Preheat the oven to 375 F. Season the pork chops with salt and pepper and place them in a baking dish. Combine the mushroom soup, mushrooms, and onion in a bowl. Pour over the pork chops. Bake for 45 minutes. Let cool.

Storage: Place in airtight containers in the refrigerator for up to 5 days (or in the freezer for up to 2 months).

Per serving: Cal 423; Carbs 12g; Fat 28g; Protein 37g

Pork Sausage & Spinach Pizza

Ingredients for 8 servings

1 lb Italian pork sausages, crumbled
½ cup grated Monterey Jack cheese
4 cups grated mozzarella   1 cup almond flour
¼ cup grated Parmesan   2 eggs
2 tbsp cream cheese, softened 1 onion, thinly sliced
1 tbsp olive oil   2 garlic cloves, minced
1 cup chopped bell peppers   1 cup baby spinach
¼ cup coconut flour   ½ cup sugar-free pizza sauce

Directions and Total Time: approx. 40 minutes

Preheat oven to 390 F. Line a pizza pan with parchment paper. Microwave 2 cups of mozzarella cheese and 2 tbsp of the cream cheese for 1 minute. Mix in sausages, coconut flour, almond flour, Parmesan cheese, and eggs. Spread the mixture on the pizza pan and bake for 15 minutes; set aside.

Heat olive oil in a skillet and sauté onion, garlic, and bell peppers for 5 minutes. Stir in baby spinach and allow wilting for 3 minutes. Spread the pizza sauce on the crust and top with the pepper mixture. Scatter mozzarella and Monterey Jack cheese on top. Bake for 5 minutes. Cool.

Storage: Place in airtight containers in the refrigerator for up to 5 days (or in the freezer for up to 2 months).

Per serving: Cal 434; Carbs 17g; Fats 28g; Protein 23g

Simple Chili Pork Chops

Ingredients for 4 servings

4 pork chops   2 tsp chili powder
¾ cup cumin powder   Salt and black pepper to taste

Directions and Total Time: approx. 15 minutes

In a bowl, combine cumin with salt, black pepper, and chili powder. Place in the pork chops and rub them well. Heat a grill over medium temperature. Add in the pork chops, cook for 5 minutes, flip, and cook for 5 minutes. Cool.

Storage: Place in airtight containers in the refrigerator for up to 5 days (or in the freezer for up to 2 months).

Per serving: Cal 349; Carbs 1g; Fat 21g; Protein 42g

Hoisin Glazed Pork Chops

Ingredients for 4 servings

4 oz hoisin sauce, sugar-free 1 tbsp brown sugar
4 pork chops   ½ tsp ginger powder
Salt and black pepper to taste 2 tsp smoked paprika

Directions and Total Time: approx. 2 hours 20 minutes

In a bowl, mix salt, pepper, brown sugar, ginger, and paprika; rub pork chops with the mixture. Cover with plastic wraps and refrigerate for 2 hours.

Preheat grill. Sear the meat for 2 minutes per side. Reduce the heat and brush with the hoisin sauce, cover, and grill for 5 minutes. Turn the meat and brush again with hoisin sauce. Cook for 5 minutes. Let cool completely.

Storage: Place in airtight containers in the refrigerator for up to 5 days (or in the freezer for up to 2 months).

Per serving: Cal 412; Carbs 11g; Fat 23g; Protein 37g

Cheddar & Pork Sausage Omelet

Ingredients for 3 servings

2 oz shredded cheddar cheese 2 oz pork sausage, crumbled
2 tbsp olive oil   1 small white onion, chopped
2 tbsp butter   6 eggs
¼ cup sliced cremini mushrooms

Directions and Total Time: approx. 30 minutes

Heat olive oil in a pan over medium heat, add in pork sausage, and fry for 10 minutes; set aside. In the same pan, sauté the onion and mushrooms, 8 minutes; set aside. Melt the butter over low heat. Beat the eggs into a bowl until smooth and frothy. Pour the eggs into the pan, swirl to spread around, and the omelet begins to firm. Top with sausages, mushroom-onion mixture, and cheddar cheese. Using a spatula, carefully remove the egg mixture around the edges of the pan and, flip over the stuffing, and cook for about 2 minutes. Let cool completely. Slice into wedges.

Storage: Place in airtight containers in the refrigerator for up to 5 days (or in the freezer for up to 2 months).

Per serving: Cal 383; Carbs 5g; Fat 31g; Protein 23g

Pork & Broccoli Pie

Ingredients for 8 servings

5 oz shredded Swiss cheese	½ celery, finely chopped
½ cup crème fraîche	2 lb ground pork
3 oz butter, melted	2 tbsp tamari sauce
2 tbsp butter, cold	2 tbsp Worcestershire sauce
1 head broccoli, cut into florets	½ tbsp hot sauce
1 whole egg	1 tsp onion powder

Directions and Total Time: approx. 45 minutes

Preheat oven to 400 F. Bring a pot of salted water to boil and cook broccoli for 3-5 minutes. Drain and transfer to a food processor; grind until rice-like. Transfer to a bowl. Add in crème fraiche, egg, celery, butter, and half of the Swiss cheese. Mix to combine. Melt the cold butter in a pot, add, and cook the pork until brown, 10 minutes. Mix in tamari, hot and Worcestershire sauces, and onion powder; cook for 3 minutes. Spread the mixture on a greased baking dish and cover it with the broccoli mix. Sprinkle with the remaining cheese and bake for 20 minutes. Let cool completely. Slice into wedges.

Storage: Place in airtight containers in the refrigerator for up to 5 days (or in the freezer for up to 2 months).

Per serving: Cal 516; Carbs 7g; Fat 39g; Protein 38g

South Asian Satay Pork Chops

Ingredients for 4 servings

2 lb boneless pork loin chops, cut into 2-inch pieces	
1/3 cup peanut butter	½ tsp onion powder
Salt and black pepper to taste	½ tsp hot sauce
1 medium white onion, sliced	1 cup chicken broth
¼ cup tamari sauce	3 tbsp xanthan gum
½ tsp garlic powder	1 tbsp chopped peanuts

Directions and Total Time: approx. 70 minutes

Season pork with salt and pepper and put into a pot with onion. In a bowl, combine peanut butter, tamari sauce, garlic and onion powders, hot sauce, and two-thirds of the chicken broth. Pour the mixture over the meat. Bring to a boil over high heat, reduce the heat, and simmer for 1 hour or until the meat becomes tender. In a bowl, combine the remaining broth and xanthan gum. Stir the mixture into the meat and simmer until the sauce thickens, 2 minutes. Garnish with peanuts and let cool completely.

Storage: Place in airtight containers in the refrigerator for up to 5 days (or in the freezer for up to 2 months).

Per serving: Cal 455; Carbs 7g; Fat 19g; Protein 57g

Bacon-Parmesan Muffins

Ingredients for 4 servings

4 eggs, separated into egg whites and egg yolks	
1 ½ cups shredded Parmesan	2 tbsp almond flour
1 cup heavy cream	4 oz bacon, chopped, cooked
2 tbsp butter, softened	

Directions and Total Time: approx. 50 minutes

Preheat oven to 350 F. Warm the butter over medium heat and mix in almond flour until well combined. Whisk in heavy cream and bring to a boil with frequent stirring. Turn the heat off and let cool for 3 minutes. Whisk in egg yolks one after another until well combined and then, mix in Parmesan cheese. Beat the egg whites until stiff peaks form. Slowly fold this mixture into the egg yolk mix until combined. Divide the mixture between 4 greased ramekins, top with bacon, and bake for 35 minutes or until slightly risen above the rim of the ramekins and golden brown. Let cool completely.

Storage: Keep in the refrigerator for up to 5 days.

Per serving: Cal 437; Carbs 8g, Fat 47g, Protein 21g

Chinese Pork with Celeriac Noodles

Ingredients for 4 servings

1 tbsp sesame oil	Salt and black pepper to taste
2 tbsp butter	1 lb pork tenderloin, cubed
3 tbsp sugar-free maple syrup	4 large celeriac, spiralized
3 tbsp coconut aminos	24 oz bok choy, chopped
1 tbsp fresh ginger paste	2 green onions, chopped
¼ tsp Chinese five spice	2 tbsp sesame seeds

Directions and Total Time: approx. 85 minutes

Preheat oven to 400 F. Line a baking sheet with foil. In a bowl, mix maple syrup, coconut aminos, ginger paste, Chinese powder, salt, and pepper. Spoon the mixture into a bowl and mix in the pork cubes; refrigerate for 25 minutes. Melt butter in a skillet and sauté celeriac for 7 minutes; set aside. Remove the pork from the marinade onto the baking sheet and bake for 40 minutes. Heat sesame oil in a skillet and sauté bok choy and celeriac pasta for 3 minutes. Transfer to airtight containers and top with pork. Garnish with green onions and sesame seeds. Drizzle with the reserved marinade. Let cool completely.

Storage: Place in the refrigerator for up to 5 days (or in the freezer for up to 2 months).

Per serving: Cal 409; Carbs 3g; Fats 18g; Protein 44g

Indian Pork Bake

Ingredients for 4 servings

1 ¼ cups coconut cream	2 tbsp garam masala
3 tbsp butter	1 green bell pepper, diced
1 lb ground pork	1 tbsp fresh cilantro, chopped

Directions and Total Time: approx. 35 minutes

Preheat oven to 400 F. Melt butter in a skillet and brown the ground pork for about 4 minutes. Stir in garam masala. Transfer the mixture to a baking dish. Mix in bell pepper, coconut cream, and cilantro and bake for 20 minutes. Cool.

Storage: Place in airtight containers in the refrigerator for up to 5 days (or in the freezer for up to 2 months).

Per serving: Cal 563; Carbs 5g; Fat 42g; Protein 35g

SEAFOOD

Greek-Style Tilapia

Ingredients for 4 servings

2 tbsp olive oil
4 tilapia fillets
2 garlic cloves, minced
½ tsp dry oregano

14 oz canned diced tomatoes
½ red onion, chopped
1 tbsp fresh parsley, chopped
¼ cup Kalamata olives

Directions and Total Time: approx. 25 minutes

Heat oil in a skillet over medium heat and cook onion for 3 minutes. Add garlic and oregano and cook for 30 seconds.

Stir in tomatoes and bring the mixture to a boil. Reduce the heat and simmer for 5 minutes. Add olives and tilapia. Cook for 8 minutes. Top with parsley. Let cool completely.

Storage: Place in airtight containers in the refrigerator for up to 5 days (or in the freezer for up to 2 months).

Per serving: Cal 182; Carbs 6g; Fat 15g; Protein 23g

Californian Tilapia Tacos

Ingredients for 4 servings

1 tbsp olive oil
1 red chili pepper, minced
1 tsp coriander seeds
4 tilapia fillets, chopped

1 tsp smoked paprika
4 zero-carb tortillas
Salt and black pepper to taste
1 lemon, juiced

Directions and Total Time: approx. 15 minutes

Season the fish with salt, pepper, and paprika. Heat olive oil in a skillet over medium heat. Add tilapia, coriander seeds, and chili pepper and stir-fry for 6 minutes. Pour in lemon juice and cook for 2 minutes. Divide the fish between the tortillas. Let cool completely.

Storage: Place in airtight containers in the refrigerator for up to 3 days.

Per serving: Cal 247; Carbs 7g; Fat 11g; Protein 24g

Delicious Cod Patties with Avocado Sauce

Ingredients for 4 servings

1 cup Swiss cheese, grated
4 tbsp olive oil
1 lb cod fillets, cubed
¼ cup mayonnaise
¼ cup almond flour
2 eggs

Salt and black pepper to taste
1 tbsp chopped dill
1 large avocado, mashed
½ cup yogurt
2 tbsp lime juice
2 tbsp fresh cilantro, chopped

Directions and Total Time: approx. 25 minutes

In a bowl, mix the cod cubes, mayonnaise, flour, eggs, salt, pepper, Swiss cheese, and dill. Warm 2 tbsp of oil in a skillet over medium heat. Fetch 2 tbsp of the fish mixture into the skillet and use the back of a spatula to flatten the top. Cook for 4 minutes, flip, and fry for 4 minutes. Remove onto a wire rack and repeat until the fish batter is over. Let cool completely.

Storage: Place in airtight containers in the refrigerator for up to 5 days (or in the freezer for up to 2 months). Before serving, reheat in the microwave for 1-2 minutes. In a small bowl, mix the avocado, lime juice, yogurt, cilantro, salt, and pepper. Pour the salsa over the fritters and enjoy!

Per serving: Cal 487; Carbs 9g; Fat 35g; Protein 33g

Parmesan Cod & Cauliflower Gratin

Ingredients for 4 servings

¼ cup grated Parmesan
1 cup crème fraiche
1 tbsp butter, melted

10 oz cauliflower florets
2 cod fillets, cubed
2 white fish fillets, cubed

Directions and Total Time: approx. 45 minutes

Preheat oven to 400 F. Coat fish cubes and broccoli with butter. Spread on a greased baking dish. Mix crème fraiche with Parmesan cheese. Smear the mixture on the fish. Bake for 25-30 minutes. Let cool completely.

Storage: Place in airtight containers in the refrigerator for up to 5 days (or in the freezer for up to 2 months).

Per serving: Cal 424; Carbs 14g; Fat 21g; Protein 38g

Cod Fillets with Hazelnut Crust

Ingredients for 2 servings

2 tbsp ghee
4 cod fillets

¼ cup roasted hazelnuts
A pinch of cayenne pepper

Directions and Total Time: approx. 20 minutes

Preheat your oven to 425 F. Line a baking dish with waxed paper. Melt the ghee and brush it over the fish. In a food processor, combine the rest of the ingredients. Coat the cod with the mixture. Transfer to the baking dish and bake for about 15 minutes. Let cool completely.

Storage: Place in airtight containers in the refrigerator for up to 5 days (or in the freezer for up to 2 months).

Per serving: Cal 367; Carbs 2g; Fat 21g; Protein 40g

Seasoned Cod Tortillas with Slaw

Ingredients for 4 servings

2 tbsp olive oil
1 tsp chili powder
4 cod fillets
1 tsp paprika
4 zero-carb tortillas

½ cup red cabbage, shredded
1 tbsp lemon juice
1 tsp apple cider vinegar
Salt and black pepper to taste

Directions and Total Time: approx. 15 minutes

Season cod fillets with chili powder, paprika, salt, and pepper. Heat half of olive oil in a skillet over medium heat. Add cod and cook until blackened, about 6 minutes. Cut into strips. Let cool. Divide the fish between the tortillas. Combine cabbage, lemon juice, vinegar, and remaining olive oil in a bowl; toss to combine. Add to the tortillas.

Storage: Keep in the refrigerator for up to 2 days.

Per serving: Cal 214; Carbs 5g; Fat 5g; Protein 24g

Creamy Salmon with Shirataki Fettucine

Ingredients for 4 servings

2 (8 oz) packs shirataki fettucine
1 ¼ cups heavy cream
4 tbsp butter
2 salmon fillets, cubed
Salt and black pepper to taste
3 garlic cloves, minced
½ cup dry white wine
1 tsp lemon zest
1 cup baby spinach

Directions and Total Time: approx. 30 minutes

Boil 2 cups of water in a pot. Strain the shirataki pasta and rinse well under hot running water. Allow proper draining and pour the shirataki pasta into the boiling water. Cook for 3 minutes and strain again. Place a dry skillet and stir-fry the shirataki pasta until visibly dry, 1-2 minutes; set aside. Melt half of the butter in a skillet over medium heat; season the salmon with salt and pepper and cook for 8 minutes; set aside. Melt remaining butter to the skillet and stir in garlic. Cook for 30 seconds. Mix in heavy cream, white wine, lemon zest, salt, and pepper. Cook over low heat for 5 minutes. Stir in spinach, let it wilt for 2 minutes and stir in shirataki fettucine and salmon. Let cool.

Storage: Place in airtight containers in the refrigerator for up to 5 days (or in the freezer for up to 2 months).

Per serving: Cal 514; Carbs 16g; Fats 33g; Protein 40g

Juicy Salmon Fillets

Ingredients for 4 servings

¼ cup heavy cream
2 tbsp butter
2 tbsp duck fat
4 salmon fillets
Salt and black pepper to taste
½ tsp tarragon, chopped

Directions and Total Time: approx. 15 minutes

Season the salmon with salt and pepper. Melt the duck fat in a pan over medium heat. Add salmon and cook for 4 minutes on both sides. Place in airtight containers.

In the same pan, melt the butter and add the tarragon. Cook for 30 seconds to infuse the flavors. Whisk in heavy cream and cook for 1 minute. Pour the sauce over the salmon. Let cool completely.

Storage: Keep in the refrigerator for up to 5 days (or in the freezer for up to 2 months).

Per serving: Cal 523; Carbs 0g; Fat 27g; Protein 63g

Trout & Zucchini Bake

Ingredients for 4 servings

¼ cup cheddar cheese, grated
Grated Parmesan for topping
1 tbsp butter, melted
4 deboned trout fillets
2 zucchinis, sliced
1 cup Greek yogurt

Directions and Total Time: approx. 40 minutes

Preheat oven to 390 F. Brush the fish and zucchini slices with melted butter. Spread them in a greased baking dish. Mix the Greek yogurt with cheddar cheese in a bowl.

Pour and smear the mixture on the fish and sprinkle with Parmesan cheese. Bake for 30 minutes until golden brown. Let cool completely.

Storage: Place in airtight containers in the refrigerator for up to 5 days (or in the freezer for up to 2 months).

Per serving: Cal 362; Carbs 5g; Fat 23g; Protein 31g

Restaurant-Style Salmon Panzanella

Ingredients for 4 servings

1 lb skinned salmon, cut into 4 steaks each
8 black olives, pitted and chopped
3 tbsp olive oil
1 cucumber, cubed
Salt and black pepper to taste
1 tbsp capers, rinsed
2 large tomatoes, diced
3 tbsp white wine vinegar
¼ cup thinly sliced red onions
2 slices zero-carb bread, cubed

Directions and Total Time: approx. 20 minutes

Preheat the grill to high. Season the salmon with salt and pepper and grill it on both sides for 8 minutes. Let cool.

Storage: Place in airtight containers in the refrigerator for up to 5 days (or in the freezer for up to 2 months). Before serving, reheat the salmon in the microwave for 1-2 minutes. In a bowl, mix cucumber, black olives, salt, pepper, capers, tomatoes, white wine vinegar, onions, olive oil, and bread cubes. Top with salmon and enjoy!

Per serving: Cal 338; Carbs 11g; Fat 21g; Protein 38g

Teriyaki Salmon with Steamed Broccoli

Ingredients for 4 servings

¼ cup grated Pecorino Romano cheese
4 salmon fillets
½ cup teriyaki sauce
1 bunch of broccoli rabe
Salt and black pepper to taste

Directions and Total Time: approx. 55 minutes

Cover the salmon with the teriyaki sauce and refrigerate for 30 minutes. Steam the broccoli rabe for 4-5 minutes until tender. Season with salt and pepper; set aside. Preheat the oven to 400 F. Remove the salmon from the fridge and place in a greased baking dish. Bake for 14-16 minutes. Top with Pecorino Romano cheese. Let cool completely.

Storage: Place in airtight containers in the refrigerator for up to 5 days (or in the freezer for up to 2 months).

Per serving: Cal 454; Carbs 8g; Fat 23g; Protein 51g

Fajita Salmon with Avocado

Ingredients for 4 servings

2 tbsp olive oil
4 salmon fillets
1 yellow onion sliced
2 mixed peppers sliced
1 tbsp fajita seasoning

Directions and Total Time: approx. 30 minutes

Preheat oven to 380 F. Arrange the salmon fillets and sliced veggies on a baking sheet. Drizzle with olive oil and sprinkle with fajita seasoning; toss the veggies to coat.

Bake for about 15-18 minutes or until the salmon is easily flaked with a fork. Divide between containers and keep in the fridges for up to 4 days. Let cool completely.

Storage: Place in airtight containers in the refrigerator for up to 5 days (or in the freezer for up to 2 months). Before serving, reheat in the microwave for 1-2 minutes. Garnish with sliced avocado, and enjoy!

Per serving: Cal 478; Carbs 6g; Fat 23g; Protein 56g

Pistachio-Crusted Baked Salmon

Ingredients for 4 servings

1 cup heavy cream
1 tbsp olive oil
4 salmon fillets
¼ cup mayonnaise
½ cup ground pistachios
1 chopped shallot
2 tsp lemon zest

Directions and Total Time: approx. 25 minutes

Preheat oven to 375 F. Spread mayonnaise on the fillets. Coat with ground pistachios. Place in a lined baking dish and bake for 15 minutes. Heat the olive oil in a saucepan and sauté the shallot for 3 minutes. Stir in heavy cream and lemon zest. Bring to a boil and cook until thickened. Pour the sauce over the salmon and let cool completely.

Storage: Place in airtight containers in the refrigerator for up to 5 days (or in the freezer for up to 2 months).

Per serving: Cal 563; Carbs 13g; Fat 31g; Protein 52g

Smoked Salmon & Parsnip Croquettes

Ingredients for 6 servings

12 oz sliced smoked salmon, finely chopped
4 tbsp olive oil   2 eggs, beaten
1 parsnip, cooked and mashed 2 tbsp pesto sauce
Salt and chili pepper to taste   1 tbsp pork rinds, crushed

Directions and Total Time: approx. 20 minutes

In a bowl, add the salmon, parsnip, eggs, pesto sauce, pork rinds, salt, and chili pepper. Mix well and make 6 compact balls. Heat olive oil in a skillet over medium heat and fry the balls for 3 minutes on each side until golden brown. Remove to a wire rack to cool completely.

Storage: Place in airtight containers in the refrigerator for up to 5 days (or in the freezer for up to 2 months).

Per serving: Cal 254; Carbs 4g; Fat 17g; Protein 21g

Salmon Caesar Salad with Poached Eggs

Ingredients for 4 servings

½ cup chopped smoked salmon
2 tbsp low-carb caesar dressing 2 cups torn romaine lettuce
8 eggs   4 pancetta slices

Directions and Total Time: approx. 30 minutes

Boil 3 cups of water in a pot over medium heat. Crack each egg into a small bowl and gently slide into the water.

Poach for 2-3 minutes, remove, and transfer to a plate. Poach the remaining eggs. Put the pancetta in a skillet and fry for 6 minutes, turning once. Cool and chop into small pieces. Toss the lettuce, smoked salmon, pancetta, and Caesar dressing in a salad bowl. Top with the eggs.

Storage: Place in airtight containers in the refrigerator for up to 2 days.

Per serving: Cal 360; Carbs 5g; Fat 21g; Protein 17g

Sheet Pan Mahi-Mahi with Dill & Cheese

Ingredients for 4 servings

½ cup grated Pecorino Romano cheese
1 cup sour cream   ½ lemon, zested and juiced
2 tbsp dill, minced   4 mahi-mahi fillets

Directions and Total Time: approx. 25 minutes

Preheat oven to 400 F. Line a baking sheet with parchment paper. In a bowl, mix sour cream, dill, and lemon zest; set aside. Drizzle the mahi-mahi with lemon juice and arrange on the baking sheet. Spread sour cream mixture on top and sprinkle with Pecorino Romano cheese. Bake for 15 minutes. Broil the top for 2 minutes until nicely brown. Let cool completely.

Storage: Place in airtight containers in the refrigerator for up to 5 days (or in the freezer for up to 2 months).

Per serving: Cal 338; Carbs 2g; Fat 23g; Protein 21g

Hazelnut-Crusted Sea Bass

Ingredients for 2 servings

2 tbsp butter   ⅓ cup roasted hazelnuts
2 sea bass fillets   A pinch of cayenne pepper

Directions and Total Time: approx. 20 minutes

Preheat oven to 420 F. Line a baking dish with waxed paper. Melt butter and brush it over the fillets. In a food processor, combine the remaining ingredients. Coat the fish with the hazelnut mixture. Bake for 15 minutes. Cool.

Storage: Place in airtight containers in the refrigerator for up to 5 days (or in the freezer for up to 2 months).

Per serving: Cal 467; Carbs 2g; Fat 31g; Protein 40g

Tuna Pickle Boats

Ingredients for 6 servings

18 oz canned and drained tuna
6 large dill pickles   ½ cup light mayonnaise
¼ tsp garlic powder   1 tsp onion powder

Directions and Total Time: approx. 40 minutes

Mix the mayo, tuna, onion powder, and garlic powder in a bowl. Cut the pickles in half, lengthwise. Top each half with the tuna mixture. Place in airtight containers.

Storage: Keep in the refrigerator for up to 5 days.

Per serving: Cal 120; Carbs 5g; Fat 4g; Protein 17g

Baked Tuna Stuffed Avocados

Ingredients for 4 servings

4 oz Colby Jack, grated
2 avocados, halved and pitted
2 oz canned tuna, flaked
2 tbsp chives, chopped
Salt and black pepper, to taste

Directions and Total Time: approx. 20 minutes

Preheat oven to 360 F. Set avocado halves in an ovenproof dish. In a bowl, mix colby Jack cheese, chives, pepper, salt, and tuna. Stuff the cheese/tuna mixture in avocado halves. Bake for 15 minutes or until the top is golden brown. Let cool completely.

Storage: Place in airtight containers in the refrigerator for up to 5 days (or in the freezer for up to 2 months).

Per serving: Cal: 316; Carbs 9g; Fat 24g; Protein 16g

Asparagus & Tuna Traybake

Ingredients for 4 servings

1 cup grated Parmesan cheese
1 bunch asparagus, trimmed and cut into 1-inch pieces
1 (15 oz) can tuna in water, drained and flaked
1 cup green beans, chopped
2 tbsp cornstarch
1 tbsp butter
1 ½ cups coconut milk
4 zucchinis, spiralized

Directions and Total Time: approx. 40 minutes

Preheat the oven to 380 F. Melt butter in a skillet and sauté green beans and asparagus until softened, about 5 minutes; set aside. In a saucepan over medium heat, mix in cornstarch with coconut milk. Bring to a boil and cook with frequent stirring until thickened, 3 minutes. Stir in half of the Parmesan cheese until melted. Mix in the green beans, asparagus, zucchini, and tuna. Transfer the mixture to a baking dish and cover with the remaining Parmesan cheese. Bake until the cheese is melted and golden, about 20 minutes. Let cool completely.

Storage: Place in airtight containers in the refrigerator for up to 5 days (or in the freezer for up to 2 months).

Per serving: Cal 470; Carbs 19g; Fats 32g; Protein 33g

Mediterranean Sardines with Bacon

Ingredients for 2 servings

2 tbsp olive oil from the sardine can
½ cup canned diced tomatoes
4 cups zoodles
2 oz cubed bacon
4 oz canned sardines, drained and chopped
1 tbsp capers
1 tbsp parsley
1 tsp minced garlic

Directions and Total Time: approx. 15 minutes

Warm the sardine oil in a pan over medium heat. Cook the garlic and bacon for 3 minutes. Stir in the tomatoes and simmer for 5 minutes. Add zoodles, capers, parsley, and sardines and cook for 3 minutes. Let cool completely.

Storage: Place in airtight containers in the refrigerator for up to 5 days (or in the freezer for up to 2 months).

Per serving: Cal 412; Carbs 6g; Fat 31g; Protein 20g

Lemony Haddock with Butter Sauce

Ingredients for 4 servings

2 tsp olive oil
4 tbsp salted butter
4 haddock fillets
Salt and black pepper to taste
4 cloves garlic, minced
¼ cup lemon juice
3 tbsp white wine
2 tbsp chopped chives

Directions and Total Time: approx. 20 minutes

Heat oil in a skillet and season the haddock with salt and black pepper. Fry the fillets for 4 minutes, flip, and cook for 1 more minute; set aside. In another skillet, melt butter and sauté garlic for 1 minute. Add in lemon juice, white wine, and chives. Season with salt and pepper and cook for 3 minutes. Put the fish in the skillet, spoon sauce over, cook for 30 seconds, and turn the heat off. Let cool.

Storage: Place in airtight containers in the refrigerator for up to 5 days (or in the freezer for up to 2 months).

Per serving: Cal 310; Carbs 3g; Fat 17g; Protein 20g

Golden Mackerel with Green Bean Salad

Ingredients for 2 servings

1 tbsp coconut oil
2 tbsp olive oil
2 mackerel fillets
2 hard-boiled eggs, sliced
2 cups green beans
1 avocado, sliced
4 cups mixed salad greens
2 tbsp lemon juice
1 tsp Dijon mustard
Salt and black pepper to taste

Directions and Total Time: approx. 25 minutes

Fill a saucepan with water and add the beans and salt. Cook over medium heat for 3 minutes. Drain and set aside. Melt the coconut oil in a pan over medium heat. Add the mackerel fillets and cook for about 4 minutes per side, or until opaque and crispy. Let cool completely. Divide the greens between airtight containers. Top with mackerel.

Storage: Keep in the refrigerator for up to 2 days. To serve, reheat in the microwave for 1-2 minutes. Top with egg and avocado slices. In a bowl, whisk lemon juice, olive oil, mustard, salt, and pepper and drizzle over the salad.

Per serving: Cal 525; Carbs 16g; Fat 32g; Protein 37g

Broccoli Mash with Anchovies

Ingredients for 4 servings

4 tbsp heavy cream
4 oz butter
1 head broccoli, cut into florets
2 anchovy fillets, chopped
¼ tsp dried thyme
½ lemon, juiced and zested

Directions and Total Time: approx. 15 minutes

Pour broccoli into a pot over high heat and cover with salted water. Bring to a boil and cook until tender, about 7 minutes. Drain and transfer to a bowl. Add in butter, thyme, lemon juice and zest, heavy cream, and anchovies. Using a blender, puree the ingredients until smooth. Cool.

Storage: Keep in the refrigerator for up to 6 days.

Per serving: Cal 376; Carbs 6g; Fat 33g; Protein 11g

Mackarel & Root Veggie Bake

Ingredients for 4 servings

2 tbsp olive oil	1 fennel bulb, sliced
4 mackerel fillets	2 shallots, cut into wedges
Salt and black pepper to taste	2 tsp lemon zest
1 daikon, sliced	2 tbsp horseradish sauce

Directions and Total Time: approx. 45 minutes

Preheat oven to 360 F. Place shallots, daikon, and fennel in a greased baking pan and drizzle with some olive oil. Season with salt and pepper. Bake for 14-16 minutes. Remove and arrange the mackerel on top. Sprinkle with salt, pepper, remaining olive oil, and lemon zest. Return to the oven and bake for another 15-20 minutes until the fish easily flakes. Let cool. Top with horseradish sauce.

Storage: Place in airtight containers in the refrigerator for up to 5 days (or in the freezer for up to 2 months).

Per serving: Cal 463; Carbs 6g; Fat 36g; Protein 27g

Rutabaga & Mackerel Fish Balls

Ingredients for 6 servings

4 smoked mackerel steaks, bones removed, flaked	
3 tbsp olive oil	3 eggs, beaten
1 rutabaga, peeled and diced	2 tbsp mayonnaise
Salt and chili pepper to taste	1 tbsp pork rinds, crushed

Directions and Total Time: approx. 20 minutes

Bring rutabaga to a boil in salted water for 8 minutes. Drain, transfer to a bowl, and mash the lumps. Add smoked mackerel, eggs, mayonnaise, rinds, salt, and chili pepper. Make 6 compact balls. Heat olive oil in a skillet and fry the patties for 3 minutes on each side. Cool completely.

Storage: Place in airtight containers in the refrigerator for up to 5 days (or in the freezer for up to 2 months).

Per serving: Cal 324; Carbs 12g; Fat 21g; Protein 23g

Original Brasilian Moqueca

Ingredients for 6 servings

1 ½ pounds shrimp, peeled and deveined	
3 tbsp olive oil	14 oz canned diced tomatoes
1 cup coconut milk	2 tbsp harissa sauce
2 tbsp lime juice	1 chopped onion
¼ cup diced roasted peppers	¼ cup chopped cilantro
1 garlic clove, minced	Salt and black pepper to taste

Directions and Total Time: approx. 20 minutes

Warm olive oil in a pot over medium heat and sauté onion and garlic for 3 minutes. Add in tomatoes and shrimp. Cook for 3-4 minutes. Stir in harissa sauce, roasted peppers, and coconut milk and cook for 2 minutes. Mix in lime juice, cilantro, salt, and pepper. Let cool completely.

Storage: Place in airtight containers in the refrigerator for up to 5 days (or in the freezer for up to 2 months).

Per serving: Cal 414; Carbs 11g; Fat 24g; Protein 26g

Peruvian Shrimp Stew

Ingredients for 6 servings

¼ cup olive oil	14 oz diced tomatoes
1 cup coconut milk	2 tbsp sriracha sauce
2 tbsp lime juice	¼ cup chopped onions
¼ cup diced roasted peppers	¼ cup chopped cilantro
1 ½ lb shrimp, deveined	Fresh dill, chopped to garnish
1 garlic clove, minced	Salt and black pepper to taste

Directions and Total Time: approx. 20 minutes

Heat olive oil in a pot over medium heat and cook onions and garlic for 3 minutes. Add in tomatoes, shrimp, and cilantro. Cook for about 3-4 minutes. Stir in roasted peppers, sriracha, and coconut milk and cook for 2 more minutes. Do not bring to a boil. Stir in lime juice and dill and season with salt and pepper. Let cool completely.

Storage: Place in airtight containers in the refrigerator for up to 5 days (or in the freezer for up to 2 months).

Per serving: Cal 394; Carbs 11g; Fat 21g, Protein 23g

Easy Chimichurri Prawns

Ingredients for 4 servings

2 tbsp olive oil	Juice of 1 lime
1 lb prawns, deveined	

Chimichurri sauce:

¼ cup olive oil	¼ cup red wine vinegar
2 garlic cloves	2 cups parsley
¼ cup red onion, chopped	Salt and chili powder to taste

Directions and Total Time: approx. 40 minutes

Combine prawns, olive oil, and lime juice in a bowl and marinate in the fridge for 30 minutes. Preheat the grill to medium heat. Add prawns and cook for 2 minutes per side. Let cool completely. Place in airtight containers.

Storage: Keep in the refrigerator for up to 5 days. Before serving, reheat in the microwave for 1-2 minutes. Process all chimichurri ingredients in your blender until smooth. Pour over the prawns. Enjoy!

Per serving: Cal 343; Carbs 5g; Fat 28g; Protein 23g

Prawn & Avocado Salad

Ingredients for 4 servings

¼ cup + 1 tbsp olive oil	2 avocados, chopped
1 cauliflower head, florets only	¼ cup lemon juice
1 lb medium-sized prawns	1 tsp lemon zest

Directions and Total Time: approx. 20 minutes

Heat 1 tbsp olive oil in a skillet and cook the prawns for 8-10 minutes. Microwave cauliflower for 5 minutes; cool. Place prawns, cauliflower, and avocado in airtight containers. Whisk together the remaining olive oil, lemon zest, and juice in a bowl. Pour the dressing over.

Storage: Keep in the refrigerator for up to 3 days.

Per serving: Cal 264; Carbs 5g; Fat 21g; Protein 15g

Garlic-lime Shrimp with Zucchini Pasta

Ingredients for 4 servings

1 cup grated Parmesan cheese	¼ cup white wine
2 tbsp butter	1 lime, zested and juiced
1 lb jumbo shrimp, deveined	3 zucchinis, spiralized
4 garlic cloves, minced	2 tbsp chopped parsley
1 pinch red chili flakes	Salt and black pepper to taste

Directions and Total Time: approx. 15 minutes

Melt butter in a skillet and cook the shrimp for 3-4 minutes. Flip and stir in garlic and red chili flakes. Cook further for 1 minute; set aside. Pour wine and lime juice into the skillet and cook until reduced by a third. Stir to deglaze the bottom. Mix in zucchini, lime zest, shrimp, and parsley. Season with salt and pepper and cook for 2 minutes. Top with Parmesan cheese. Let cool completely.

Storage: Place in airtight containers in the refrigerator for up to 5 days (or in the freezer for up to 2 months).

Per serving: Cal 275; Carbs 12g; Fat 16g; Protein 23g

Shrimp Sushi Rolls

Ingredients for 3 servings

4 cups cooked shrimp	12 hand roll nori sheets
2 tbsp Sriracha sauce	½ cup mayonnaise
1 small cucumber, julienned	2 tbsp fresh dill, chopped

Directions and Total Time: approx. 10 minutes

Chop the shrimp and combine with mayonnaise, dill, and sriracha sauce in a bowl. Place a single nori sheet on a flat surface and spread about a fifth of the shrimp mixture; add the cucumber. Roll the nori sheet as desired. Repeat with the rest of the ingredients. Place in airtight containers.

Storage: Keep in the refrigerator for up to 3 days.

Per serving: Cal 310; Carbs 4g; Fat 21g; Protein 18g

Shrimp Scampi Pizza

Ingredients for 4 servings

¼ cup grated Parmesan	2 garlic cloves, minced
2 cups grated cheese blend	¼ cup white wine
3 tbsp olive oil	½ tsp dried basil
2 tbsp butter	½ tsp dried parsley
½ cup almond flour	½ lemon, juiced
¼ tsp salt	½ lb shrimp, deveined
2 tbsp ground psyllium husk	½ tsp Italian seasoning

Directions and Total Time: approx. 30 minutes

Preheat oven to 390 F. Line a baking sheet with parchment paper. In a bowl, mix almond flour, salt, psyllium powder, 1 tbsp of olive oil, and 1 cup of lukewarm water until dough forms. Spread the mixture on the baking sheet and bake for 10 minutes. Heat butter and the remaining olive oil in a skillet. Sauté garlic for 30 seconds. Mix in white wine and cook until it reduces by half. Stir in basil, parsley, and lemon juice. Stir in shrimp and cook for 3 minutes.

Mix in the cheese blend and Italian seasoning. Let the cheese melt, 3 minutes. Spread the shrimp mixture on the crust and top with Parmesan cheese. Bake for 5 minutes or until Parmesan melts. Let cool completely. Slice.

Storage: Place in airtight containers in the refrigerator for up to 5 days (or in the freezer for up to 2 months).

Per serving: Cal 423; Carbs 3g; Fat 34g; Protein 23g

Simple Shrimp Shirataki Noodles

Ingredients for 4 servings

2 (8 oz) packs angel hair shirataki noodles	
½ cup grated Asiago cheese	1 lb shrimp, deveined
1 ½ cups heavy cream	6 garlic cloves, minced
1 tbsp olive oil	½ cup dry white wine
2 tbsp unsalted butter	2 tbsp chopped fresh parsley

Directions and Total Time: approx. 15 minutes

Heat olive oil in a skillet over medium heat and cook the shrimp on both sides, 2 minutes; set aside. Melt butter in the skillet and sauté garlic. Stir in wine and cook until reduced by half, scraping the bottom of the pan to deglaze. Stir in heavy cream. Let simmer for 1 minute and stir in Asiago cheese to melt. Return the shrimp to the sauce and sprinkle the parsley on top. Bring 2 cups of water to a boil. Strain shirataki pasta and rinse under hot running water. Allow proper draining and pour the shirataki pasta into the boiling water. Cook for 3 minutes and strain again. Place a dry skillet and stir-fry the pasta until dry, 1-2 minutes. Top with the shrimp sauce. Let cool completely.

Storage: Place in airtight containers in the refrigerator for up to 5 days (or in the freezer for up to 2 months).

Per serving: Cal 493; Carbs 6g; Fats 32g; Protein 33g

Shrimp in Creamy Sauce

Ingredients for 2 servings

½ oz grated Parmesan cheese	¼ tsp curry powder
½ ounce cheddar cheese	2 tsp almond flour
½ cup heavy cream	12 shrimp, shelled
2 tbsp butter	2 tbsp curry leaves
3 tbsp coconut oil	½ onion, diced
1 egg, beaten in a bowl	Salt and black pepper to taste

Directions and Total Time: approx. 15 minutes

Combine Parmesan cheese, curry, and almond flour in a bowl. Melt the coconut oil in a skillet over medium heat. Dip the shrimp in the egg first and then coat with the dry mixture. Fry until golden and crispy. In another skillet, melt the butter. Add onion and cook for 3 minutes. Add in curry leaves and cook for 30 seconds. Stir in heavy cream and cheddar cheese and cook until thickened. Add the shrimp and coat well. Adjust the seasoning. Let cool.

Storage: Place in airtight containers in the refrigerator for up to 5 days (or in the freezer for up to 2 months).

Per serving: Cal 476; Carbs 11g; Fat 36g; Protein 31g

Garlic and Parsley Scallops

Ingredients for 6 servings

½ cup ghee, divided — 1 garlic clove, minced
2 lb large sea scallops — 3 tbsp water
Salt and black pepper to taste — 1 lemon, zested and juiced
¼ tsp paprika — 2 tbsp chopped parsley

Directions and Total Time: approx. 15 minutes

Melt half of the ghee in a skillet, season the scallops with salt, pepper, paprika, and add to the skillet. Stir in garlic and cook for 4 minutes on both sides. Remove to a bowl. Put the remaining ghee in the skillet; add lemon zest, juice, and water. Add in the scallops and cook for 2 minutes on low heat. Let cool completely. Sprinkle with parsley.

Storage: Place in airtight containers in the refrigerator for up to 5 days (or in the freezer for up to 2 months).

Per serving: Cal 318; Carbs 2g; Fat 22g; Protein 27g

Coconut-Curry Calamari Rings

Ingredients for 4 servings

2 tbsp Parmesan, grated — ½ tsp curry powder
2 tbsp mozzarella, shredded — 2 tsp coconut flour
½ cup coconut cream — 2 lb calamari rings
2 tbsp butter — 2 tbsp curry leaves
3 tbsp coconut oil — 1 onion, chopped
1 egg, beaten

Directions and Total Time: approx. 15 minutes

In a bowl, combine Parmesan cheese, curry powder, and coconut flour and mix to combine. Warm coconut oil in a skillet over medium heat. Dip the calamari in the egg first and then coat with the dry mixture. Fry until golden and crispy. In another skillet, melt butter and sauté onion for 3 minutes. Add in curry leaves, coconut cream, and mozzarella cheese and stir until thickened, about 3-4 minutes. Add the calamari to coat thoroughly. Let cool.

Storage: Place in airtight containers in the refrigerator for up to 5 days (or in the freezer for up to 2 months).

Per serving: Cal 442; Carbs 8g; Fat 36g; Protein 33g

Coconut Snack Crab Balls

Ingredients for 4 servings

2 tbsp coconut oil — 2 tsp wasabi sauce
1 lime, juiced — 1 egg, beaten
8 oz lump crab meat — 1 tbsp coconut flour

Directions and Total Time: approx. 15 minutes

Mix together the crab meat, wasabi sauce, lime juice, coconut flour, and egg in a bowl. Make balls out of the mixture. Melt coconut oil over medium heat and fry the crab balls for 5-6 minutes in total until crispy. Let cool.

Storage: Place in airtight containers in the refrigerator for up to 5 days (or in the freezer for up to 2 months).

Per serving: Cal 277; Carbs 6g; Fat 11g; Protein 24g

Shrimp Curry with Asparagus

Ingredients for 4 servings

2 tbsp ghee — 2 tbsp red curry paste
1 lb jumbo shrimp, deveined — 1 cup coconut milk
2 tsp ginger-garlic puree — 1 bunch asparagus

Directions and Total Time: approx. 20 minutes

Melt ghee in a saucepan over medium heat and add in the shrimp. Sauté for 3 minutes; remove to a plate. Add ginger-garlic puree and red curry paste to the saucepan and cook for 2 minutes. Stir in coconut milk and 3 cups water. Add the shrimp and asparagus. Cook for 4 minutes. Reduce the heat and simmer for 3 more minutes. Let cool.

Storage: Place in airtight containers in the refrigerator for up to 5 days (or in the freezer for up to 2 months).

Per serving: Cal 445; Carbs 10g; Fat 35g, Protein 21g

Curry Steamed Clams

Ingredients for 6 servings

5 tbsp sesame oil — 12 oz coconut milk
1 onion, chopped — 16 oz white wine
2 lb clams, cleaned — 2 tsp red curry powder
2 garlic cloves, minced — 2 tbsp cilantro, chopped

Directions and Total Time: approx. 20 minutes

Warm the sesame oil in a saucepan over medium heat and cook onion and garlic for 3 minutes. Pour in white wine, coconut milk, and curry powder and cook for 5 minutes.

Add clams, turn off the heat, and cover the saucepan. Steam the clams until the shells open up, 5 minutes. Discard any closed clams. Top with cilantro. Let cool completely.

Storage: Place in airtight containers in the refrigerator for up to 5 days (or in the freezer for up to 2 months).

Per serving: Cal 423; Carbs 17g; Fat 16g; Protein 28g

Shrimp & Crab Cakes

Ingredients for 4 servings

½ lb shrimp, peeled, deveined, and chopped
2 tbsp coconut oil — 2 tsp Dijon mustard
1 cup lump crab meat — 1 egg, beaten
1 tbsp lemon juice — 1 ½ tbsp coconut flour
2 tbsp parsley — Salt and black pepper to taste

Directions and Total Time: approx. 15 minutes

Place crab meat and shrimp in a bowl. Add the remaining ingredients, except for coconut oil. Mix well to combine.

Make 8 balls out of the mixture and flatten them into patties with your hands. Melt the coconut oil in a skillet. Add the cakes and cook for 2-3 minutes per side. Let cool.

Storage: Place in airtight containers in the refrigerator for up to 5 days (or in the freezer for up to 2 months).

Per serving: Cal 265; Carbs 3g; Fat 14g; Protein 27g

Dijon Crab Patties

Ingredients for 4 servings

2 tbsp coconut oil	2 tsp Dijon mustard
1 tbsp lime juice	1 egg, beaten
1 cup lump crab meat	1 ½ tbsp coconut flour

Directions and Total Time: approx. 15 minutes

In a bowl, add all the ingredients, except for the oil, and mix well to combine. Make patties out of the mixture.

Melt coconut oil in a skillet over medium heat. Cook the crab meat patties for about 3-4 minutes per side. Let cool.

Storage: Place in airtight containers in the refrigerator for up to 5 days (or in the freezer for up to 2 months).

Per serving: Cal 225; Carbs 9g; Fat 11g; Protein 15g

Crabmeat Avocado Boats

Ingredients for 4 servings

3 oz plain yogurt, strained overnight in a cheesecloth

1 cup crabmeat	¼ cup almonds, chopped
2 avocados, halved and pitted	Salt and black pepper, to taste

Directions and Total Time: approx. 25 minutes

Set oven to 425 F. In a bowl, mix crabmeat, yogurt, salt, and pepper. Fill avocado halves with crabmeat mixture and place in a greased baking pan. Bake for 18 minutes. Decorate with almonds. Let cool completely.

Storage: Place in airtight containers in the refrigerator for up to 5 days (or in the freezer for up to 2 months).

Per serving: Cal 264; Carbs 11g; Fat 24g; Protein 14g

Mediterranean Scallops with Chorizo

Ingredients for 4 servings

1 cup Parmesan, grated	8 ounces chorizo, chopped
2 tbsp ghee	1 red bell pepper, sliced
16 fresh scallops	1 cup red onions, chopped

Directions and Total Time: approx. 15 minutes

Melt the ghee in a skillet and cook onion and bell pepper for 5 minutes. Add in chorizo and stir-fry for another 3 minutes; set aside. Sear the scallops in the same skillet for 2 minutes on each side. Stir in the chorizo mixture and transfer to an airtight container. Top with Parmesan. Cool.

Storage: Keep in the refrigerator for up to 5 days (or in the freezer for up to 2 months).

Per serving: Cal 491; Carbs 5g; Fat 32g; Protein 36g

Seafood Taco Bowls

Ingredients for 4 servings

2 cups broccoli, riced	Salt and chili pepper to taste
2 tsp ghee	¼ head red cabbage, shredded
4 tilapia fillets, cut into cubes	1 ripe avocado, chopped
¼ tsp taco seasoning	1 tsp dill

Directions and Total Time: approx. 20 minutes

Sprinkle broccoli in a bowl with a little bit of water and microwave for 3 minutes. Fluff with a fork and let cool. Melt ghee in a skillet over medium heat, rub the tilapia with taco seasoning, salt, dill, and chili, and fry until brown on all sides, 8 minutes in total. Let cool completely. In 4 airtight containers, share the broccoli and fish.

Storage: Keep in the refrigerator for up to 5 days. To serve, reheat the food for 1 minute. Top with cabbage and avocado.

Per serving: Cal 269; Carbs 4g; Fat 23g; Protein 18g

Steamed Mussels with Chili Shirataki

Ingredients for 4 servings

2 (8 oz) packs angel hair shirataki pasta

1 ½ cups heavy cream	6 garlic cloves, minced
4 tbsp olive oil	2 tsp red chili flakes
1 lb mussels	½ cup fish stock
1 cup white wine	2 tbsp chopped fresh parsley
3 shallots, finely chopped	Salt and black pepper to taste

Directions and Total Time: approx. 20 minutes

Bring 2 cups of water to a boil in a pot. Strain the pasta and rinse well under hot running water. Drain and transfer to the boiling water. Cook for 3 minutes and strain again. Place a large skillet and stir-fry the pasta until visibly dry, 2 minutes; set aside. Pour mussels and wine into a pot over medium heat, cover, and cook for 3-4 minutes. Strain mussels and reserve the cooking liquid. Let cool, discard any closed mussels, and remove the meat out of ¾ of the mussel shells. Set aside with the remaining mussels in the shells. Heat the oil in a skillet and sauté shallots, garlic, and chili for 3 minutes. Mix in reduced wine and stock. Let boil and whisk in heavy cream; season. Mix in pasta and mussels. Top with parsley. Let cool completely.

Storage: Keep in the refrigerator for up to 5 days.

Per serving: Cal 471; Carbs 13g; Fat 34g; Protein 25g

Seafood Risotto

Ingredients for 4 servings

¾ cup grated Parmesan	1 red onion, finely chopped
2 tbsp butter	1 head broccoli, grated
1 lb mussels	1 cup water
2 garlic cloves, minced	Salt and black pepper to taste

Directions and Total Time: approx. 45 minutes

Melt butter in a saucepan over medium heat and sauté garlic and onion for 3 minutes. Mix in broccoli, 1 cup water, white wine, salt, and pepper and simmer for 10 minutes. Mix in mussels and simmer for 5 minutes. Stir in Parmesan and let cool completely.

Storage: Place in airtight containers in the refrigerator for up to 5 days (or in the freezer for up to 2 months).

Per serving: Cal 472; Carbs 12g; Fat 33g; Protein 15g

LUNCH & DINNER

Garlicky Cauliflower & Bacon Stew

Ingredients for 4 servings

1 head cauliflower, cut into florets
1 cup grated mozzarella	½ tsp onion powder
¼ cup heavy cream	Salt and black pepper to taste
2 cups chicken broth	4 garlic cloves, minced
½ tsp garlic powder	1 cup chopped bacon

Directions and Total Time: approx. 35 minutes

In a pot over medium heat, sauté bacon until crispy, about 5 minutes; reserve. Add broth, cauliflower, salt, and pepper to the pot and cook for 15 minutes. Stir in heavy cream, garlic, mozzarella cheese, onion powder, and garlic powder and cook for 5 minutes. Top with bacon. Cool.

Storage: Place in airtight containers in the refrigerator for up to 5 days (or in the freezer for up to 2 months).

Per serving: Cal 380; Carbs 16g; Fat 25g; Protein 23g

Pumpkin & Beef Stew

Ingredients for 6 servings

1 tbsp olive oil	½ cup white wine
1 tbsp peanut butter	1 tsp lemon juice
1 cup pumpkin puree	¼ cup brown sugar
2 lb chopped beef stew meat	¼ tsp cardamom powder
4 tbsp chopped peanuts	¼ tsp allspice
1 garlic clove, minced	2 cups water
½ cup chopped onion	2 cups chicken stock

Directions and Total Time: approx. 45 minutes

Heat olive oil in a saucepan over medium heat and sauté onion and garlic for 3 minutes. Add in beef and cook for 5-6 minutes. Pour in white wine and cook for 1 minute. Add in the remaining ingredients, except for the lemon juice and peanuts. Bring to a boil and cook for 5 minutes. Reduce the heat to low and simmer for 30 minutes. Stir in the lemon juice. Let cool. Place in airtight containers.

Storage: Keep in the refrigerator for up to 5 days (or in the freezer for up to 2 months). To serve, reheat the stew in the microwave for 1-2 minutes and top with peanuts.

Per serving: Cal 431, Carbs: 14g, Fat: 33g, Protein: 27g

Chicken & Egg Lettuce Wraps

Ingredients for 4 servings

6 tbsp cream cheese	4 large eggs
1 tbsp olive oil	2 tomatoes, seeded, chopped
2 chicken breasts, cubed	1 head lettuce, leaves separated

Directions and Total Time: approx. 30 minutes

Preheat oven to 400 F. Put the chicken in a bowl and coat it with olive oil. Transfer to a greased baking sheet. Bake for 8 minutes, turning once; let cool. Bring eggs to a boil in salted water for 10 minutes. Run the eggs in cold water

Peel, and chop into small pieces. Mix them with the baked chicken, tomatoes, and cream cheese and mix evenly. Lay 2 lettuce leaves each in cups and fill with 2 tbsp of egg salad each. Place in airtight containers.

Storage: Keep in the refrigerator for up to 3 days.

Per serving: Cal 325; Carbs 8g; Fat 21g; Protein 26g

Texas-Style Pizza

Ingredients for 4 servings

3 cups shredded mozzarella	2 tbsp almond meal
3 tbsp cream cheese, softened	1 tbsp dry Ranch seasoning
¼ cup half and half	3 bacon slices, chopped
1 tbsp butter	2 chicken breasts
¾ cup almond flour	6 fresh basil leaves

Directions and Total Time: approx. 45 minutes

Preheat oven to 390 F. Line a pizza pan with parchment paper. Microwave 2 cups of mozzarella cheese and 2 tbsp of the cream cheese for 30 seconds. Mix in almond flour and almond meal. Spread the "dough" on the pan and bake for 15 minutes. In a bowl, mix butter, remaining cream cheese, half and half, and ranch mix; set aside. Heat a grill pan and cook the bacon for 5 minutes; set aside. Grill the chicken in the pan on both sides for 10 minutes. Remove to a plate, allow cooling, and cut into thin slices. Spread the ranch sauce on the pizza crust, followed by the chicken and bacon, and then the remaining mozzarella cheese and basil. Bake for 5 minutes. Let cool completely.

Storage: Place in airtight containers in the refrigerator for up to 5 days (or in the freezer for up to 2 months).

Per serving: Cal 478; Carbs 14g; Fats 28g; Protein 52g

Vegetarian Lasagna

Ingredients for 4 servings

2 cups cream cheese	Salt and black pepper to taste
2 cups tofu cheese, shredded	3 cups tomato sauce
2 zucchinis, sliced	1 cup packed baby spinach

Directions and Total Time: approx. 60 minutes

Preheat oven to 370 F. Mix cream cheese, tofu, salt, and black pepper to combine evenly. Spread ¼ cup of the mixture in the bottom of a greased baking dish.

Lay a third of the zucchini slices on top, spread 1 cup of tomato sauce over, and scatter one-third cup of spinach on top. Repeat the layering process two more times to exhaust the ingredients while finishing with the last ¼ cup of cheese mixture. Grease one end of foil with cooking spray and cover the baking dish with the foil. Bake for 35 minutes, remove the foil, and bake further for 10 minutes. Let sit for 5 minutes, make slices, and let cool completely.

Storage: Place in airtight containers in the refrigerator for up to 5 days (or in the freezer for up to 2 months).

Per serving: Cal 422; Carbs 12g; Fat 33g; Protein 17g

Stuffed Lamb Leg

Ingredients for 4 servings

½ cup rosemary, chopped
1 lb rolled lamb leg, boneless
5 tbsp pine nuts, chopped
½ cup green olives, chopped
3 cloves garlic, minced
Salt and black pepper to taste

Directions and Total Time: approx. 1 hour 10 minutes

Preheat oven to 400 F. In a bowl, combine rosemary, pine nuts, olives, and garlic. Season with salt and pepper. Untie the lamb flat onto a chopping board, and rub rosemary mixture all over the meat. Roll lamb over the spices and tie it together using four strings of butcher's twine. Place lamb on a baking dish and bake for 10 minutes. Cook for 40 minutes. Transfer to a clean chopping board; let it rest for 10 minutes before slicing. Let cool completely.

Storage: Place in airtight containers in the refrigerator for up to 5 days (or in the freezer for up to 2 months).

Per serving: Cal 477; Carbs 2g; Fat 31g; Protein 33g

Spinach & Blue Cheese Salad

Ingredients for 2 servings

1 ½ cups gorgonzola cheese
4 cups spinach
4 strawberries, sliced
½ cup flaked almonds
4 tbsp raspberry vinaigrette

Directions and Total Time: approx. 30 minutes

Preheat oven to 400 F. Crumble gorgonzola cheese onto 2 pieces of parchment paper. Bake for 10 minutes. Set 2 airtight containers, upside down, and put 2 parchment papers on top to give the cheese a container-like shape. Cool for 15 minutes. Top with spinach.

Storage: Keep in the refrigerator for up to 5 days. To serve, drizzle with vinaigrette; top with almonds and strawberries.

Per serving: Cal 415; Carbs: 12g; Fat: 36g; Protein: 16g

Montana's Veal Stew

Ingredients for 6 servings

2 tbsp olive oil
2 lb veal shoulder, cubed
1 onion, chopped
1 garlic clove, minced
1 ½ cups red wine
12 oz canned tomato sauce
1 carrot, chopped
1 cup mushrooms, chopped
½ cup green beans
Salt and black pepper to taste

Directions and Total Time: approx. 130 minutes

Warm the oil in a pot over medium heat and brown veal for 5 minutes. Stir in onion and garlic and cook for 3 minutes. Pour in red wine, carrot, salt, pepper, tomato sauce, 1 cup water, and mushrooms and bring to a boil. Reduce the heat and cook for 1 hour and 45 minutes. Add in green beans and cook for 5 minutes. Let cool completely.

Storage: Place in airtight containers in the refrigerator for up to 5 days (or in the freezer for up to 2 months).

Per serving: Cal 423, Carbs 17g, Fat 27g, Protein 36g

Braised Sage-Flavored Lamb Chops

Ingredients for 6 servings

2 tbsp olive oil
1 onion, sliced
3 garlic cloves, minced
12 lamb chops
1 tbsp sage
1 tsp thyme
½ cup white wine
Salt and black pepper to taste

Directions and Total Time: approx. 1 hour 15 minutes

Heat the olive oil in a pan. Add onion and garlic and cook for 3 minutes, until soft; set aside. Rub sage, thyme, salt, and pepper onto the lamb and sear it in the pan for 3 minutes per side; reserve. Deglaze the pan with white wine and pour in 1 cup of water. Bring the mixture to a boil. Cook until the liquid reduces by half. Add the lamb, lower the heat, and let simmer for 1 hour. Let cool completely.

Storage: Place in airtight containers in the refrigerator for up to 5 days (or in the freezer for up to 2 months).

Per serving: Cal 140; Carbs 2g; Fat 7g; Protein 16g

Avocado Dip with Garlicky Turnip Chips

Ingredients for 6 servings

2 avocados, mashed
2 tsp lime juice
2 tbsp olive oil
2 garlic cloves, minced

For turnip chips

1 tbsp olive oil
1 ½ pounds turnips, sliced
Salt to taste
½ tsp garlic powder

Directions and Total Time: approx. 20 minutes

Stir avocado in lime juice, 2 tbsp of olive oil, and garlic until well combined. Remove to a glass jar. Preheat oven to 300 F. Set turnip slices on a greased baking sheet; toss with garlic powder, 1 tbsp of olive oil, and salt. Bake for 15 minutes. Let cool completely. Place in airtight containers.

Storage: Keep in the refrigerator for up to 5 days. Before serving, microwave for 1 minute. Enjoy with avocado dip!

Per serving: Cal 289; Carbs: 19g; Fat: 22g; Protein: 3g

Spaghetti Squash a la Primavera

Ingredients for 4 servings

¼ cup Parmesan cheese
1 tbsp butter
1 cup cherry tomatoes
2 tbsp parsley
4 bacon slices
3 tbsp scallions, chopped
1 cup sugar snap peas
1 tsp lemon zest
2 cups cooked spaghetti squash
Salt and black pepper to taste

Directions and Total Time: approx. 15 minutes

Melt the butter in a saucepan and cook bacon until crispy. Add the tomatoes and peas, and cook for 5 more minutes. Stir in parsley, zest, and scallions and remove the pan from heat. Stir in spaghetti and Parmesan cheese. Let cool.

Storage: Place in airtight containers in the refrigerator for up to 5 days (or in the freezer for up to 2 months).

Per serving: Cal 229; Carbs 18g; Fat 11g; Protein 9g

Avocado & Yogurt Gyros

Ingredients for 4 servings

2 cups cauli rice
2 cups Greek yogurt
6 zero-carb flatbread
1 ½ cups tomato herb salsa
2 avocados, sliced

Directions and Total Time: approx. 10 minutes

Pour the cauli rice into a bowl. Sprinkle with water and microwave for 2 minutes. On flatbread, spread the Greek yogurt all over and distribute the salsa on top. Top with cauli rice and scatter the avocado evenly on top. Fold and tuck the burritos and cut them in two.

Storage: Place in airtight containers in the refrigerator for up to 5 days (or in the freezer for up to 2 months).

Per serving: Cal 313; Carbs 16g; Fat 25g; Protein 8g

Bacon & Feta Salad

Ingredients for 4 servings

2 (8 oz) pack mixed salad greens
1 ½ cups feta cheese, crumbled
3 tbsp extra virgin olive oil
8 strips bacon
1 tbsp white wine vinegar
Salt and black pepper to taste

Directions and Total Time: approx. 15 minutes

Pour the salad greens into an airtight container; set aside. Fry the bacon strips in a skillet for 6 minutes until browned and crispy; let cool. Chop it and scatter it over the salad. Add in half of the feta cheese and toss to coat.

Storage: Keep in the refrigerator for up to 3 days. To serve, in a small bowl, whisk white wine vinegar, olive oil, salt, and black pepper until well combined. Drizzle dressing over the salad, toss, and top with the remaining cheese.

Per serving: Cal 265; Carbs 10g; Fat 20g; Protein 11g

Homemade Biryani with Mushrooms

Ingredients for 4 servings

1 cup sliced cremini mushrooms
1 cup diced paneer cheese
2 tbsp olive oil
3 tbsp ghee
6 cups cauli rice
Salt and black pepper to taste
3 white onions, chopped
6 garlic cloves, minced
1 tsp ginger puree
1 tbsp turmeric powder
2 cups chopped tomatoes
1 habanero pepper, minced
1 tbsp tomato puree
½ cup spinach, chopped
½ cup kale, chopped
¼ cup chopped parsley
1 cup Greek yogurt

Directions and Total Time: approx. 1 hour 10 minutes

Preheat oven to 400 F. Microwave cauli rice for 1 minute. Remove and season with salt and black pepper; set aside. Melt ghee in a pan over medium heat and sauté onions, garlic, ginger puree, and turmeric. Cook for 15 minutes, stirring regularly. Add in tomatoes, habanero pepper, and tomato puree; cook for 5 minutes. Stir in mushrooms, paneer cheese, spinach, kale, and 1/3 cup water.

Simmer for 15 minutes or until the mushrooms soften. Turn the heat off and stir in yogurt. Spoon half of the stew into a bowl. Sprinkle half of the parsley over the stew in the pan, half of the cauli rice and dust with turmeric. Repeat the layering a second time, including the reserved stew. Drizzle with olive oil and bake for 25 minutes. Cool.

Storage: Place in airtight containers in the refrigerator for up to 7 days (or in the freezer for up to 2 months).

Per serving: Cal 316; Carbs 2g; Fat 21g; Protein 16g

Red Wine Lamb in Butter Sauce

Ingredients for 4 servings

3 oz butter, melted
1 ¼ pounds rack of lamb
3 cloves garlic, minced
3 oz red wine
A handful of mint, chopped

Butter Sauce

2 tbsp olive oil
2 oz butter
1 cup vegetable broth
1 zucchini, chopped
2 cloves garlic, minced
Salt and white pepper to taste

Directions and Total Time: approx. 1 hour 35 minutes

In a bowl, mix melted butter with red wine, salt, and 3 garlic cloves; brush the mixture all over the lamb. Top with chopped mint, cover the bowl with plastic wrap, and refrigerate for 1 hour. Preheat grill to high and cook the lamb for 6 minutes on both sides. Let cool before slicing.

Heat olive oil in a pan and sauté 2 garlic cloves and zucchini for 5 minutes. Pour in the broth and continue cooking until the liquid reduces by half, 10 minutes. Add in 2 oz of butter, salt, and pepper. Stir to melt the butter and turn the heat off. Puree the ingredients in a food processor until smooth and strain the sauce through a fine mesh into a glass jar. Let cool. Place in airtight containers.

Storage: Keep the lamb and sauce in the refrigerator for up to 5 days (or in the freezer for up to 2 months). To serve, reheat the lamb and the sauce in the microwave for 1-2 minutes. Pour the sauce over the lamb and enjoy!

Per serving: Cal 553; Carbs 3g; Fat 47g; Protein 30g

Turnip Pasta with Chicken Ham

Ingredients for 4 servings

1 lb turnips, spiralized
4 tbsp olive oil
4 oz chicken ham, chopped
1 tbsp smoked paprika
Salt and black pepper to taste

Directions and Total Time: approx. 15 minutes

Preheat oven to 450 F. Pour turnips into a bowl and add paprika, salt, and pepper; toss to coat. Spread the mixture on a greased baking sheet, scatter ham on top, and drizzle with olive oil. Bake for 10 minutes. Let cool completely.

Storage: Place in airtight containers in the refrigerator for up to 5 days (or in the freezer for up to 2 months).

Per serving: Cal 274; Carbs 16g; Fat 15g; Protein 15g

Colby Cheese & Cauliflower Bake

Ingredients for 4 servings

10 oz cauliflower florets	1 white onion, chopped
1 ½ cups grated Colby cheese	¼ almond milk
¼ cup butter, cubed	½ cup almond flour
2 tbsp melted butter	Salt and black pepper to taste

Directions and Total Time: approx. 30 minutes

Preheat oven to 350 F. Microwave the cauli florets for 4-5 minutes. Melt the butter cubes in a saucepan and sauté onion for 3 minutes. Add in cauliflower, season with salt and pepper, and mix in almond milk. Simmer for 3 minutes. Mix the remaining melted butter with almond flour. Stir in the cauliflower as well as half of the cheese. Sprinkle the top with the remaining cheese and bake for 10 minutes. Let cool completely.

Storage: Place in airtight containers in the refrigerator for up to 5 days (or in the freezer for up to 2 months).

Per serving: Cal 315; Carbs 14g; Fat 25g; Protein 15g

Smothered Chicken Breasts with Bacon

Ingredients for 4 servings

½ cup heavy cream	Salt and black pepper to taste
4 strips bacon, chopped	5 sprigs fresh thyme
2 chicken breasts, halved	¼ cup chicken broth

Directions and Total Time: approx. 25 minutes

Cook bacon in a skillet for 5 minutes; remove to a plate. Season chicken breasts with salt and pepper and brown in the bacon fat for 4 minutes on each side. Remove to the bacon plate. Stir thyme, chicken broth, and heavy cream in the skillet and simmer for 5 minutes. Return the chicken and bacon and cook for 2 minutes. Let cool completely.

Storage: Place in airtight containers in the refrigerator for up to 5 days (or in the freezer for up to 2 months).

Per serving: Cal 325; Carbs 3g; Fat 17g; Protein 37g

Curried Bell Pepper & Cauliflower Bake

Ingredients for 4 servings

1 lb cauliflower, cut into florets	
¼ cup olive oil	Salt and black pepper to taste
1 yellow bell pepper, halved	½ tsp cayenne pepper
1 red bell pepper, halved	1 tsp curry powder

Directions and Total Time: approx. 35 minutes

Preheat oven to 425 F. Line a parchment paper to a baking sheet. Sprinkle olive oil to the peppers and cauliflower alongside curry powder, pepper, salt, and cayenne pepper. Set the vegetables on the baking sheet. Roast for 30 minutes as you toss in intervals until they start to brown. Let cool completely.

Storage: Place in airtight containers in the refrigerator for up to 5 days (or in the freezer for up to 2 months).

Per serving: Cal 186; Carbs: 17g; Fat: 14g; Protein: 3g

Classic Carbonara with Avocado Sauce

Ingredients for 8 servings

¼ cup grated Parmesan	1 avocado, peeled and pitted
1 ½ cups cream cheese	Juice of ½ lemon
1 ½ cups coconut cream	1 teaspoon onion powder
¼ cup olive oil	½ teaspoon garlic powder
8 tbsp flax seed powder	Salt and black pepper to taste
4 tbsp psyllium husk	4 tbsp toasted pecans

Directions and Total Time: approx. 30 minutes

Preheat oven to 300 F. In a bowl, mix flax seed powder with 1 ½ cups water and let sit to thicken for 5 minutes. Add cream cheese, 1 tsp salt, and psyllium husk. Whisk until smooth batter forms. Line a baking sheet with parchment paper, pour in the batter, and cover with another parchment paper. Use a rolling pin to flatten the dough into the sheet. Bake for 12 minutes. Remove, take off the parchment papers, and slice the "pasta" into thin strips lengthwise.

Cut each piece into halves, pour into a bowl, and set aside. In a blender, combine avocado, coconut cream, lemon juice, onion, and garlic powders and puree until smooth. Pour olive oil over the pasta and stir to coat. Pour avocado sauce on top and mix. Sprinkle with salt, pepper, and Parmesan cheese. Let cool completely.

Storage: Place in airtight containers in the refrigerator for up to 5 days (or in the freezer for up to 2 months). To serve, microwave the pasta and top with pecans.

Per serving: Cal 427; Carbs 8g; Fat 36g; Protein 8g

Pork Kabobs with Squash Purée

Ingredients for 6 servings

2 oz grated Parmesan	Juice of ½ a lemon
2/3 cup olive oil	4 tbsp capers
½ cup butter	Salt and black pepper to taste
1 cup fresh cilantro, chopped	1 lb pork tenderloin, cubed
4 tbsp fresh basil, chopped	½ tbsp sugar-free BBQ sauce
2 garlic cloves	3 cups butternut squash, cubed

Directions and Total Time: approx. 30 minutes

In a blender, add cilantro, basil, garlic, lemon juice, capers, olive oil, salt, and pepper and process until smooth. Transfer to a glass jar and place in the refrigerator.

Thread pork cubes on skewers. Season with salt and brush with BBQ sauce. Melt 1 tbsp butter in a grill pan and sear the skewers until browned on both sides; let cool.

Pour squash into a pot, add salted water, and bring to a boil for 15 minutes. Drain and pour the squash into a bowl. Add in the remaining butter, Parmesan cheese, salt, and pepper and mash everything. Let cool completely.

Storage: Place the skewers and mash in airtight containers in the refrigerator for up to 5 days. Before serving, reheat in the microwave for 1-2 minutes. Top with salsa verde.

Per serving: Cal 446; Carbs 25g; Fat 21g; Protein 31g

Vegetarian Mushroom Stroganoff

Ingredients for 4 servings

½ cup grated Pecorino Romano cheese
3 tbsp butter | ½ cup heavy cream
1 white onion, chopped | 1 ½ tbsp dried mixed herbs
4 cups mushrooms, chopped | Salt and black pepper to taste

Directions and Total Time: approx. 15 minutes

Melt butter in a saucepan and sauté onion for 3 minutes. Stir in mushrooms and cook for 3 minutes. Add 2 cups water and bring to a boil; cook for 4 minutes. Pour in heavy cream and Pecorino Romano cheese. Stir to melt the cheese. Also, mix in dried herbs. Season with salt and pepper. Ladle stroganoff over spaghetti squash. Let cool.

Storage: Place in airtight containers in the refrigerator for up to 5 days (or in the freezer for up to 2 months).

Per serving: Cal 284; Carbs 15g; Fat 23g; Protein 8g

Balsamic Tofu Sautée with Hazelnuts

Ingredients for 4 servings

1 tbsp tomato paste with garlic and onion
1 tbsp olive oil | Salt and black pepper to taste
1 (8 oz) firm tofu, cubed | ½ tsp mixed dried herbs
1 tbsp balsamic vinegar | 1 cup chopped raw hazelnuts

Directions and Total Time: approx. 15 minutes

Heat oil in a skillet and cook tofu for 3 minutes. In a bowl, mix tomato paste with the balsamic vinegar and add to the tofu. Stir, season with salt and black pepper, and cook for another 4 minutes. Add the herbs and hazelnuts. Stir and cook on low heat for 3 minutes until fragrant. Let cool.

Storage: Place in airtight containers in the refrigerator for up to 5 days (or in the freezer for up to 2 months).

Per serving: Cal 322; Carbs 4g; Fat 24g; Protein 13g

Cauliflower & Sausage Bake

Ingredients for 8 servings

1 cauliflower head, cut into florets
1 ½ cups coconut cream | 1 lb sausages, sliced
4 tbsp butter, melted | 2 tbsp red curry paste
Salt and black pepper to taste | ½ cup fresh parsley, chopped

Directions and Total Time: approx. 30 minutes

Preheat oven to 400 F. Arrange sausages on a greased baking dish and drizzle with butter. In a bowl, mix curry paste with coconut cream and parsley. Pour the mixture over the sausages and bake for 20 minutes; cool. Season cauliflower with salt and pepper and microwave for 3 minutes until soft and tender within. Let cool.

Storage: Place the food in airtight containers in the refrigerator for up to 5 days (or in the freezer for up to 2 months).

Per serving: Cal 417; Carbs 10g; Fat 36g; Protein 23g

British Mushroom & Cheese Pie

Ingredients for 6 servings

For the pie crust

¼ cup butter, cold and crumbled
¼ cup almond flour | 3 tbsp brown sugar
3 tbsp coconut flour | 1 ½ tsp vanilla extract
½ tsp salt | 4 whole eggs

For the filling

2 cups mixed mushrooms, chopped
1 cup green beans, cut into 3 pieces each
1 cup grated Monterey Jack | 1 green bell pepper, diced
¼ cup heavy cream | Salt and black pepper to taste
1/3 cup sour cream | ½ cup almond milk
2 tbsp butter | 2 eggs, lightly beaten
1 yellow onion, chopped | ¼ tsp nutmeg powder
2 garlic cloves, minced | 1 tbsp chopped parsley

Directions and Total Time: approx. 2 hours 10 minutes

Preheat oven to 350 F. In a bowl, mix almond and coconut flours and salt. Add in butter and mix until crumbly. Stir in brown sugar and vanilla extract. Pour in the eggs one after another while mixing until formed into a ball. Flatten the dough on a clean, flat surface, cover with plastic wrap, and refrigerate for 1 hour. Dust a clean flat surface with almond flour, unwrap the dough and roll out into a large rectangle. Fit into a greased pie pan and with a fork, prick the base of the crust. Bake for 15 minutes; let cool. For the filling, melt butter in a skillet over medium heat and sauté onion and garlic for 3 minutes. Add in mushrooms, bell pepper, and green beans; cook for 5 minutes. In a bowl, beat heavy cream, sour cream, almond milk, and eggs. Season with salt, pepper, and nutmeg. Stir in parsley and cheese. Spread the mushroom mixture on the baked pastry and spread the cheese filling on top. Place the pie in the oven and bake for 35 minutes. Let cool completely. Slice.

Storage: Place in airtight containers in the refrigerator for up to 5 days (or in the freezer for up to 2 months).

Per serving: Cal 433; Carbs 16g; Fat 33g; Protein 16g

Lamb Koftas

Ingredients for 4 servings

1 egg | 1 grated onion
1 pound ground lamb | Salt and black pepper to taste
¼ tsp cinnamon | 2 tbsp mint, chopped

Directions and Total Time: approx. 15 minutes

Place all ingredients in a bowl; mix to combine. Divide the meat into 4 pieces. Shape all of the meat portions around skewers. Preheat grill to medium heat. Grill the koftas for 5 minutes per side until browned all over. Cool completely.

Storage: Place in airtight containers in the refrigerator for up to 5 days (or in the freezer for up to 2 months).

Per serving: Cal 417; Carbs 3g; Fat 37g; Protein 27g

Tofu Zoodles in Pesto Sauce

Ingredients for 4 servings

2/3 cup grated Pecorino Romano cheese
½ cup shredded mozzarella   1 red bell pepper, sliced
2 tbsp olive oil   4 zucchinis, spiralized
1 white onion, chopped   Salt and black pepper to taste
1 garlic clove, minced   ¼ cup basil pesto
14 oz tofu, pressed and cubed   Toasted pine nuts to garnish

Directions and Total Time: approx. 20 minutes

Heat olive oil in a pot and sauté onion and garlic for 3 minutes. Add in tofu and cook until golden on all sides, then pour in the bell pepper and cook for 4 minutes. Mix in zucchini, pour pesto on top, and season with salt and pepper. Cook for 3-4 minutes. Stir in the Pecorino cheese. Top with mozzarella and pine nuts. Let cool completely.

Storage: Place in airtight containers in the refrigerator for up to 5 days (or in the freezer for up to 2 months).

Per serving: Cal 477; Carbs 14g; Fat 32g; Protein 20g

Grilled Pork with Broccoli Patties

Ingredients for 4 servings

4 oz halloumi cheese   1 tsp salt and cayenne pepper
2 tbsp olive oil   4 pork chops
2 tbsp butter   1 head broccoli, grated
2 eggs   3 tbsp almond flour
1 tbsp soy sauce   ½ tsp onion powder
1 tbsp grated ginger   Salt and black pepper to taste
2 tbsp fresh lime juice

Directions and Total Time: approx. 40 minutes

In a bowl, combine soy sauce, olive oil, grated ginger, lime juice, salt, and cayenne pepper. Brush the pork chops with the mixture. Heat a grill pan and grill the pork on both sides until golden brown; let cool.

Put broccoli in a bowl and grate halloumi cheese on top. Add in eggs, almond flour, onion powder, salt, and pepper. Mix and form 12 patties out of the mixture. Melt butter in a skillet and fry the patties until golden brown. Let cool completely.

Storage: Place in airtight containers in the refrigerator for up to 5 days (or in the freezer for up to 2 months).

Per serving: Cal 497; Carbs 16g; Fat 26g; Protein 42g

Indian Cauliflower Dip

Ingredients for 4 servings

¼ cup olive oil   1 tbsp sesame paste
1 cauliflower head, chopped   1 tbsp fresh lemon juice
Salt and black pepper to taste   ½ tsp garam masala
1 garlic clove, smashed

Directions and Total Time: approx. 15 minutes

Steam cauliflower until tender for 7 minutes. Transfer to a blender and pulse until you attain a rice-like consistency.

Place in garam masala, olive oil, black paper, fresh lemon juice, garlic, salt, and sesame paste. Blend the mixture until well combined. Let cool completely.

Storage: Place in airtight containers in the refrigerator for up to 5 days (or in the freezer for up to 2 months).

Per serving: Cal 123; Carbs: 17g; Fat: 6g; Protein: 4g

Pizza Cups with Mushrooms & Avocado

Ingredients for 4 servings

1 cup grated Monterey Jack   2 large tomatoes, chopped
1 cup grated mozzarella   1 small red onion, chopped
1 tbsp olive oil   1 tsp dried oregano
1 ½ cups cauli rice   2 jalapeño peppers, chopped
2 tbsp water   Salt and black pepper to taste
2 cups pizza sauce   1 avocado, chopped
½ cup sliced mushrooms   ¼ cup chopped cilantro

Directions and Total Time: approx. 30 minutes

Preheat oven to 400 F. Microwave cauli rice for 2 minutes. Fluff with a fork and set aside. Brush 4 ramekins with olive oil and spread half of the pizza sauce at the bottom.

Top with half of cauli rice and half of the cheeses. In a bowl, mix mushrooms, tomatoes, onion, oregano, jalapeños, salt, and pepper. Spoon half of the mixture into the ramekins and repeat the layering process, finishing off with cheese. Bake for 20 minutes. Let cool completely.

Storage: Place in airtight containers in the refrigerator for up to 5 days (or in the freezer for up to 2 months). To serve, reheat the pizza cups in the microwave for 1-2 minutes and top with avocado and cilantro. Enjoy!

Per serving: Cal 428; Carbs 14g; Fat 30g; Protein 21g

No-Meat Florentine Pizza

Ingredients for 4 servings

1 cup shredded provolone cheese
1 (7 oz) can sliced mushrooms, drained
½ cup grated mozzarella   2/3 cup tomato sauce
8 eggs   2 cups chopped kale, wilted
1 tsp Italian seasoning

Directions and Total Time: approx. 35 minutes

Preheat oven to 400 F. Line a pizza-baking pan with parchment paper. Whisk 6 eggs with provolone cheese and Italian seasoning. Spread the mixture on a pizza-baking pan and bake for 15 minutes; let cool for 2 minutes. Increase the oven's temperature to 450 F. Spread tomato sauce on the crust, top with kale, mozzarella cheese, and mushrooms. Bake for 8 minutes. Crack the remaining eggs on top and continue baking until the eggs are set, 3 minutes. Let cool completely. Slice.

Storage: Place in airtight containers in the refrigerator for up to 5 days (or in the freezer for up to 2 months).

Per serving: Cal 343; Carbs 14g; Fat 26g; Protein 18g

Tomato Bites with Vegan Cheese

Ingredients for 6 servings

5 tomatoes, sliced
¼ cup olive oil

2 spring onions, chopped
1 tbsp seasoning mix

For vegan cheese

½ cup pepitas seeds
1 tbsp nutritional yeast

Salt and black pepper to taste
1 tsp garlic puree

Directions and Total Time: approx. 15 minutes

Drizzle tomatoes with olive oil. Preheat oven to 400 F. In a food processor, add all vegan cheese ingredients and pulse until the desired consistency is attained. Combine vegan cheese and seasoning mix. Toss in the tomato slices to coat. Set tomato slices on a baking pan and bake for 10 minutes. Top with spring onions. Let cool completely.

Storage: Place in airtight containers in the refrigerator for up to 5 days (or in the freezer for up to 2 months).

Per serving: Cal 161; Carbs: 7g; Fat: 14g; Protein: 5g

Dijon Brussel Sprout & Cabbage Salad

Ingredients for 4 servings

1 cup Parmesan, grated
3 tbsp olive oil
2 lb Brussels sprouts, halved
Salt and black pepper to taste

2 ½ tbsp balsamic vinegar
¼ red cabbage, shredded
1 tbsp Dijon mustard
2 tbsp pumpkin seeds, toasted

Directions and Total Time: approx. 35 minutes

Preheat oven to 400 F. Line a baking sheet with foil. Toss Brussels sprouts with olive oil, salt, pepper, and balsamic vinegar in a bowl and spread on the baking sheet. Bake for 20-25 minutes. Let cool. Transfer to an airtight container and mix in red cabbage, mustard, and half of the cheese. Sprinkle with the remaining cheese and pumpkin seeds.

Storage: Keep in the refrigerator for up to 5 days.

Per serving: Cal 233; Carbs 13g; Fat 18g; Protein 8g

Mustard Eggplant Boats with Prosciutto

Ingredients for 3 servings

3 eggplants, cut into halves
1 tbsp deli mustard
3 prosciutto slices, chopped

6 eggs
Salt and black pepper to taste
¼ tsp dried parsley

Directions and Total Time: approx. 40 minutes

Scoop flesh from eggplant halves to make shells. Set the eggplant boats on a greased baking pan. Spread mustard on the bottom of every eggplant half. Split the prosciutto among eggplant boats. Crack an egg in each half, sprinkle with parsley, pepper, and salt. Set oven to 400 F. Bake for 30 minutes or until boats become tender. Let cool.

Storage: Place in airtight containers in the refrigerator for up to 5 days (or in the freezer for up to 2 months).

Per serving: Cal 326; Carbs 15g; Fat 23g; Protein 15g

Herby Broccoli Gratin

Ingredients for 4 servings

1 cup Manchego cheese, grated
2 tbsp olive oil
1 head broccoli, cut into florets

1 garlic clove, minced
1 rosemary sprig, chopped
1 thyme sprig, chopped

Directions and Total Time: approx. 25 minutes

Add broccoli to boiling salted water over medium heat and cook for 8 minutes. Remove to a casserole dish and mix in olive oil, garlic, rosemary, and thyme. Scatter the cheese all over. Preheat oven to 380 F. Insert the casserole and bake for 10 minutes until the cheese is melted. Cool.

Storage: Place in airtight containers in the refrigerator for up to 5 days (or in the freezer for up to 2 months).

Per serving: Cal 231; Carbs: 7g; Fat: 17g; Protein: 12g

Farmers' Lamb Stew

Ingredients for 4 servings

2 tbsp olive oil
1 lb lamb chops
1 garlic clove, minced
1 parsnip, chopped
1 onion, chopped
1 celery stalk, chopped
Salt and black pepper to taste

2 cups vegetable stock
2 carrots, chopped
½ tbsp rosemary, chopped
1 tbsp sweet paprika
1 leek, chopped
1 tbsp tomato paste
½ fennel bulb, chopped

Directions and Total Time: approx. 1 hour 15 minutes

Warm olive oil in a pot over medium heat and cook celery, onion, garlic, leek, and garlic for 5 minutes. Add in lamb chops, and cook for 4 minutes. Add in paprika, carrots, parsnip, fennel, vegetable stock, and tomato paste and let simmer for 1 hour. Adjust the seasoning and top with rosemary. Let cool completely. Place in airtight containers.

Storage: Keep in the refrigerator for up to 5 days (or in the freezer for up to 2 months). Microwave for 2 minutes to serve.

Per serving: Cal 343; Carbs 16g; Fat 17g; Protein 20g

Flank Steak Pinwheels with Spinach & Ricotta

Ingredients for 6 servings

1 cup ricotta, crumbled
1 ½ lb flank steak
½ loose cup baby spinach

1 jalapeño pepper, chopped
¼ cup chopped basil leaves

Directions and Total Time: approx. 45 minutes

Preheat oven to 400 F. Wrap steak in plastic wrap, place on a flat surface, and run a rolling pin over to flatten. Take off the wraps. Sprinkle with half of the ricotta cheese, top with spinach, jalapeño pepper, basil, and remaining cheese. Roll the steak over on the stuffing and secure with toothpicks. Place on a greased baking sheet and cook for 30 minutes, flipping once. Let cool completely. Slice into pinwheels.

Storage: Place in airtight containers in the refrigerator for up to 5 days (or in the freezer for up to 2 months).

Per serving: Cal 488; Carbs 4g; Fat 33g; Protein 35g

Colby Cauli Mash with Pancetta

Ingredients for 4 servings

¼ cup Colby cheese, grated
2 tbsp melted butter
½ cup buttermilk
1 head cauliflower, chopped

6 slices pancetta
2 cups water
2 tbsp chopped chives

Directions and Total Time: approx. 25 minutes

Preheat oven to 350 F. Fry pancetta in a skillet over medium heat for 5 minutes. Let cool and crumble. Keep the pancetta fat. Boil cauli head in water in a pot for 7 minutes. Drain and put in a food processor. Add in butter and buttermilk and puree until smooth and creamy. Grease a casserole with the pancetta fat and spread the mash inside. Sprinkle with Colby cheese and place under the broiler for 4 minutes. Top with pancetta and chives. Cool.

Storage: Place in airtight containers in the refrigerator for up to 5 days (or in the freezer for up to 2 months).

Per serving: Cal 342; Carbs 11g; Fat 25g; Protein 14g

Blue Cheese Stuffed Chicken in Pancetta Wrap

Ingredients for 8 servings

1 tbsp fresh chives, chopped
8 ounces blue cheese
1 lb chicken breasts, halved

12 pancetta slices
2 tomatoes, chopped
Salt and black pepper to taste

Directions and Total Time: approx. 40 minutes

In a bowl, stir chives, blue cheese, tomatoes, pepper, and salt. Use a meat tenderizer to flatten the chicken breasts well, season with salt and pepper, and spread the blue cheese mixture on top. Roll them up and wrap them in pancetta slices. Transfer to a greased baking dish and roast in the oven at 370 F for 30 minutes. Let cool completely.

Storage: Place in airtight containers in the refrigerator for up to 5 days (or in the freezer for up to 2 months).

Per serving: Cal 345; Carbs 3g; Fat 28g; Protein 23g

Effortless Garlic & Thyme Spinach

Ingredients for 4 servings

2 tbsp almond oil
½ tsp red pepper flakes
2 lb spinach, chopped

1 tsp garlic, minced
½ tsp thyme

Directions and Total Time: approx. 10 minutes

Add spinach to a pot with salted water over medium heat and cook for 3 minutes. Drain and set aside. Place a sauté pan over medium heat and warm the almond oil. Cook in garlic until soft, 1 minute. Stir in spinach, red pepper flakes, and thyme for 2 minutes. Let cool completely.

Storage: Place in airtight containers in the refrigerator for up to 5 days (or in the freezer for up to 2 months).

Per serving: Cal 118; Carbs: 13g; Fat: 7g; Protein: 3g

Provençal-Style Baked Veal

Ingredients for 4 servings

2 fennel bulbs, sliced
3 tbsp olive oil
12 ounces veal rack

Salt and black pepper to taste
½ cup apple cider vinegar
1 tsp herbs de Provence

Directions and Total Time: approx. 50 minutes

Preheat oven to 400 F. In a bowl, mix fennel with 2 tbsp of oil and vinegar, toss to coat, and set to a baking dish. Season with herbs de Provence and bake for 15 minutes.

Sprinkle pepper and salt on the veal, place into a greased pan over medium-high heat, and cook for a couple of minutes. Place the veal in the baking dish with the fennel, and bake for 20 minutes. Let cool completely.

Storage: Place in airtight containers in the refrigerator for up to 5 days (or in the freezer for up to 2 months).

Per serving: Cal 373; Carbs 7g; Fat 17g; Protein 33g

Venison Tenderloin Stuffed with Cheese

Ingredients for 8 servings

2 pounds venison tenderloin
½ cup Gorgonzola cheese
½ cup feta cheese
3 tbsp olive oil

2 garlic cloves, minced
2 tbsp chopped almonds
1 tsp chopped onion

Directions and Total Time: approx. 50 minutes

Preheat oven to 360 F. Slice the tenderloin lengthwise to make a pocket for the filling. In a skillet, heat the oil and brown the meat on all sides, 8-10 minutes in total. Combine the rest of the ingredients in a bowl. Stuff the tenderloin with the filling. Shut the meat with skewers. Transfer to a baking dish along with the oil and half cup of water and cook for 25-30 minutes until cooked through. Cool.

Storage: Place in airtight containers in the refrigerator for up to 5 days (or in the freezer for up to 2 months).

Per serving: Cal 234; Carbs 4g; Fat 12g; Protein 25g

Asparagus & Chicken Prosciutto Wraps

Ingredients for 4 servings

2 tbsp Romano cheese, grated
4 tbsp olive oil
4 chicken breasts

8 prosciutto slices
1 lb asparagus spears
Salt and black pepper to taste

Directions and Total Time: approx. 50 minutes

Preheat oven to 400 F. Season chicken with salt and pepper and wrap 2 prosciutto slices around each chicken breast. Arrange on a lined baking sheet with parchment paper, drizzle with oil, and bake for 25-30 minutes. Preheat the grill to high heat. Brush asparagus spears with olive oil and grill them for 8-10 minutes, frequently turning until slightly charred. Let cool completely. Top with cheese.

Storage: Place in airtight containers in the refrigerator for up to 5 days (or in the freezer for up to 2 months).

Per serving: Cal 438; Carbs 12g; Fat 26g; Protein 43g

Valencian Paella the Healthy Way

Ingredients for 4 servings

2 tbsp olive oil
½ pound chicken drumsticks
½ lb rabbit, cut into pieces
1 white onion, chopped
2 garlic cloves, minced
1 red bell pepper, chopped
½ cup thyme, chopped

1 tsp smoked paprika
2 tbsp tomato puree
½ cup white wine
1 cup chicken broth
2 cups cauli rice
1 cup green beans, chopped
A pinch of saffron

Directions and Total Time: approx. 50 minutes

Preheat oven to 350 F. Warm olive oil in a pan. Fry chicken and rabbit on all sides for 8 minutes; remove to a plate. Add onion and garlic to the pan and sauté for 3 minutes. Include tomato puree, bell pepper, and smoked paprika, and let simmer for 2 minutes. Pour in broth and simmer for 6 minutes. Stir in cauli rice, white wine, green beans, saffron, and thyme, and lay the meat on top. Transfer the pan to the oven and cook for 20 minutes. Season. Let cool.

Storage: Place in airtight containers in the refrigerator for up to 5 days (or in the freezer for up to 2 months).

Per serving: Cal 328; Carbs 13g; Fat 12g; Protein 37g

Pizza Margherita

Ingredients for 4 servings

1 ½ cups almond flour
2 tbsp ghee
¼ tsp salt
2 small eggs
1/3 cup tomato sauce

4 fresh mozzarella slices
4 fresh basil leaves
2 tbsp grated Parmesan
1 tsp dried oregano

Directions and Total Time: approx. 30 minutes

Preheat oven to 350 F. In a bowl, mix almond flour, ghee, salt, and eggs until a dough forms. Mold the dough into a ball and place it between 2 wide parchment paper pieces on a flat surface. Use a pin to roll it out into a circle of a quarter-inch thickness. Slide the dough into the pizza pan and remove the parchment paper. Bake for 20 minutes. Spread a thin layer of tomato sauce over the pizza crust and top with oregano and mozzarella slices. Bake further an additional 7-8 minutes, or until cheese is melted and pizza is bubbly. Top with basil. Let cool completely.

Storage: Place in airtight containers in the refrigerator for up to 5 days (or in the freezer for up to 2 months).

Per serving: Cal 325; Carbs 16g; Fat 18g; Protein 17g

Zucchini Boats Filled with Cheese & Nuts

Ingredients for 4 servings

1 cup grated Monterey Jack
2 tbsp olive oil
1 cup cauliflower rice
¼ cup vegetable broth
1 ¼ cup diced tomatoes
1 red onion, chopped

¼ cup pine nuts
¼ cup hazelnuts
4 tbsp chopped cilantro
1 tbsp balsamic vinegar
1 tbsp smoked paprika
2 zucchinis, halved

Directions and Total Time: approx. 35 minutes

Preheat oven to 350 F. Pour cauli rice and broth into a pot and cook for 5 minutes. Fluff the cauli rice and allow it to cool. Scoop the flesh out of the zucchini halves using a spoon and chop the pulp. Brush the zucchini shells with some olive oil. In a bowl, mix cauli rice, tomatoes, red onion, pine nuts, hazelnuts, cilantro, vinegar, paprika, and zucchini pulp. Spoon the mixture into the zucchini halves, drizzle with remaining olive oil, and sprinkle the cheese on top. Bake for 20 minutes until the cheese melts. Cool.

Storage: Place in airtight containers in the refrigerator for up to 5 days (or in the freezer for up to 2 months).

Per serving: Cal 363; Carbs 12g; Fat 28g; Protein 12g

Cheesy Strawberry Pizza

Ingredients for 4 servings

2 cups shredded mozzarella
2 tbsp cream cheese, softened
1 tbsp olive oil
¾ cup almond flour
2 tbsp almond meal

1 celery stalk, chopped
1 tomato, chopped
2 tbsp balsamic vinegar
1 cup strawberries, halved
1 tbsp chopped mint leaves

Directions and Total Time: approx. 35 minutes

Preheat oven to 390 F. Line a pizza pan with parchment paper. Microwave 2 cups of mozzarella cheese and cream cheese for 1 minute. Remove and mix in almond flour and almond meal. Spread the mixture on the pizza pan and bake for 10 minutes. Spread the remaining mozzarella cheese on the crust. In a bowl, toss celery, tomato, olive oil, and balsamic vinegar. Spoon the mixture onto the mozzarella cheese and arrange the strawberries on top. Top with mint leaves. Bake for 15 minutes. Let cool completely. Slice.

Storage: Place in airtight containers in the refrigerator for up to 5 days (or in the freezer for up to 2 months).

Per serving: Cal 326; Carbs 14g; Fat 23g; Protein 12g

Cauliflower Pizza with Salami

Ingredients for 4 servings

4 cups cauliflower rice
2 cups grated mozzarella
1 tbsp dried thyme

¼ cup tomato sauce
4 oz salami slices

Directions and Total Time: approx. 30 minutes

Preheat oven to 390 F. Microwave cauliflower rice mixed with 1 tbsp of water for 1 minute. Remove and mix in 1 cup of mozzarella cheese and thyme. Pour the mixture into a greased baking dish, spread out, and bake for 5 minutes. Remove the dish and spread the tomato sauce on top. Scatter the remaining mozzarella cheese on the sauce and then arrange salami slices on top. Bake for 15 minutes. Let cool completely.

Storage: Place in airtight containers in the refrigerator for up to 5 days (or in the freezer for up to 2 months).

Per serving: Cal 336; Carbs 16g; Fat 26g; Protein 17g

Asian-Inspired Chicken Skewers

Ingredients for 6 servings

1 (13.5-oz) can coconut milk	2 green onions, thinly sliced
1 tbsp oyster sauce	Salt and black pepper to taste
¼ cup sugar-free maple syrup	1 ½ lb chicken breasts, cubed
2 limes, juiced	24 cherry tomatoes
2 tsp freshly grated ginger	24 small mushrooms

Directions and Total Time: approx. 50 minutes

Preheat oven to 370 F. In a medium bowl, whisk together the oyster sauce, maple syrup, coconut milk, lime juice, ginger, salt, and black pepper. Put the chicken in a large bowl. Pour 1 cup of the coconut mixture over the chicken and toss to coat. Cover and chill for at least 30 minutes.

Thread the chicken, cherry tomatoes, and mushrooms alternately on skewers. Discard the used marinade. Place the skewers on a greased baking sheet in a single layer. Bake for 20 minutes. Cool the skewers completely.

Heat the remaining coconut mixture in a small saucepan over medium heat for 5 minutes until bubbling. Let cool. With a fork, slide the food off the skewers into an airtight container. Top with the coconut mixture.

Storage: Keep in airtight containers in the refrigerator for up to 7 days. Microwave for 1-2 minutes before serving.

Per serving: Cal 328; Carbs 17g; Fat 23g; Protein 13g

Minty Grilled Lamb Chops

Ingredients for 4 servings

8 lamb chops	2 tbsp fresh mint
¼ cup olive oil	3 garlic cloves, pressed
2 tbsp favorite spice mix	2 tbsp lemon zest
1 tsp red pepper flakes	¼ cup parsley
2 tbsp lemon juice	½ tsp smoked paprika

Directions and Total Time: approx. 15 minutes

Preheat grill to medium heat. Rub the lamb with oil and sprinkle with spices. Grill for 3 minutes per side. Let cool.

Storage: Place in airtight containers in the refrigerator for up to 5 days (or in the freezer for up to 2 months). To serve, whisk the remaining oil, lemon juice and zest, mint, garlic, parsley, and paprika. Top the chops with the dressing.

Per serving: Cal 242; Carbs 2g; Fat 13g; Protein 26g

Caprese Casserole

Ingredients for 4 servings

1 cup mozzarella cheese, cubed	
2 oz Parmesan cheese	2 tbsp basil pesto
4 tbsp olive oil	1 cup mayonnaise
1 cup cherry tomatoes, halved	1 cup arugula

Directions and Total Time: approx. 30 minutes

Preheat oven to 350 F. In a baking dish, mix cherry tomatoes, mozzarella cheese, basil pesto, mayonnaise, and half of the Parmesan cheese. Level the ingredients with a spatula and sprinkle the remaining Parmesan cheese on top. Bake for 20 minutes until the top is golden brown; let cool. Slice and place in airtight containers.

Storage: in the refrigerator for up to 5 days (or in the freezer for up to 2 months). To serve, reheat in the microwave for 1-2 minutes and top with arugula and olive oil. Enjoy!

Per serving: Cal 346; Carbs 5g; Fat 27g; Protein 12g

Broccoli Pizza Crust with Mushrooms

Ingredients for 2 servings

2 ½ oz cremini mushrooms, sliced	
¼ cup shredded cheddar	Salt and black pepper to taste
¼ cup Parmesan cheese	½ tsp Italian seasoning
½ cup cottage cheese	6 tbsp tomato sauce
½ tbsp olive oil	1 small red onion, sliced
1 head broccoli, riced	A handful of fresh basil
4 eggs	

Directions and Total Time: approx. 40 minutes

Preheat oven 400 F. Line a baking sheet with parchment paper. Microwave broccoli for 2 minutes; let cool. Crack in the eggs, add cheeses, salt, pepper, and Italian seasoning and whisk until evenly combined. Spread the mixture on the baking sheet and bake for 15 minutes. Allow cooling of the crust for 2 minutes. Spread tomato sauce on the crust, scatter with mushrooms, onion, and cottage cheese, drizzle with olive oil. Place the pan in the oven to bake for 15 minutes. Let cool completely. Scatter with basil leaves.

Storage: Place in airtight containers in the refrigerator for up to 5 days (or in the freezer for up to 2 months).

Per serving: Cal 292; Carbs 8g; Fat 22g; Protein 13g

Quick Cabbage Roast with Grana Padano

Ingredients for 4 servings

1 cup grated Grana Padano	1 tsp garlic powder
4 tbsp melted butter	Salt and black pepper to taste
1 head green cabbage	1 tbsp parsley, chopped

Directions and Total Time: approx. 30 minutes

Preheat oven to 400 F. Line a baking sheet with foil. Cut cabbage into wedges. Mix butter, garlic, salt, and pepper in a bowl. Brush the mixture on all sides of the wedges and sprinkle with some cheese. Bake for 20 minutes. Sprinkle with remaining cheese and parsley. Let cool completely.

Storage: Place in airtight containers in the refrigerator for up to 5 days (or in the freezer for up to 2 months).

Per serving: Cal 318; Carbs 13g; Fat 23g; Protein 15g

Yummy Veal Chops in Raspberry Sauce

Ingredients for 4 servings

3 tbsp olive oil	¼ cup water
2 lb veal chops	1 ½ tbsp Italian Herb mix
Salt and black pepper to taste	3 tbsp balsamic vinegar
2 cups raspberries	2 tsp Worcestershire sauce

Directions and Total Time: approx. 20 minutes

Heat oil in a skillet over medium heat, season veal with salt and pepper, and cook for 5 minutes on each side. Put on serving plates and reserve the veal drippings. Mash the raspberries in a bowl until jam-like. Pour into a saucepan, add water and herb mix. Bring to boil on low heat for 4 minutes. Stir in veal drippings, balsamic vinegar, and Worcestershire sauce. Simmer for 1 minute. Spoon sauce over the veal chops and let cool completely.

Storage: Place in airtight containers in the refrigerator for up to 5 days (or in the freezer for up to 2 months).

Per serving: Cal 413; Carbs 11g; Fat 32g; Protein 26g

Mushroom-Mascarpone Muffins

Ingredients for 6 servings

1 ½ cups heavy cream	3 eggs, beaten
5 ounces mascarpone cheese	2 cups mushrooms, chopped
1 tbsp butter, softened	2 garlic cloves, minced

Directions and Total Time: approx. 55 minutes

Preheat oven to 320 F. In a pan over medium heat, warm heavy cream. Set heat to low and stir in mascarpone cheese; cook until melted. Place beaten eggs in a bowl and place in 3 tbsp of the hot cream mixture; mix well. Place the mixture back in the pan with the hot cream/cheese mixture. Spoon the mixture into 6 ramekins. Place them into a large pan. Add in boiling water up to 1-inch depth. Bake for 40 minutes. Melt butter in a pan and add garlic and mushrooms; sauté for 5-6 minutes. Top the muffins with the mushrooms. Let cool completely.

Storage: Place in airtight containers in the refrigerator for up to 5 days (or in the freezer for up to 2 months).

Per serving: Cal 283; Carbs: 11g; Fat: 22g; Protein: 10g

South Korean Tofu & Cabbage Dish

Ingredients for 4 servings

½ cup grated coconut	1 tsp yellow curry powder
2 tbsp coconut oil	Salt and onion powder to taste
4 oz butter	2 cups Napa cabbage
2 cups extra firm tofu, cubed	Lemon wedges for serving

Directions and Total Time: approx. 25 minutes

In a bowl, mix grated coconut, curry powder, salt, and onion powder. Toss in tofu. Heat coconut oil in a skillet and fry tofu until golden brown; transfer to a plate. In the same skillet, melt half of the butter and sauté the cabbage until slightly caramelized. Place the cabbage into plates with tofu and lemon wedges. Melt the remaining butter in the skillet and drizzle over the cabbage and tofu. Let cool.

Storage: Place in airtight containers in the refrigerator for up to 5 days (or in the freezer for up to 2 months).

Per serving: Cal 476; Carbs 11g; Fat 41g; Protein 23g

Tasty Chicken Cordon Bleu Casserole

Ingredients for 4 servings

1 ¼ cups grated cheddar	1 tbsp mustard powder
1 cup cream cheese	1 tbsp plain vinegar
1 lb chicken breasts, cubed	½ cup baby spinach

Directions and Total Time: approx. 25 minutes

Preheat oven to 400 F. Mix cream cheese, mustard powder, plain vinegar, chicken, baby spinach, and cheddar cheese in a greased baking dish. Bake until golden brown, about 20 minutes. Let cool completely.

Storage: Place in airtight containers in the refrigerator for up to 5 days (or in the freezer for up to 2 months).

Per serving: Cal 531; Carbs 3g; Fat 42g; Protein 37g

Baked Avocados Stuffed with Cheese

Ingredients for 4 servings

3 avocados, halved and pitted, skin on	
½ cup mozzarella, shredded	3 eggs, beaten
½ cup Swiss cheese, grated	1 tbsp fresh cilantro, chopped

Directions and Total Time: approx. 25 minutes

Preheat oven to 360 F. Lay avocado halves in an ovenproof dish. In a bowl, mix both types of cheeses and eggs. Split the mixture into the avocado halves. Bake for 15-18 minutes. Let cool completely. Decorate with cilantro.

Storage: Place in airtight containers in the refrigerator for up to 5 days (or in the freezer for up to 2 months).

Per serving: Cal 383; Carbs: 14g; Fat: 28g; Protein: 16g

Savory Beef Cakes with Mashed Broccoli

Ingredients for 6 servings

1 lb ground beef	½ white onion, chopped
2 tbsp olive oil	1 lb broccoli
5 tbsp butter, softened	Salt and black pepper to taste
1 egg	2 tbsp lemon juice

Directions and Total Time: approx. 30 minutes

In a bowl, add ground beef, egg, onion, salt, and pepper. Mix and mold about 6 cakes out of the mixture. Warm olive oil in a skillet and fry the patties for 6-8 minutes on both sides. Remove to a plate and let them cool.

Pour lightly salted water into a pot over medium heat, bring to a boil, and add broccoli. Cook until tender, 6-8 minutes. Drain and transfer to a bowl. Use an immersion blender to puree the broccoli until smooth and creamy; stir in 3 tbsp of the butter, salt, and pepper. Let cool.

Storage: Place in airtight containers in the refrigerator for up to 5 days (or in the freezer for up to 2 months). To serve, reheat the patties and mash in the microwave for 1-2 minutes. To make the lemon butter, mix the remaining butter with lemon juice, salt, and pepper in a bowl. Enjoy!

Per serving: Cal 294; Carbs 3g; Fat 21g; Protein 24g

Leafy Greens & Cheddar Quesadillas

Ingredients for 4 servings

5 oz grated cheddar cheese	1½ tsp cornstarch
½ cup cream cheese	1 tbsp coconut flour
1 tbsp butter, softened	½ tsp salt
3 eggs	1 oz leafy greens

Directions and Total Time: approx. 30 minutes

Preheat oven to 400 F. In a bowl, whisk the eggs with cream cheese. In another bowl, combine psyllium husk, coconut flour, and salt. Add in the egg mixture and mix until fully incorporated. Let sit for a few minutes. Line a baking sheet with parchment paper and pour in half of the mixture. Bake the tortilla for 7 minutes until brown around the edges. Repeat with the remaining batter.

Grease a skillet with the butter and place in a tortilla. Sprinkle with cheddar cheese, leafy greens and cover with another tortilla. Brown each side for 1 minute. Let cool.

Storage: Place in airtight containers in the refrigerator for up to 5 days (or in the freezer for up to 2 months).

Per serving: Cal 481; Carbs 4g; Fat 38g; Protein 19g

Spicy Spaghetti Squash Gratin

Ingredients for 4 servings

1 cup grated mozzarella	2 lb spaghetti squash
2 oz grated Parmesan	Salt and black pepper to taste
1 cup coconut cream	½ tbsp garlic powder
2 oz cream cheese	½ tsp chili powder
1 tbsp coconut oil	2 tbsp fresh cilantro, chopped
2 tbsp melted butter	

Directions and Total Time: approx. 45 minutes

Preheat oven to 350 F. Cut squash in halves lengthwise and spoon out the seeds and fiber. Place the halves on a baking dish, brush each with coconut oil and season with salt and pepper. Bake for 30 minutes. Remove and use two forks to shred the flesh into strands.

Empty the spaghetti strands into a bowl and mix with butter, garlic powder, chili powder, coconut cream, cream cheese, half of the mozzarella cheese, and Parmesan cheese. Spoon the mixture into the squash cups and sprinkle with the remaining mozzarella cheese.

Bake further for 5 minutes or until the cheese is golden brown. Let cool completely. Sprinkle with cilantro.

Storage: Place in airtight containers in the refrigerator for up to 5 days (or in the freezer for up to 2 months).

Per serving: Cal 477; Carbs 27g; Fat 36g; Protein 18g

Bell Pepper & Feta Loaf

Ingredients for 4 servings

1 white onion, chopped	1 lb feta, cubed
3 tbsp olive oil	2 tbsp soy sauce
4 garlic cloves, minced	¾ cup chopped walnuts
Salt and black pepper	1 tbsp sesame seeds
1 tbsp Italian mixed herbs	1 green bell pepper, chopped
½ tsp brown sugar	1 red bell pepper, chopped
¼ cup corn flour	½ cup tomato sauce

Directions and Total Time: approx. 55 minutes

Preheat oven to 350 F. In a bowl, combine onion, olive oil, garlic, feta, soy sauce, walnuts, salt, pepper, Italian herbs, brown sugar, and corn flour and mix with your hands. Pour the mixture into a bowl and stir in sesame seeds and bell peppers. Transfer the mixture into a greased loaf and spoon tomato sauce on top. Bake for 45 minutes. Turn onto a chopping board, slice, and let cool completely.

Storage: Place in airtight containers in the refrigerator for up to 5 days (or in the freezer for up to 2 months).

Per serving: Cal 382; Carbs 18g; Fat 29g; Protein 16g

Spiralized Carrots with Kale

Ingredients for 4 servings

¼ cup vegetable broth	1 garlic clove, minced
4 tbsp butter	1 cup chopped kale
2 carrots, spiralized	Salt and black pepper to serve

Directions and Total Time: approx. 15 minutes

Pour broth into a saucepan over low heat and add in carrot noodles to simmer for 3 minutes; strain and set aside. Melt butter in a skillet and sauté garlic and kale until the kale is wilted. Pour in carrots, season with salt and pepper, and stir-fry for 4 minutes. Let cool completely.

Storage: Place in airtight containers in the refrigerator for up to 5 days (or in the freezer for up to 2 months).

Per serving: Cal 235; Carbs 8g; Fat 17g; Protein 6g

Vegetable Steaks with Green Salad

Ingredients for 2 servings

4 oz cheddar cheese, cubed	8 Kalamata olives
¼ cup coconut oil	2 tbsp pecans
1/3 eggplant, sliced	1 oz mixed salad greens
½ zucchini, sliced	½ cup mayonnaise
Juice of ½ lemon	½ tsp Cayenne pepper

Directions and Total Time: approx. 35 minutes

Set the oven to broil and line a baking sheet with parchment paper. Arrange zucchini and eggplant slices on the sheet. Brush with coconut oil and sprinkle with cayenne pepper. Broil until golden brown, about 18-20 minutes. Let cool completely and drizzle with lemon juice.

Storage: Place in airtight containers in the refrigerator for up to 5 days (or in the freezer for up to 2 months). To serve, reheat the vegetable steaks in the microwave for 1-2 minutes. Arrange cheddar cheese, olives, pecans, and mixed greens next to grilled veggies. Top with mayonnaise. Enjoy!

Per serving: Cal 412g; Carbs 8g; Fat 31g; Protein 17g

Easy Pepperoni Fat Head Pizza

Ingredients for 4 servings

2 tbsp cream cheese, softened	1 tsp dried oregano
1 ½ cups grated mozzarella	4 tbsp tomato sauce
1 egg, beaten	½ cup sliced pepperoni
¾ cup almond flour	

Directions and Total Time: approx. 30 minutes

Preheat oven to 420 F. Line a round pizza pan with parchment paper. Microwave the cream cheese and mozzarella cheese for 1 minute. Stir in egg and add in the almond flour; mix well. Transfer the pizza "dough" onto a flat surface and knead until smooth. Spread it on the pizza pan. Bake for 6 minutes. Top with tomato sauce, remaining mozzarella, oregano, and pepperoni. Bake for 15 minutes. Let cool completely. Slice.

Storage: Place in airtight containers in the refrigerator for up to 5 days (or in the freezer for up to 2 months).

Per serving: Cal 379; Carbs 16g; Fat 27g; Protein 16g

Pesto & Arugula Pizza with Pecans

Ingredients for 4 servings

1 cup grated mozzarella	1 tomato, thinly sliced
1 tbsp olive oil	1 zucchini, cut into half-moons
½ cup almond flour	1 cup baby arugula
2 tbsp ground psyllium husk	2 tbsp chopped pecans
1 cup basil pesto	¼ tsp red chili flakes

Directions and Total Time: approx. 35 minutes

Preheat oven to 390 F. Line a baking sheet with parchment paper. In a bowl, mix almond flour, psyllium powder, olive oil, and 1 cup of lukewarm water until dough forms. Spread the mixture on the sheet and bake for 10 minutes.

Spread the pesto on the crust and top with mozzarella cheese, tomato slices, and zucchini. Bake until the cheese melts, 15 minutes. Top with arugula, pecans, and red chili flakes. Let cool completely.

Storage: Place in airtight containers in the refrigerator for up to 5 days (or in the freezer for up to 2 months).

Per serving: Cal 286; Carbs 11g; Fat 21g; Protein 11g

Simple Scrambled Eggs

Ingredients for 4 servings

12 eggs, beaten	Salt and black pepper to taste
2 tbsp butter	¼ tsp chili powder

Directions and Total Time: approx. 20 minutes

Melt the butter in a skillet over medium heat. Add the beaten eggs and cook them for 5-6 minutes, gently stirring until the eggs are set. Season with salt and black pepper and sprinkle with chili powder. Let cool completely.

Storage: Place in airtight containers in the refrigerator for up to 3 days (or in the freezer for up to 3 months).

Per serving: Cal 243; Carbs 1g; Fat 18g; Protein 17g

Parmesan Cauliflower Bake

Ingredients for 4 servings

4 oz grated Parmesan	1 green bell pepper, chopped
2 oz butter, melted	1 head cauliflower, chopped
1 white onion, finely chopped	1 cup mayonnaise
½ cup celery stalks, chopped	1 tsp red chili flakes

Directions and Total Time: approx. 30 minutes

Preheat oven to 400 F. In a bowl, mix cauliflower, mayonnaise, butter, and chili flakes. Pour the mixture into a greased baking dish and distribute the onion, celery, and bell pepper evenly on top. Sprinkle with Parmesan cheese and bake until golden, 20 minutes. Let cool completely.

Storage: Place in airtight containers in the refrigerator for up to 5 days (or in the freezer for up to 2 months).

Per serving: Cal 364; Carbs 12g; Fat 27g; Protein 16g

Asian Bok Choy & Tofu Stir-Fry

Ingredients for 4 servings

2 ½ cups baby bok choy, quartered lengthwise	
5 oz butter	1 tbsp plain vinegar
2 cups extra firm tofu, cubed	2 garlic cloves, minced
Salt and black pepper to taste	1 tsp chili flakes
1 tsp garlic powder	1 tbsp fresh ginger, grated
1 tsp onion powder	3 green onions, sliced

Directions and Total Time: approx. 15 minutes

Melt half of the butter in a wok over medium heat, add bok choy, and stir-fry until softened. Season with salt, pepper, garlic and onion powders, and plain vinegar. Sauté for 2 minutes and set aside. Melt the remaining butter in the wok and sauté garlic, chili flakes, and ginger until fragrant. Put in tofu and cook until browned. Add in green onions and bok choy and cook for 2 minutes. Cool.

Storage: Place in airtight containers in the refrigerator for up to 5 days (or in the freezer for up to 2 months).

Per serving: Cal 436; Carbs 10g; Fat 37g; Protein 23g

Feta & Cheddar Omelet with Parsley

Ingredients for 2 servings

2 tbsp olive oil	½ cup feta cheese, crumbled
6 eggs, beaten	2 tbsp parsley, chopped
½ cup cheddar cheese, grated	Salt and black pepper to taste
½ jalapeño pepper, minced	¼ tsp garlic powder

Directions and Total Time: approx. 20 minutes

Heat the olive oil in a skillet over medium heat. Add the jalapeño pepper and sauté for 3 minutes, then add the beaten eggs. Season with salt, pepper, and garlic powder. Top with feta cheese. Cook for 8-10 minutes, flipping once until the edges barely start setting. Sprinkle with cheddar cheese and cook for 2 more minutes. Let cool completely.

Storage: Place in airtight containers in the refrigerator for up to 3 days (or in the freezer for up to 3 months).

Per serving: Cal 330; Carbs 2g; Fat 26g; Protein 22g

Grilled Zucchini with Avocado Sauce

Ingredients for 4 servings

3 oz spinach, chopped	1 garlic clove, minced
¾ cup olive oil	2 oz pecans
2 tbsp melted butter	Salt and black pepper to taste
1 avocado, chopped	2 zucchinis, sliced
Juice of 1 lemon	

Directions and Total Time: approx. 15 minutes

Place spinach in a food processor along with avocado, half of the lemon juice, garlic, olive oil, and pecans, and blend until smooth; season with salt and pepper. Pour the pesto into a glass jar and set it in the refrigerator. Season zucchini with the remaining lemon juice, salt, pepper, and butter. Preheat a grill pan and cook the zucchini slices until browned. Let cool completely.

Storage: Place zucchini in airtight containers and place in the refrigerator. Keep for up to 5 days.

Per serving: Cal 347; Carbs 11g; Fat 26g; Protein 15g

Eggplant Fries with Chili Aioli & Salad

Ingredients for 8 servings

2 cups almond flour	2 garlic cloves, minced
1 cup olive oil	½ tsp red chili flakes
2 tbsp butter, melted	2 tbsp lemon juice
1 egg, beaten in a bowl	3 tbsp yogurt
2 eggplants, sliced	3 ½ oz cooked beets, shredded
Salt and black pepper to taste	3 ½ oz red cabbage, shredded
2 egg yolks	2 tbsp fresh cilantro, chopped

Directions and Total Time: approx. 25 minutes

Preheat oven to 400 F. On a deep plate, mix almond flour, salt, and pepper. Dip eggplants into the egg, then in the flour. Place in a greased baking sheet and brush with butter. Bake for 15 minutes. Cool. Place in an airtight container.

To make aioli, whisk egg yolks with garlic. Gradually pour in ¾ cup olive oil while whisking. Stir in chili flakes, salt, pepper, 1 tbsp of lemon juice, and yogurt. Transfer to a glass jar and put in the refrigerator. In a separate airtight container, mix beets, cabbage, cilantro, remaining oil, remaining lemon juice, salt, and pepper; toss to coat.

Storage: Keep the fries and salad in the refrigerator for up to 3 days. Microwave the fries for 1 minute and serve with beet salad and chili aioli. Enjoy!

Per serving: Cal 434; Carbs 15g; Fat 39g; Protein 6g

Savory Cauliflower with Parsnip Mash

Ingredients for 6 servings

½ cup grated cheddar cheese	¼ tsp cayenne pepper
1 cup coconut cream	½ cup almond breadcrumbs
2 tbsp sesame oil	1 ¼ lb cauliflower florets
3 tbsp melted butter	1 lb parsnips, quartered
½ cup almond milk	A pinch nutmeg
¼ cup coconut flour	1 tsp cumin powder

Directions and Total Time: approx. 55 minutes

Preheat oven to 425 F. Line a baking sheet with parchment paper. In a bowl, combine almond milk, coconut flour, and cayenne. In another bowl, mix breadcrumbs and cheddar cheese. Dip each cauliflower floret into the milk mixture and then into the cheese mixture. Place breaded cauliflower on the baking sheet and bake for 30 minutes, turning once. Let cool completely.

Pour 4 cups of slightly salted water into a pot and add in parsnips. Bring to boil and cook for 15 minutes. Drain and transfer to a bowl. Add in melted butter, cumin, nutmeg, and coconut cream. Mash the ingredients using a potato mash. Drizzle with sesame oil. Let cool.

Storage: Place in airtight containers in the refrigerator for up to 5 days (or in the freezer for up to 2 months).

Per serving: Cal 385; Carbs 8g; Fat 35g; Protein 6g

Sesame Roasted Asparagus in Peanut Sauce

Ingredients for 4 servings

2 tbsp olive oil	3 tbsp sesame seeds
Salt and garlic powder to taste	1 ½ lb asparagus spears
3 tbsp peanut butter, softened	2 tbsp lemon juice
1 tbsp soy sauce	1 tsp red chili flakes

Directions and Total Time: approx. 15 minutes

Preheat oven to 400 F. In a bowl, whisk the olive oil, garlic powder, soy sauce, and sesame seeds. Add in the asparagus and stir to combine. Transfer the asparagus to a large baking dish and place in the oven. Roast for 10-12 minutes or until lightly charred and tender. Let cool.

Storage: Place in airtight containers in the refrigerator for up to 5 days (or in the freezer for up to 2 months). To serve, reheat the asparagus in the microwave for 1-2 minutes. In a small bowl, combine the peanut butter, lemon juice, and salt and stir until smooth. Drizzle the dressing over roasted asparagus, top with chili flakes, and enjoy!

Per serving: Cal 245; Carbs 7g; Fat 18g; Protein 8g

Baked Chicken & Brussels Sprouts

Ingredients for 6 servings

1 ¼ cups grated cheddar	1 lb chicken breasts, cubed
¼ cup grated Parmesan	1 lb halved Brussels sprouts
1 cup coconut cream	5 garlic cloves, minced
3 tbsp butter	Salt and black pepper to taste

Directions and Total Time: approx. 30 minutes

Preheat oven to 400 F. Melt butter in a skillet and sauté chicken cubes for 6 minutes; remove to a plate. Pour the Brussels sprouts and garlic into the skillet and sauté until nice color forms. Mix in coconut cream, salt, and pepper and simmer for 4 minutes. Mix in chicken cubes. Pour the sauté into a baking dish, sprinkle with cheddar and Parmesan cheeses. Bake for 10 minutes. Let cool.

Storage: Place in airtight containers in the refrigerator for up to 5 days (or in the freezer for up to 2 months).

Per serving: Cal 448; Carbs 11g; Fat 32g; Protein 28g

Mouthwatering Zoodles a la Bolognese

Ingredients for 4 servings

3 oz olive oil	2 tbsp tomato paste
2 tbsp butter	1 ½ cups crushed tomatoes
1 white onion, chopped	Salt and black pepper to taste
1 garlic clove, minced	1 tbsp dried basil
1 carrot, chopped	1 tbsp Worcestershire sauce
½ lb ground pork	2 lbs zucchini, spiralized

Directions and Total Time: approx. 30 minutes

Heat olive oil in a saucepan and sauté onion, garlic, and carrot for 3 minutes. Pour in ground pork, tomato paste, tomatoes, salt, pepper, basil, some water, and Worcestershire sauce. Stir and cook for 15 minutes. Melt butter in a skillet and toss in zoodles quickly, about 1 minute; season. Let cool completely. Top with the sauce.

Storage: Place in airtight containers in the refrigerator for up to 5 days (or in the freezer for up to 2 months).

Per serving: Cal 425; Carbs 12g; Fat 33g; Protein 20g

Santorini-Style Pizza

Ingredients for 4 servings

1 cup crumbled feta cheese	¼ tsp red chili flakes
1 tbsp olive oil	¼ tsp dried Greek seasoning
½ cup almond flour	3 plum tomatoes, sliced
¼ tsp salt	6 Kalamata olives, chopped
2 tbsp ground psyllium husk	5 basil leaves, chopped

Directions and Total Time: approx. 30 minutes

Preheat oven to 390 F. Line a baking sheet with parchment paper. In a bowl, mix almond flour, salt, psyllium powder, olive oil, and 1 cup of lukewarm water until dough forms.

Spread the mixture on the baking sheet and bake for 10 minutes. Sprinkle the red chili flakes and Greek seasoning on the crust and top with the feta cheese.

Arrange the tomatoes and olives on top. Bake for 10 minutes. Let cool completely. Garnish with basil and slice.

Storage: Place in airtight containers in the refrigerator for up to 5 days (or in the freezer for up to 2 months).

Per serving: Cal 276; Carbs 12g; Fat 24g; Protein 10g

Jalapeño & Avocado Pie

Ingredients for 6 servings

½ cup cream cheese	1 tbsp cornstarch
1¼ cups grated Parmesan	1 tsp baking powder
3 tbsp coconut oil	2 ripe avocados, chopped
1 egg	1 cup mayonnaise
4 tbsp coconut flour	2 tbsp fresh parsley, chopped
4 tbsp chia seeds	1 jalapeño pepper, chopped
¾ cup almond flour	½ tsp onion powder

Directions and Total Time: approx. 60 minutes

Preheat oven to 350 F. In a food processor, add coconut flour, chia seeds, almond flour, psyllium husk, baking powder, coconut oil, and 4 tbsp water. Blend until the resulting dough forms into a ball.

Line a springform pan with parchment paper and spread the dough. Bake for 15 minutes. In a bowl, put avocado, mayonnaise, egg, parsley, jalapeño pepper, onion powder, cream cheese, and Parmesan cheese; mix well. Remove the pie crust when ready and fill with the creamy mixture. Bake for 35 minutes until lightly golden brown. Let cool.

Storage: Place in airtight containers in the refrigerator for up to 5 days (or in the freezer for up to 2 months).

Per serving: Cal 476; Carbs 18g; Fat 37g; Protein 16g

Romano & Walnut Stuffed Mushrooms

Ingredients for 4 servings

½ cup grated Pecorino Romano cheese
12 button mushrooms, stemmed

¼ cup olive oil	2 tbsp chopped fresh parsley
¼ cup pork rinds	Salt and black pepper to taste
2 garlic cloves, minced	¼ cup ground walnuts

Directions and Total Time: approx. 30 minutes

Preheat oven to 400 F. In a bowl, mix pork rinds, Pecorino Romano cheese, garlic, parsley, salt, and pepper.

Brush a baking sheet with some oil. Spoon the cheese mixture into the mushrooms and arrange on the baking sheet. Top with the ground walnuts and drizzle the remaining olive oil on the mushrooms. Bake for 20 minutes or until golden. Let cool completely.

Storage: Place in airtight containers in the refrigerator for up to 5 days (or in the freezer for up to 2 months).

Per serving: Cal 312; Carbs 13g; Fat 24g; Protein 8g

Italian-Style Turkey Meatballs

Ingredients for 4 servings

½ cup shredded mozzarella	2 tbsp olive oil
2 tbsp chopped sun-dried tomatoes	
1 lb ground turkey	1 egg
2 tbsp chopped basil	¼ cup almond flour
½ tsp garlic powder	Salt and black pepper to taste

Directions and Total Time: approx. 15 minutes

Place everything except for the oil in a bowl; mix well. Form 16 meatballs out of the mixture. Heat the olive oil in a skillet. Cook the meatballs for about 6 minutes. Cool.

Storage: Place in airtight containers in the refrigerator for up to 5 days (or in the freezer for up to 2 months).

Per serving: Cal 332; Carbs 2g; Fat 26g; Protein 22g

DESSERTS

Coffee-Chocolate Cake

Ingredients for 4 servings

2 tbsp heavy cream	¼ cup cocoa powder
1 tbsp melted butter	¼ tsp salt
¼ cup organic coconut oil	½ tsp espresso powder
1 cup almond flour	1/3-½ cup coconut sugar
2 tbsp coconut flour	¼ tsp xanthan gum
1 tsp baking powder	2 eggs
3 tbsp corn flour	

Directions and Total Time: approx. 30 minutes

Preheat oven to 400 F. Grease a springform pan with melted butter. In a bowl, mix almond flour, corn flour, coconut flour, baking powder, cocoa powder, salt, espresso, coconut sugar, and xanthan gum. In another bowl, whisk coconut oil, heavy cream, and eggs. Combine both mixtures until smooth batter forms. Pour the batter into the pan and bake until a toothpick comes out clean, 20 minutes. Transfer to a wire rack. Let cool completely. Cover the cake loosely with plastic wrap.

Storage: Place in airtight containers in the refrigerator for up to 5 days (or in the freezer for up to 2 months).

Per serving: Cal 232; Carbs 11g; Fat 22g; Protein 7g

Peanut Butter Fat Bombs

Ingredients for 4 servings

½ cup coconut oil	4 tbsp cocoa powder
½ cup peanut butter	½ cup brown sugar

Directions and Total Time: approx. 5 minutes

Melt butter and coconut oil in the microwave for 45 seconds, stirring twice until properly melted. Mix in cocoa powder and brown sugar until completely combined. Pour into muffin molds and freeze until hardened.

Storage: Keep in the freezer for up to 3 months.

Per serving: Cal 213; Carbs 8g; Fat 18g; Protein 4g

Coconut & Chocolate Barks with Almonds

Ingredients for 6 servings

½ cup coconut butter	¼ tsp salt
½ cup almonds	½ cup coconut flakes
3 tbsp brown sugar	4 ounces dark chocolate

Directions and Total Time: approx. 15 minutes

Preheat oven to 350 F. Place almonds on a baking sheet and toast for 5 minutes. Melt together the butter and chocolate. Stir in sugar. Line a cookie sheet with waxed paper and spread the chocolate evenly. Scatter the almonds and coconut flakes on top and sprinkle with salt. Refrigerate.

Storage: Keep in the refrigerator for up to 5 days.

Per serving: Cal 201; Carbs 9g; Fat 15g; Protein 4g

Chocolate Cake in a Mug

Ingredients for 4 servings

4 tbsp ghee	2 tbsp cornstarch
3 tbsp cocoa powder	3 tsp coconut flour
3 tbsp brown sugar	1 tsp baking powder
2 eggs	A pinch of salt
3 tbsp almond flour	

Directions and Total Time: approx. 5 minutes

In a bowl, whisk the ghee, cocoa powder, and sugar until a thick mixture forms. Whisk in the egg until smooth, and then add in almond flour, psyllium husk, coconut flour, baking powder, and salt. Pour the mixture into 4 mugs and microwave for 70 to 90 seconds or until set. Cool.

Storage: Keep in the refrigerator for up to 5 days.

Per serving: Cal 260; Carbs 11g; Fat 17g; Protein 8g

Raspberry & Coconut Cake

Ingredients for 8 servings

1 cup coconut cream	2 cups corn flour
1 cup whipping cream	1 cup almond meal
½ cup melted butter	1 lemon, juiced
2 cups fresh raspberries	1 cup coconut flakes

Directions and Total Time: approx. 30 minutes

Preheat oven to 400 F. In a bowl, mix corn flour, almond meal, and butter. Spread the mixture on the bottom of a baking dish. Bake for 20 minutes until the mixture is crusty. Allow cooling. In another bowl, mash 1 ½ cups of the raspberries and mix with the lemon juice. Spread the mixture on the crust. Carefully spread the coconut cream on top, scatter with the coconut flakes and add the whipped cream all over. Garnish with the remaining raspberries. Cover the cake loosely with plastic wrap.

Storage: Keep in the refrigerator for up to 7 days.

Per serving: Cal 443; Carbs 42g; Fat 35g; Protein 7g

Mom's Berry Clafoutis

Ingredients for 6 servings

2 tsp coconut oil	1 cup almond flour
4 eggs	¼ cup brown sugar
2 cups berries	½ tsp vanilla powder
1 cup coconut milk	1 tbsp powdered brown sugar

Directions and Total Time: approx. 45 minutes

Preheat oven to 350 F. Place all ingredients except for the coconut oil, berries and powdered brown sugar in a blender; pulse until smooth. Gently fold in the berries. Grease a flan dish with coconut oil and pour in the mixture. Bake for 35 minutes. Sprinkle with powdered sugar and cool. Cover the cake loosely with plastic wrap.

Storage: Keep in the refrigerator for up to 5 days (or in the freezer for up to 2 months).

Per serving: Cal 310; Carbs 29g; Fat 18g; Protein 10g

Chocolate Mousse with Strawberries

Ingredients for 4 servings

1 cup heavy cream	1 cup dark chocolate chips
1 cup fresh strawberries, sliced	1 vanilla extract
3 eggs	1 tbsp brown sugar

Directions and Total Time: approx. 20 minutes

Melt the chocolate in a microwave-safe bowl in the microwave oven for 1 minute; let cool for 8 minutes. In a bowl, whip the heavy cream until very soft. Whisk in the eggs, vanilla extract, and brown sugar. Fold in the cooled chocolate. Divide the mousse between glasses, top with the strawberry, and cover with lids.

Storage: Keep in the refrigerator for up to 5 days.

Per serving: Cal 387; Carbs 7g; Fat 25g; Protein 8g

Coconut-Lemon Panna Cotta

Ingredients for 4 servings

1 cup heavy cream	3 tsp agar agar
½ cup coconut milk	¼ cup warm water
¼ cup brown sugar	3 tbsp water
5 tbsp sugar-free maple syrup	½ lemon, juiced

Directions and Total Time: approx. 20 minutes

Heat the coconut milk and heavy cream in a pot over low heat. Stir in brown sugar, 3 tbsp maple syrup, and 2 tsp agar agar. Continue cooking for 3 minutes. Divide the mixture between 4 dessert cups and let chill in the refrigerator. In a bowl, soak the remaining agar agar with warm water. Allow blooming for 5 minutes. In a small pot, heat the water with lemon juice. Mix in the remaining maple syrup and add agar agar mixture. Whisking while cooking until no lumps form; let cool for 2 minutes. Remove the cups, pour in the mixture, and put in the refrigerator.

Storage: Keep in the refrigerator for up to 5 days.

Per serving: Cal 248; Carbs 12g; Fat 18g; Protein 4g

Dark Chocolate Barks

Ingredients for 6 servings

10 oz unsweetened dark chocolate, chopped
¼ cup toasted peanuts, chopped
¼ cup dried cranberries, chopped
½ cup brown sugar

Directions and Total Time: approx. 2 hours 10 minutes

Line a baking sheet with parchment paper. Pour chocolate and brown sugar in a bowl and microwave for 25 seconds. Stir in cranberries, and peanuts, reserving a few cranberries and peanuts for garnishing. Pour the mixture on the baking sheet and spread out. Sprinkle with remaining cranberries and peanuts. Refrigerate for 2 hours to set.

Storage: Keep in the refrigerator for up to 5 days (or in the freezer for up to 3 months). Cut into bite-size pieces to serve.

Per serving: Cal 325; Carbs 13g; Fat 25g; Protein 6g

Lime-Yogurt Mousse

Ingredients for 4 servings

1 cup whipped cream + extra for garnish
24 oz plain yogurt, strained overnight in a cheesecloth
2 cups Confectioner's brown sugar
2 limes, juiced and zested

Directions and Total Time: approx. 1 hour 5 minutes

Whip the plain yogurt in a bowl with a hand mixer until light and fluffy. Mix in the brown sugar and lime juice. Fold in the whipped cream to combine. Spoon the mousse into dessert cups. Swirl with extra whipped cream and garnish with lime zest. Cover with lids.

Storage: Keep in the refrigerator for up to 5 days.

Per serving: Cal 353; Carbs 23g; Fat 24g; Protein 12g

Cardamom & Saffron Coconut Bars

Ingredients for 4 servings

10 saffron threads	1 ¾ cups shredded coconut
1 oz ghee	4 tbsp brown sugar
1 ⅓ cups coconut milk	1 tsp cardamom powder

Directions and Total Time: approx. 15 minutes

Combine the shredded coconut with 1 cup of coconut milk. In another bowl, mix the remaining coconut milk with the brown sugar and saffron. Let sit for 30 minutes, and then combine the two mixtures. Heat the ghee in a wok. Add in the mix and cook for 5 minutes on low heat, stirring continuously. Mix in cardamom and cook for 5 more minutes. Spread the mixture onto a baking pan.

Storage: Keep in the freezer for up to 3 months. Cut into bars to serve.

Per serving: Cal 370; Carbs 18g; Fat 32g; Protein 4g

Coconut Cheesecake with Raspberries

Ingredients for 6 servings

1 cup whipped cream	3 tbsp brown sugar
24 ounces cream cheese	3 cups desiccated coconut
1 tsp coconut oil	3 tbsp lemon juice
¼ cup melted butter	6 ounces raspberries
2 egg whites	

Directions and Total Time: approx. 35 minutes

Preheat oven to 350 F. Grease a baking pan with coconut oil and line with parchment paper. Mix egg whites, 2 tbsp brown sugar, coconut, and butter until a crust forms and pour into the pan. Bake for 25 minutes. Let cool. Beat the cream cheese until soft. Add lemon juice and the remaining sugar. Fold the whipped cream into the cheese cream mixture; stir in raspberries. Spread the filling onto the baked crust. Cover loosely with plastic wrap.

Storage: Keep in the refrigerator for up to 5 days.

Per serving: Cal 327; Carbs 17g; Fat 25g; Protein 5g

Classic Spanish Flan

Ingredients for 4 servings

2 cups heavy whipping cream
⅓ cup brown sugar, for caramel
2 cups almond milk
4 eggs
1 tbsp vanilla
1 tbsp lemon zest
½ cup brown sugar, for custard
Mint leaves, to serve

Directions and Total Time: approx. 55 minutes

Heat the sugar for the caramel in a pan. Add 2-3 tbsp of water and bring to a boil. Reduce the heat and cook until the caramel turns golden brown. Carefully divide between 4 metal cups. Let them cool. In a bowl, mix eggs, remaining sugar, lemon zest, and vanilla. Add almond milk and beat again until combined. Pour the custard into caramel-lined cups and place them into a baking tin. Pour enough hot water into the baking tin to halfway up the sides of cups. Bake at 345 F for 45 minutes. Let cool completely.

Storage: Keep in the refrigerator for up to 5 days. To serve, take a knife and slowly run around the edges to invert onto dishes. Garnish with dollops of cream and mint leaves.

Per serving: Cal 469; Carbs 47g; Fat 26g; Protein 10g

Quick Blackberry Sherbet

Ingredients for 4 servings

4 tbsp heavy whipping cream
½ tsp vanilla extract
2 packet gelatine
1 cup mashed blackberries
3 cups crushed ice
2 cups cold water

Directions and Total Time: approx. 10 minutes

Put the gelatin in boiling water until dissolved. Place the remaining ingredients in a blender and add gelatin. Blend until the mixture is fluffy. Pour sherbet into a metal dish.

Storage: Freeze for about 3 hours before serving. Keep in the freezer for up to 2 months.

Per serving: Cal 173; Carbs 7g; Fat 10g; Protein 4g

Chocolate Ice Cream Bars

Ingredients for 8 servings

¼ cup cocoa butter pieces, chopped
2 cups heavy whipping cream
½ cup coconut oil
½ cup peanut butter, softened
1 ½ cups almond milk
1 tbsp butter
6 tbsp brown sugar
2 oz unsweetened chocolate

Directions and Total Time: approx. 4 hours 20 minutes

Blend heavy cream, peanut butter, almond milk, and half of the brown sugar until smooth. Place in an ice cream maker and follow the instructions. Spread the ice cream into a lined pan and freeze for 4 hours. Mix coconut oil, cocoa butter, chocolate, and remaining brown sugar and microwave until melted; let cool. Slice the ice cream into 8 bars. Dip into the chocolate mixture.

Storage: Keep in the freezer for up to 2 months.

Per serving: Cal 475 Carbs 15g; Fat 37g; Protein 3g

Dark Chocolate-Walnut Biscuits

Ingredients for 8 servings

4 tbsp brown sugar
4 oz butter, softened
1 cup dark chocolate chips
2 eggs
1 tsp vanilla extract
1 cup almond flour
½ tsp baking soda
½ cup chopped walnuts

Directions and Total Time: approx. 25 minutes

Preheat oven to 350 F. In a bowl, whisk butter, brown sugar, and brown sugar until smooth. Beat in the egg and mix in the vanilla extract. In another bowl, combine almond flour with baking soda and mix into the wet ingredients. Fold in chocolate chips and walnuts. Spoon tablespoons full of the batter onto a greased baking sheet, leaving 2-inch spaces between each spoon. Press down each dough to flatten slightly. Bake for 15 minutes. Transfer to a wire rack to cool completely.

Storage: Place in airtight containers in the refrigerator for up to 5 days (or in the freezer for up to 3 months).

Per serving: Cal 360; Carbs 15g; Fat 29g; Protein 12g

Ricotta & Strawberry Parfait

Ingredients for 4 servings

1 cup ricotta cheese
2 cups strawberries, chopped
2 tbsp sugar-free maple syrup
2 tbsp balsamic vinegar

Directions and Total Time: approx. 10 minutes

Divide half of the strawberries between 4 small glasses and top with ricotta cheese. Drizzle with maple syrup, balsamic vinegar and finish with the remaining strawberries.

Storage: Keep in the refrigerator for up to 3 days.

Per serving: Cal 184; Carbs 13g; Fat 8g; Protein 7g

Holiday Cookies

Ingredients for 8 servings

1 cup butter, softened
½ cup brown sugar, divided
2 cups almond flour
2 tsp cocoa powder
¼ cup Confectioner's brown sugar
1 tsp vanilla extract
1 cup pecans, finely chopped
½ tsp salt
2 tbsp water

Directions and Total Time: approx. 35 minutes

Preheat oven to 325 F. Line a baking sheet with parchment paper. In a bowl, using a hand mixer, cream the butter and brown sugar. Fold in almond flour, cocoa powder, vanilla, pecans, salt, and water. Mold 1 tbsp cookie dough from the mixture and place on the sheet. Chill for 1 hour. Transfer to the sheet and bake for 25 minutes or until the cookies look dry and colorless. Let cool. Sprinkle with sugar.

Storage: Place in airtight containers in the refrigerator for up to 5 days (or in the freezer for up to 3 months).

Per serving: Cal 273; Carbs 13g; Fat 24g; Protein 3g

Traditional Granny Smith Apple Tart

Ingredients for 6 servings

¼ cup + 6 tbsp butter	1 cup brown sugar
2 cups almond flour	2 cups sliced Granny Smith
1 ¼ tsp cinnamon	½ tsp lemon juice

Directions and Total Time: approx. 45 minutes

Preheat oven to 375 F. Combine 6 tbsp of butter, almond flour, 1 tsp of cinnamon, and ⅓ cup of brown sugar in a bowl. Press this mixture into a greased pan. Bake for 5 minutes. Combine apples and lemon juice in a bowl and arrange them on top of the crust. Combine the remaining butter and brown sugar and brush over the apples. Bake for 30 minutes. Let cool completely. Dust with remaining cinnamon. Cover the cake loosely with plastic wrap.

Storage: Place in airtight containers in the refrigerator for up to 5 days (or in the freezer for up to 2 months).

Per serving: Cal 402; Carbs 17g; Fat 32g; Protein 7g

Favorite Strawberry Mousse

Ingredients for 4 servings

2 cups whipped cream	2 tbsp brown sugar
2 cups frozen strawberries	1 large egg white

Directions and Total Time: approx. 10 minutes

Pour 1 ½ cups strawberries into a blender and process until smooth. Add brown sugar and process further. Pour in the egg white and transfer the mixture to a bowl. Use an electric hand mixer to whisk until fluffy. Spoon the mixture into dessert glasses and top with whipped cream and strawberries.

Storage: Keep in the refrigerator for up to 5 days.

Per serving: Cal 185; Carbs 12g; Fats 12g; Protein 3g

Nutty Ice Cream

Ingredients for 4 servings

1 tbsp olive oil	½ tsp salt
2 cups heavy cream	2 egg yolks
½ cup smooth almond butter	½ cup almonds, chopped
1 tbsp brown sugar	½ cup brown sugar
1 tbsp vanilla extract	

Directions and Total Time: approx. 40 minutes

Warm the heavy cream with butter, olive oil, sugar, and salt in a pan over low heat without boiling for 3 minutes. Beat the egg yolks until creamy in color. Stir the eggs into the cream mixture. Refrigerate the cream mixture for 30 minutes. Remove and stir in brown sugar. Pour the mixture into the ice cream machine and churn it according to the manufacturer's instructions. Stir in almonds and vanilla and spoon the mixture into a loaf pan. Freeze.

Storage: Keep in the freezer for up to 3 months.

Per serving: Cal 432; Carbs 17g; Fat 29g; Protein 9g

Vanilla Maple-Lemon Cake

Ingredients for 6 servings

1 cup sour cream	2 tsp baking powder
4 eggs	½ cup brown sugar
2 lemons, zested and juiced	1 tsp cardamom powder
1 tsp vanilla extract	½ tsp ground ginger
2 cups almond flour	A pinch of salt
2 tbsp coconut flour	¼ cup maple syrup

Directions and Total Time: approx. 35 minutes

Preheat oven to 400 F. Grease a cake pan with melted butter. In a bowl, beat eggs, sour cream, lemon juice, and vanilla extract until smooth. In another bowl, whisk almond and coconut flour, baking powder, brown sugar, cardamom, ginger, salt, lemon zest, and half of the maple syrup. Combine both mixtures until smooth and pour the batter into the pan. Bake for 25 minutes or until a toothpick inserted comes out clean. Transfer to a wire rack, let cool and drizzle with the remaining maple syrup. Cover the cake loosely with plastic wrap.

Storage: Keep in the refrigerator for up to 5 days (or in the freezer for up to 2 months).

Per serving: Cal 340; Carbs 15g; Fat 21g; Protein 13g

Lemon-Blueberry Sorbet

Ingredients for 4 servings

1 cup brown sugar	½ lemon, juiced
4 cups frozen blueberries	½ tsp salt

Directions and Total Time: approx. 2 hours 30 minutes

In a blender, add blueberries, brown sugar, lemon juice, and salt; process until smooth. Strain through a colander into a bowl. Chill for 2 hours. Pour the chilled juice into an ice cream maker and churn until the mixture resembles ice cream, 10-15 minutes. Spoon into freezable containers.

Storage: Keep in the freezer for up to 3 months.

Per serving: Cal 123; Carbs 23g; Fat 1g; Protein 1g

Simple Walnut Cookies

Ingredients for 12 servings

1 tbsp ghee	¼ cup brown sugar
1 egg	½ tsp baking soda
2 cups ground pecans	20 walnuts, chopped

Directions and Total Time: approx. 25 minutes

Preheat oven to 350 F. In a bowl, mix all the ingredients, except for walnuts, until combined. Make balls out of the mixture and press them with your thumb onto a lined cookie sheet. Top with walnuts. Bake for 12 minutes. Let cool completely. Place in airtight containers.

Storage: Keep in the refrigerator for up to 5 days (or in the freezer for up to 2 months).

Per serving: Cal 121; Carbs: 5g; Fat: 9g; Protein: 2g

Caramel Cake

Ingredients for 8 servings

½ cup sugar-free caramel sauce + extra for topping
2 ½ cups almond flour ⬩ 1 cup brown sugar
¼ cup coconut flour ⬩ 4 large eggs
¼ cup whey protein powder ⬩ 1 tsp vanilla extract
1 tbsp baking powder ⬩ 1 cup almond milk
½ tsp salt

Directions and Total Time: approx. 30 minutes

Preheat oven to 400 F. In a bowl, mix almond and coconut flour, protein and baking powders, and salt. In another bowl, mix brown sugar, eggs, vanilla, almond milk, and ½ cup of caramel sauce. Combine both mixtures until smooth batter forms. Pour batter into a greased pan; bake for 22 minutes. Cool and top with caramel sauce. Cover the cake loosely with plastic wrap.

Storage: Keep in the refrigerator for up to 5 days (or in the freezer for up to 3 months).

Per serving: Cal 176; Carbs 21g; Fat 7g; Protein 6g

Mocha Coffee Ice Bombs

Ingredients for 4 servings

½ lb cream cheese ⬩ 2 oz strong coffee
1 oz cocoa butter, melted ⬩ 2 tbsp cocoa powder
4 tbsp powdered brown sugar ⬩ 2 ½ oz dark chocolate, melted

Directions and Total Time: approx. 10 minutes

Combine cream cheese, brown sugar, coffee, and cocoa powder in a food processor. Roll 2 tbsp of the mixture and place on a lined tray. Mix the melted cocoa butter and chocolate and coat the bombs with it. Freeze them up.

Storage: Keep in the freezer for up to 3 months.

Per serving: Cal 247; Carbs 17g; Fat 18g; Protein 5g

Coconut Ice Cream

Ingredients for 6 servings

½ cup smooth coconut butter ⬩ 3 cups half and half
½ cup brown sugar ⬩ 1 tsp vanilla extract

Directions and Total Time: approx. 10 minutes

Beat coconut butter and brown sugar in a bowl with a hand mixer until smooth. Gradually whisk in half and half until thoroughly combined. Mix in vanilla. Pour the mixture into a loaf pan and freeze.

Storage: Keep in the freezer for up to 3 months.

Per serving: Cal 215; Carbs 16g; Fat 14g; Protein 7g

Easy Matcha Fat Bombs

Ingredients for 4 servings

¼ cup coconut oil ⬩ 4 tbsp matcha powder
¼ cup almond butter ⬩ ½ cup brown sugar

Directions and Total Time: approx. 5 minutes

Melt almond butter and coconut oil in a saucepan over low heat, stirring until properly melted and mixed. Mix in matcha powder and brown sugar until combined. Pour into muffin molds and freeze to harden.

Storage: Keep in the refrigerator for up to 5 days (or in the freezer for up to 3 months).

Per serving: Cal 284; Carbs 8g; Fat 26g; Protein 4g

Tasty Gingerbread Cheesecake

Ingredients for 8 servings

For the crust:

2 cups corn flour
6 tbsp melted butter ⬩ A pinch of salt
¼ cup brown sugar

For the filling

8 oz cream cheese, softened ⬩ 1 tsp pure vanilla extract
¼ cup sour cream ⬩ 2 tsp smooth ginger paste
¾ cup brown sugar ⬩ 1 tsp cinnamon powder
¼ cup sugar-free maple syrup ⬩ ¼ tsp nutmeg powder
3 large eggs ⬩ ¼ tsp salt
2 tbsp almond flour ⬩ A pinch of cloves powder

Directions and Total Time: approx. 80 minutes

Preheat oven to 325 F. In a bowl, mix corn flour, butter, brown sugar, and salt. Pour and fit the mixture into a greased pan using a spoon. Bake the crust for 15 minutes or until firm. Using an electric mixer, beat cream cheese, brown sugar, and maple syrup in a bowl until smooth. Whisk one after the other the eggs, sour cream, almond flour, vanilla extract, ginger paste, cinnamon, nutmeg, salt, and clove powder. Pour the mixture onto the crust while shaking to release any bubbles. Cover with foil and bake for 55 minutes until the center of the cake jiggles slightly. Let cool completely. Garnish with ginger powder. Cover the cake loosely with plastic wrap.

Storage: Keep in the refrigerator for up to 5 days (or in the freezer for up to 3 months).

Per serving: Cal 453; Carbs 53g; Fat 22g; Protein 7g

Cardamom Chia Pudding

Ingredients for 4 servings

1 cup coconut cream ⬩ ½ tsp vanilla extract
½ cup sour cream ⬩ ¼ tsp cardamon powder
4 tbsp chia seeds ⬩ 1 tbsp brown sugar
½ cup almond milk

Directions and Total Time: approx. 10 minutes

Add all the ingredients to a mixing bowl and stir to combine. Leave to rest for 20 minutes. Apportion the mixture among airtight containers. Refrigerate.

Storage: Keep in the refrigerator for up to 5 days.

Per serving: Cal 278; Carbs: 2g; Fat: 24g; Protein: 5g

Mascarpone & Rum Bombs

Ingredients for 4 servings

1 cup mascarpone cheese	1 tbsp dark rum
2 tbsp butter, melted	2 tbsp cocoa powder
4 tbsp brown sugar	2 oz dark chocolate, melted

Directions and Total Time: approx. 10 minutes

Blitz mascarpone cheese, brown sugar, rum, and cocoa powder in a food processor until mixed. Roll 2 tbsp of the mixture and place on a lined tray. Mix melted butter and chocolate, and coat the bombs with it. Freeze.

Storage: Keep in the freezer for up to 2 months.

Per serving: Cal 286; Carbs 7g; Fat 23g; Protein 10g

Coconut Rhubarb Galette

Ingredients for 8 servings

For the crust:

3 oz butter, melted	1/3 cup brown sugar
6 oz almond flour	2 tbsp shredded coconut

For the rhubarb filling:

4 ¼ oz butter, softened	3 eggs
½ cup brown sugar	1 tsp vanilla extract
¾ cups almond flour	7 oz rhubarb, spiralized
1 cup almond milk	

Directions and Total Time: approx. 45 minutes

Preheat oven to 350 F. In a food processor, blend the almond flour, brown sugar, butter, and coconut. Spread the dough in a greased tart tin and bake in the oven for 15 minutes; let cool. For the filling, in a bowl, whisk butter, brown sugar, almond flour, almond milk, eggs, and vanilla. Pour the filling into the crust, gently tap on a flat surface to release air bubbles, and press rhubarb spirals into the filling. Bake further for 35 minutes until the filling sets. Let cool. Cover the cake loosely with plastic wrap.

Storage: Place in airtight containers in the refrigerator for up to 5 days (or in the freezer for up to 3 months).

Per serving: Cal 380; Carbs 23g; Fat 26g; Protein 11g

Sesame Chocolate Crunch Bars

Ingredients for 8 servings

¼ cup melted butter	½ cup sugar-free maple syrup
¼ cup almond butter	1 tbsp sesame seeds
1 ½ cups chocolate chips	1 cup chopped walnuts

Directions and Total Time: approx. 1 hour 10 minutes

Line a baking sheet with parchment paper. In a bowl, mix chocolate chips, almond butter, maple syrup, butter, seeds, and walnuts. Spread the mixture onto the sheet and refrigerate until firm, about 1 hour. Cut into bars.

Storage: Place in airtight containers in the refrigerator for up to 5 days (or in the freezer for up to 3 months).

Per serving: Cal 273; Carbs 17g; Fat 19g; Protein 5g

Cheesecake Bites with Chocolate Chips

Ingredients for 8 servings

20 oz cream cheese, softened	
10 oz unsweetened dark chocolate chips	
½ cup half and half	1 tsp vanilla extract
½ cup brown sugar	

Directions and Total Time: approx. 10 minutes

In a saucepan, melt the chocolate with half and a half over low heat for 1 minute. Turn the heat off. In a bowl, whisk the cream cheese, brown sugar, and vanilla with a hand mixer until smooth. Stir into the chocolate mixture. Spoon into silicone muffin tins and freeze until firm.

Storage: Keep in the freezer for up to 3 months.

Per serving: Cal 231; Carbs 8g; Fat 21g; Protein 5g

Orange Cardamom Cookies

Ingredients for 8 servings

½ cup butter, softened	1 tbsp grated orange zest
2 cups almond flour	¾ cup brown sugar
½ tsp baking soda	1 tbsp vanilla extract
Coating	
2 tbsp brown sugar	1 tsp ground cardamom

Directions and Total Time: approx. 25 minutes

Preheat oven to 350 F. Combine all cookie ingredients in a bowl. Make balls out of the mixture and flatten them with your hands. Combine the cardamom and brown sugar. Dip the cookies in the cardamom mixture and arrange them on a lined cookie sheet. Cook for 15 minutes until crispy. Let cool completely. Place in airtight containers.

Storage: Keep in airtight containers in the refrigerator for up to 5 days (or in the freezer for up to 3 months).

Per serving: Cal 181; Carbs: 11g; Fat: 13g; Protein: 3g

Easy Cheesecake Cookies

Ingredients for 12 servings

2 oz softened cream cheese	1 large egg
1 tbsp sour cream	2 tsp vanilla extract
¼ cup softened butter	¼ tsp salt
1/3 cup brown sugar	3 cups blanched almond flour

Directions and Total Time: approx. 25 minutes

Preheat oven to 350 F. Line a baking sheet with parchment paper. Using an electric mixer, whisk butter, cream cheese, and sugar in a bowl until fluffy and light in color. Beat in egg, vanilla, salt, and sour cream until smooth. Add in flour and mix until smooth batter forms. With a cookie scoop, arrange 1 tbsp of batter onto the sheet at 2-inch intervals. Bake for 15 minutes until lightly golden. Cool.

Storage: Place in airtight containers in the refrigerator for up to 5 days (or in the freezer for up to 3 months).

Per serving: Cal 165; Carbs 8g; Fat 11g; Protein 3g

Raspberry-Chocolate Cake

Ingredients for 8 servings

½ cup butter, softened	1 tsp baking powder
2 cups blanched almond flour	1 tsp vanilla extract
1 cup brown sugar	2 eggs
½ cup cocoa powder	1 cup almond milk

For the frosting:

1 cup fresh raspberries, mashed	
8 oz cream cheese, softened	3 tbsp cocoa powder
2 tbsp heavy whipping cream	1/3 cup powdered brown sugar
½ cup butter, softened	1 tsp vanilla extract

Directions and Total Time: approx. 40 minutes

Preheat oven to 350 F. In a bowl, mix almond flour, brown sugar, cocoa powder, and baking powder until fully combined. Mix in butter and vanilla. Crack the eggs into the bowl and whisk until completely combined; stir in almond milk. Prepare three 6-inch round cake pans and generously grease with butter. Divide the batter into the 3 cake pans. Place all the pans in the oven and bake for 25 minutes or until the cakes are set. Remove them to a wire rack to cool. In a bowl, whip cream cheese, butter, raspberries, cocoa powder, heavy cream, brown sugar, and vanilla extract until smooth. To assemble: place the first cake on a flat surface and spread ⅓ of the frosting over the top. Place the second cake layer, add and smoothen the frosting, and then do the same for the last cake. Cover the cake loosely with plastic wrap.

Storage: Keep in the refrigerator for up to 5 days (or in the freezer for up to 3 months).

Per serving: Cal 446; Carbs 18g; Fat 31g; Protein 7g

Maple Cinnamon Cake

Ingredients for 8 servings

2 tsp cream cheese, softened	¼ cup almond flour
2 tbsp heavy cream	1 ½ tsp baking powder
6 eggs	1 tsp cinnamon powder
1 tsp vanilla extract	½ tsp salt
8 tbsp butter, melted and cooled	
½ cup sugar-free maple syrup + extra for topping	

Directions and Total Time: approx. 35 minutes

Preheat oven to 400 F. Grease a cake pan with melted butter. In a bowl, beat the eggs, butter, cream cheese, vanilla, heavy cream, and maple syrup until smooth. In another bowl, mix almond flour, baking powder, cinnamon, and salt. Combine both mixtures until smooth, and pour the batter into the cake pan. Bake for 25 minutes or until a toothpick inserted comes out clean. Transfer the cake to a wire rack to cool and drizzle with maple syrup. Cover the cake loosely with plastic wrap.

Storage: Keep in the refrigerator for up to 5 days (or in the freezer for up to 2 months).

Per serving: Cal 412; Carbs 11g; Fat 31g; Protein 12g

Crunchy Almond Squares

Ingredients for 2 servings

1 cup butter, softened	1 cup brown sugar
2 ¼ cups almond flour	1 large egg
1 tsp baking powder	¾ tsp almond extract

Directions and Total Time: approx. 35 minutes

Preheat oven to 400 F. Line a baking sheet with parchment paper. In a bowl, mix almond flour and baking powder. In another bowl, mix butter, brown sugar, egg, and almond extract until well smooth. Combine both mixtures until smooth dough forms. Lay a parchment paper on a flat surface, place the dough, and cover with another parchment paper. Using a rolling pin, flatten it into a ½-inch thickness and cut it into 12 squares. Arrange on the baking sheet with 1-inch intervals and bake in the oven until the edges are set and golden brown, 25 minutes. Let cool.

Storage: Place in airtight containers in the refrigerator for up to 5 days (or in the freezer for up to 2 months).

Per serving: Cal 176; Carbs 7g; Fat 14g; Protein 4g

Very Berry Mug Cakes

Ingredients for 4 servings

4 tbsp cream cheese	2 tsp vanilla extract
2 tbsp butter, melted	½ tsp baking powder
4 tbsp coconut flour	2 eggs
2 tbsp brown sugar	½ cup mixed berries, mashed

Directions and Total Time: approx. 5 minutes

In a bowl, whisk butter, cream cheese, coconut flour, brown sugar, baking powder, egg, vanilla, and mashed berries. Pour the mixture into 4 mugs and microwave for 80 seconds or until set. Let them cool before consuming.

Storage: Keep in the refrigerator for up to 5 days.

Per serving: Cal 108; Carbs 11g; Fat 6g; Protein 3g

Luscious Blueberry Tart

Ingredients for 4 servings

2 tsp coconut oil	1 cup almond flour
4 eggs	¼ cup brown sugar
2 cups blueberries	½ tsp vanilla powder
1 cup coconut milk	1 tbsp powdered brown sugar

Directions and Total Time: approx. 45 minutes

Preheat oven to 350 F. Place all ingredients except coconut oil, berries, and powdered brown sugar in a blender and blend until smooth. Gently fold in the berries. Pour the mixture into a greased dish and bake for 35 minutes. Let cool completely. Sprinkle with powdered brown sugar. Cover the cake loosely with plastic wrap.

Storage: Keep in the refrigerator for up to 5 days (or in the freezer for up to 3 months).

Per serving: Cal 311; Carbs 26g; Fat 19g; Protein 8g

Effortless Coconut Cake

Ingredients for 8 servings

2 tsp cream cheese, softened	5 oz coconut flour
2 tbsp coconut cream	1 ½ tsp baking powder
5 oz butter, melted	2 tbsp coconut flakes
6 eggs	½ tsp salt
1 tsp vanilla extract	2 tbsp coconut flakes
½ cup brown sugar	

Directions and Total Time: approx. 35 minutes

Preheat oven to 400 F. In a bowl, beat the eggs and butter until smooth. Whisk in the cream cheese, vanilla, and coconut cream. In another bowl, mix brown sugar, coconut flour, baking powder, coconut flakes, and salt. Combine both mixtures until smooth and pour the batter into a greased pan. Bake for 24 minutes or until a toothpick inserted comes out clean. Top with coconut flakes. Let cool completely. Cover the cake loosely with plastic wrap.

Storage: Place in airtight containers in the refrigerator for up to 5 days (or in the freezer for up to 3 months).

Per serving: Cal 233; Carbs 15g; Fat 18g; Protein 5g

Almond Cookies

Ingredients for 8 servings

½ cup peanut butter, softened	1 cup brown sugar
2 cups almond flour	A pinch of salt
½ tsp baking soda	1 tsp ground cardamom pods

Directions and Total Time: approx. 30 minutes

Combine peanut butter, almond flour, baking soda, ¾ cup of brown sugar, and salt in a bowl. Form balls out of the mixture and flatten them. Combine cardamom and remaining sugar. Dip in the biscuits and arrange them on a lined cookie sheet. Cook in the oven for 15-20 minutes at 350 F. Let cool completely. Place in airtight containers.

Storage: Keep in the refrigerator for up to 5 days.

Per serving: Cal 226; Carbs 19g; Fat 14g; Protein 6g

Maple-Ginger Cookies

Ingredients for 8 servings

4 tbsp coconut oil	1/3 cup brown sugar
2 tbsp sugar-free maple syrup	2 tsp ginger powder
1 egg	1 tsp cinnamon powder
2 tbsp water	½ tsp nutmeg powder
2 ½ cups almond flour	1 tsp baking soda

Directions and Total Time: approx. 25 minutes

Preheat oven to 350 F. Line a baking sheet with wax paper. Using an electric mixer, mix coconut oil, maple syrup, egg, and water in a bowl. In a separate bowl, mix almond flour, brown sugar, ginger, cinnamon, nutmeg, and baking soda. Combine both mixtures until smooth. Roll the dough into 1 ½-inch balls and arrange on the sheet at 2-inch intervals. Bake for 15 minutes until lightly golden. Let cool.

Storage: Place in airtight containers in the refrigerator for up to 5 days (or in the freezer for up to 3 months).

Per serving: Cal 242; Carbs 11g; Fat 19g; Protein 7g

Speedy Coffee Balls

Ingredients for 6 servings

1 ½ cups mascarpone cheese	¼ cup brown sugar
½ cup melted ghee	6 tbsp brewed coffee
3 tbsp cocoa powder	

Directions and Total Time: approx. 10 minutes

Whisk mascarpone, ghee, cocoa powder, brown sugar, and coffee with a hand mixer until creamy and fluffy, about 1 minute. Fill in muffin tins and freeze.

Storage: Keep in the freezer for up to 3 months.

Per serving: Cal 215; Carbs 12g; Fat 14g; Protein 4g

Banana Chia Pudding

Ingredients for 4 servings

2 ripe bananas, mashed	2 tbsp maple syrup
½ cup chia seeds	1 tsp vanilla extract
2 cups almond milk	2 tbsp chopped nuts
3 tbsp cocoa powder	

Directions and Total Time: approx. 10 minutes

In a bowl, combine mashed bananas, chia seeds, almond milk, cocoa powder, maple syrup or honey, vanilla extract, and a pinch of salt. Stir well to combine. Cover the bowl and refrigerate for at least 2 hours or overnight to allow the chia seeds to absorb the liquid and thicken.

Storage: Divide into 8 serving jars. Keep in the refrigerator for up to 5 days. Before serving, reheat in the microwave for 1-2 minutes. Top with chopped nuts to serve.

Per serving: Cal 240; Carbs 34g; Fat 11g; Protein 8g

Chocolate Shortbread Cookies

Ingredients for 12 servings

¼ cup sugar-free caramel sauce

1 cup butter	1 cup chopped dark chocolate
1 cup brown sugar	Sea salt flakes
2 cups almond flour	

Directions and Total Time: approx. 25 minutes

Preheat oven to 350 F. Line a baking sheet with parchment paper. In a bowl, using an electric mixer, whisk butter, brown sugar, and caramel sauce. Mix in flour and chocolate until well combined. Using a scoop, arrange 1 tbsp of the batter onto the sheet at 2-inch intervals and sprinkle salt flakes on top. Bake for 15 minutes until lightly golden. Let cool. Cover the cake loosely with plastic wrap.

Storage: Keep in the refrigerator for up to 5 days (or in the freezer for up to 3 months).

Per serving: Cal 317; Carbs 26g; Fat 23g; Protein 5g

Homestyle Samoa Cookies

Ingredients for 8 servings

For the crust:

¼ cup butter, melted   ¼ cup brown sugar
1 ¼ cups almond flour   ¼ tsp salt

For the filling and drizzle:

2 tbsp butter   4 oz dark chocolate

For the coconut caramel topping:

¾ cup heavy whipping cream   ¼ cup brown sugar
3 tbsp butter   ½ tsp vanilla extract
1 ½ cups shredded coconut   ¼ tsp salt

Directions and Total Time: approx. 1 hour 35 minutes

For the crust:

Preheat oven to 325 F. Line a baking sheet with parchment paper. In a bowl, mix almond flour, sugar, and salt. Stir in melted butter until well combined. Spread the mixture onto the sheet and bake for 18 minutes until golden brown. Allow complete cooling while you make the filling.

For the filling and drizzle:

Microwave the chocolate and butter for 30-40 seconds until fully melted. Spread two-thirds of the mixture over the cooled crust and reserve the rest. Set aside.

For the coconut topping:

Toast shredded coconut in a skillet over medium heat until golden brown; set aside. Add butter and brown sugar to a pot and melt over low heat, 3 minutes. Turn the heat off. Whisk in heavy cream, vanilla, and salt until smoothly combined. Pour the mixture into a bowl; chill for 1 hour. Stir in toasted coconut. Spread the mixture over the chocolate-covered crust. Let cool and cut into squares.

Storage: Keep in the refrigerator for up to 5 days (or in the freezer for up to 3 months). To serve, reheat the remaining chocolate mixture and drizzle over the bars.

Per serving: Cal 413; Carbs 23g; Fat 33g; Protein 6g

Dark Chocolate Nut Bars

Ingredients for 12 servings

1 cup macadamia nuts, chopped
¼ cup coconut oil   ½ cup sugar-free maple syrup
½ cup cashew butter   1 cup walnuts, chopped
1 cup dark chocolate chips

Directions and Total Time: approx. 1 hour 10 minutes

Line a baking sheet with parchment paper. In a bowl, mix chocolate chips, cashew butter, maple syrup, coconut oil, and nuts. Spread the mixture onto the sheet and refrigerate until firm, at least 1 hour. Cut into bars.

Storage: Place in airtight containers in the refrigerator for up to 5 days (or in the freezer for up to 3 months).

Per serving: Cal 234; Carbs 7g; Fat 27g; Protein 3g

Valentine's Red Velvet Cakes

Ingredients for 8 servings

½ cup butter   ½ cup coconut flour
6 eggs   2 tbsp cocoa powder
1 tsp vanilla extract   2 tbsp baking powder
1 cup Greek yogurt   ¼ tsp salt
1 cup brown sugar   1 tbsp red food coloring
1 cup almond flour

For the frosting

1 cup mascarpone cheese   ½ cup brown sugar
2 tbsp heavy cream   1 tsp vanilla extract

Directions and Total Time: approx. 40 minutes

Preheat oven to 400 F. Grease 2 heart-shaped cake pans with butter. In a bowl, beat butter, eggs, vanilla, Greek yogurt, and brown sugar until smooth. In another bowl, mix the almond and coconut flour, cocoa, salt, baking powder, and red food coloring. Combine both mixtures until smooth and divide the batter between the two cake pans. Bake in the oven for 25 minutes or until a toothpick inserted comes out clean. In a bowl, using an electric mixer, whisk the mascarpone cheese and brown sugar until smooth. Mix in vanilla and heavy cream. Transfer to a wire rack, let cool, and spread the frosting on top.

Storage: Place in airtight containers in the refrigerator for up to 5 days (or in the freezer for up to 3 months).

Per serving: Cal 484; Carbs 27g; Fat 31g; Protein 10g

Cranberry Cheesecake Bars

Ingredients for 8 servings

For the crust:

2 tbsp confectioner's brown sugar
8 tbsp melted butter   1 ¼ cups almond flour

For the cheesecake layer:

1/3 cup confectioner's brown sugar
8 oz cream cheese   2 tsp pure vanilla extract
1 egg yolk

For the cranberry layer:

1 cup unsweetened cranberry sauce

Directions and Total Time: approx. 40 minutes

For the crust, preheat oven to 350 F. Line a baking sheet with parchment paper. In a bowl, mix butter, almond flour, and brown sugar. Spread and press the mixture onto the baking sheet and bake for 13 minutes or until golden brown. For the cheesecake layer, whisk cream cheese, egg yolk, brown sugar, and vanilla in a bowl using an electric hand mixer until smooth. Spread the mixture on the crust when ready. Bake further for 15 minutes or until the filling sets. Remove from the oven, spread cranberry sauce on top, and let cool completely. Cut into bars.

Storage: Place in airtight containers in the refrigerator for up to 5 days (or in the freezer for up to 3 months).

Per serving: Cal 274; Carbs 15g; Fat 26g; Protein 5g

Healthy Snickerdoodle Muffins

Ingredients for 12 servings

For the muffin batter:

½ cup sour cream	1 tsp cinnamon powder
1/3 cup butter, melted	3 large eggs
2 ½ cups almond flour	1/3 cup almond milk
½ cup brown sugar	1 tsp vanilla extract
2 tsp baking powder	

For the topping:

1 tbsp Confectioner's brown sugar
¼ tsp cinnamon powder

Directions and Total Time: approx. 35 minutes

Preheat oven to 350 F. Line a 12-cup muffin pan with paper liners. In a bowl, mix almond flour, brown sugar, baking powder, and cinnamon. In another bowl, whisk eggs, butter, almond milk, sour cream, and vanilla. Combine both mixtures and spoon into the muffin cups, two-thirds way up. For the topping, mix brown sugar and cinnamon in a bowl and sprinkle the batter. Bake muffins for 25 minutes or until a toothpick inserted into the muffins comes out clean. Let cool completely.

Storage: Place in airtight containers in the refrigerator for up to 5 days (or in the freezer for up to 3 months).

Per serving: Cal 221; Carbs 12g; Fat 18g; Protein 7g

Classic Pumpkin Scones

Ingredients for 8 servings

¼ cup heavy cream	½ tsp cornstarch
2 tbsp coconut oil, melted	¼ tsp salt
1 cup almond flour	½ cup pumpkin puree
6 tbsp coconut flour	1 large egg
¼ cup brown sugar	1 tbsp pumpkin pie spice
½ tsp baking powder	1 tsp sugar-free maple syrup

Directions and Total Time: approx. 30 minutes

Preheat oven to 350 F. Line a baking sheet with parchment paper. In a bowl, mix almond and coconut flours, brown sugar, baking powder, cornstarch, and salt. In another bowl, mix heavy cream, pumpkin puree, oil, egg, pumpkin spice, and maple syrup. Combine both mixtures until smooth. Pour and spread the mixture on the baking sheet. Cut into 8 wedges and bake for 20 minutes or until set and golden brown. Let cool completely.

Storage: Place in airtight containers in the refrigerator for up to 5 days (or in the freezer for up to 3 months).

Per serving: Cal 199; Carbs 14g; Fat 14g; Protein 4g

Minty Sweet Bars

Ingredients for 8 servings

1 ½ cups shredded coconut flakes	
½ cup melted coconut oil	¼ cup sugar-free maple syrup
1 tsp mint extract	

Directions and Total Time: approx. 2 hours 10 minutes

Line loaf pan with parchment paper and set aside. In a bowl, mix coconut flakes, coconut oil, mint, and maple syrup until a thick batter forms. Pour the mixture into the loaf pan and press to fit. Refrigerate for 2 hours or until hardened. Remove from the fridge and cut into bars.

Storage: Place in airtight containers in the refrigerator for up to 5 days (or in the freezer for up to 3 months).

Per serving: Cal 216; Carbs 15g; Fat 16g; Protein 2g

No-Bake Coconut & Hemp Seed Cookies

Ingredients for 8 servings

¾ cup coconut oil	1 tsp vanilla extract
¾ cup peanut butter	1 ½ cup coconut flakes
¼ cup cocoa powder	2 tbsp hulled hemp seeds
1 cup brown sugar	

Directions and Total Time: approx. 25 minutes

Preheat oven to 350 F. Line two baking sheets with parchment paper. Add coconut oil and peanut butter to a pot. Melt the mixture over low heat until smoothly combined. Stir in cocoa powder, brown sugar, and vanilla until smooth. Slightly increase the heat and simmer the mix with occasional stirring until slowly boiling. Turn the heat off. Mix in coconut flakes and hemp seeds. Set the mixture aside to cool. Spoon the batter into silicone muffin cups and freeze until set.

Storage: Keep in the freezer for up to 3 months.

Per serving: Cal 215; Carbs 23g; Fat 13g; Protein 3g

Country Cookies

Ingredients for 12 servings

1 cup butter, softened	1 tbsp cinnamon powder
½ cup brown sugar	1 tsp salt
1 tbsp vanilla extract	1 cup dark chocolate chips
2 large eggs	1 cup peanut butter chips
1 ½ cups almond flour	1 ½ cups corn flour
1 tsp baking powder	1 ½ cups coconut flakes
1 tsp baking soda	1 cup chopped walnuts

Directions and Total Time: approx. 30 minutes

Preheat oven to 375 F. Line a baking sheet with parchment paper. In a large bowl, using a hand mixer, cream the butter and brown sugar until light and fluffy. Slowly beat in the vanilla and eggs until smooth. In a separate bowl, mix almond flour, baking powder, baking soda, cinnamon, and salt. Combine both mixtures and fold in the chocolate chips, peanut butter chips, corn flour, coconut flakes, and walnuts. Roll the dough into 1 ½-inch balls and arrange on the baking sheet at 2-inch intervals. Bake for 10 to 12 minutes or until lightly golden. Cool.

Storage: Keep in the refrigerator for up to 5 days.

Per serving: Cal 382; Carbs 25g; Fat 27g; Protein 8g

Chocolate Silk Tart with Coconut Crust

Ingredients for 8 servings

For the crust:

1 tbsp olive oil	¼ tsp salt
½ cup cold butter, cubed	2/3 cup coconut flour
2 eggs	1/3 cup almond flour
1 tsp vanilla extract	5 tbsp cold water
¼ cup brown sugar	

For the filling:

2 tsp Confectioner's brown sugar
16 oz cream cheese, softened 1 tsp vanilla extract
1 cup coconut cream ½ cup brown sugar
4 tbsp sour cream ½ cup cocoa powder
4 tbsp butter

Directions and Total Time: approx. 90 minutes

For the pie crust:

In a bowl, whisk eggs, olive oil, and vanilla until combined. In another bowl, mix brown sugar, salt, coconut flour, and almond flour. Combine both mixtures into a stand mixer and blend until smooth dough forms. Add in butter and mix until a breadcrumb-like mixture forms. Add one tbsp of water, and mix further until the dough begins to come together. Keep adding water until it sticks well together.

Lightly flour a working surface, turn the dough onto it, and knead a few times until formed into a ball, and comes together smoothly. Divide into half and flatten each piece into a disk. Wrap in plastic and refrigerate for 1 hour. Preheat oven to 375 F. Lightly grease a 9-inch pie pan with olive oil. Remove the dough from the fridge, let it stand at room temperature, and roll one piece into a 12-inch round. Fit this piece into the bottom and walls to the rim of the pie pan while shaping to take the pan's form. Roll out the other dough into an 11-inch round; set aside.

For the filling:

In a bowl, using an electric mixer, whisk cream cheese, sour cream, butter, vanilla, Confectioner's brown sugar, and cocoa powder until smooth. In a separate bowl, whisk the coconut cream and brown sugar. Gently fold the cocoa powder mixture into the cream cheese mix until well combined. Fill the pie dough in the pie pan with the cream-cocoa mixture and make sure to level well. Brush the overhanging pastry with water and attach the top pastry on top of the filling.

Press the edges to merge the dough ends and then trim the overhanging ends to 1-inch. Fold the edge under itself and decoratively crimp. Cut 4 slits on the top crust. Bake the pie for 75 minutes or until the bottom crust is golden and the filling is bubbling. Let cool completely.

Storage: Place in airtight containers in the refrigerator for up to 5 days (or in the freezer for up to 3 months).

Per serving: Cal 443; Carbs 25g; Fat 33g; Protein 7g

Perfect Strawberry Scones

Ingredients for 8 servings

2 tbsp coconut oil	¼ tsp salt
1 cup blanched almond flour	¼ cup almond milk
¼ cup coconut flour	1 large egg
3 tbsp brown sugar	1 tsp vanilla extract
½ tsp baking powder	½ cup chopped strawberries

For the glaze:

1 tsp Confectioner's brown sugar
1 tbsp coconut oil 2 tbsp mashed strawberries

Directions and Total Time: approx. 30 minutes

Preheat oven to 350 F. Line a baking sheet with parchment paper. In a bowl, mix almond and coconut flour, brown sugar, baking powder, and salt. In another bowl, whisk almond milk, coconut oil, egg, and vanilla. Combine both mixtures and fold in the strawberries. Pour and spread the mixture on the baking sheet. Cut into 8 wedges like a pizza and place the baking sheet in the oven. Bake for 20 minutes until set and golden brown. Remove and let cool. For the glaze, in a bowl, whisk brown sugar, coconut oil, and strawberries until smoothly combined. Swirl the glaze over the scones.

Storage: Place in airtight containers in the refrigerator for up to 5 days (or in the freezer for up to 3 months).

Per serving: Cal 161; Carbs 12g; Fat 11g; Protein 2g

Cashew Scones with Maple Glaze

Ingredients for 8 servings

½ cup heavy cream	½ tsp salt
2 ½ tbsp cold butter, cubed	1 tbsp baking powder
1 ½ cups almond flour	1 large egg
½ cup coconut flour	3 tsp sugar-free maple syrup
¼ cup brown sugar	2/3 cup chopped cashew nuts
2 tbsp protein powder	

For the glaze:

1 tbsp heavy cream
½ cups Confectioner's brown sugar
1 tsp sugar-free maple syrup

Directions and Total Time: approx. 30 minutes

Preheat oven to 350 F. Line a baking sheet with parchment paper. In a bowl, mix almond and coconut flour, brown sugar, protein powder, salt, and baking powder. In another bowl, mix heavy cream, egg, butter, and maple syrup. Combine both mixtures until smooth. Fold in cashew nuts. Pour and spread the mixture on the sheet. Cut into 8 wedges and bake for 20 minutes or until set and golden brown. Remove from the oven and let cool. For the glaze, in a bowl, whisk brown sugar, maple syrup, heavy cream, and 2 tsp of water. Swirl the glaze all over the scones.

Storage: Place in airtight containers in the refrigerator for up to 5 days (or in the freezer for up to 3 months).

Per serving: Cal 283; Carbs 17g; Fat 23g; Protein 6g

Chocolate-Glazed Donuts

Ingredients for 8 servings

¼ cup heavy cream
4 tbsp melted butter
1 cup almond flour
¼ cup brown sugar

2 tsp baking powder
¼ tsp salt
2 large eggs
½ tsp vanilla extract

Chocolate glaze:

1 cup Confectioner's brown sugar
¼ cup cocoa powder
½ cup water

1 tsp vanilla extract
A pinch salt

Directions and Total Time: approx. 25 minutes

Preheat oven to 350 F. Grease an 8-cup donut pan. In a bowl, mix almond flour, brown sugar, baking powder, and salt. In another bowl, mix butter, heavy cream, eggs, and vanilla. Combine both mixtures until smooth. Pour the batter into the donut cups and bake for 15 minutes or until set. Remove, flip the donut onto a wire rack, and let cool.

For the glaze, in a bowl, whisk brown sugar, cocoa powder, water, vanilla extract, and salt until smooth. Swirl the glaze over the cooled donuts.

Storage: Place in airtight containers in the refrigerator for up to 5 days (or in the freezer for up to 3 months).

Per serving: Cal 212; Carbs 15g; Fat 18g; Protein 5g

Danish-Style Butter Cookies

Ingredients for 8 servings

¾ cup Confectioner's brown sugar
½ cup butter, softened
½ oz cocoa butter
2 cups almond flour

1 large egg
1 tsp vanilla extract
3 oz dark chocolate

Directions and Total Time: approx. 25 minutes

Preheat oven to 350 F. Line a baking sheet with parchment paper. In a food processor, mix almond flour, and brown sugar. Add butter and process until resembling coarse breadcrumbs. Add egg, vanilla, and process until smooth. Pour the batter into a piping bag and press mounds of the batter onto the baking sheets at 1-inch intervals. Bake for 10 to 12 minutes. Microwave dark chocolate and cocoa butter for 50 seconds, mixing at every 10-second interval. When the cookies are ready, transfer to a rack to cool and swirl the chocolate mixture.

Storage: Place in airtight containers in the refrigerator for up to 5 days (or in the freezer for up to 3 months).

Per serving: Cal 273; Carbs 14g; Fat 24g; Protein 2g

Coconut Bars

Ingredients for 8 servings

1 ¼ cups coconut cream
3 tbsp melted coconut oil
1 ½ cups almond flour
2 tbsp brown sugar

¼ tsp salt
¾ cup mini chocolate chips
¼ cup chopped almonds
2/3 cup coconut flakes

Directions and Total Time: approx. 60 minutes

Preheat oven to 350 F. Line a baking sheet with parchment paper. In a bowl, mix almond flour, brown sugar, coconut oil, and salt. Spread and press the mixture onto the baking sheet. Scatter chocolate chips, almonds, and coconut flakes on top. Drizzle with coconut cream. Bake for 35 minutes. Let cool completely and cut into bars.

Storage: Place in airtight containers in the refrigerator for up to 5 days (or in the freezer for up to 3 months).

Per serving: Cal 236; Carbs 17g; Fat 18g; Protein 4g

Vanilla Cookies

Ingredients for 8 servings

3 oz unsweetened white chocolate chips
½ cup unsalted butter
¾ cup brown sugar
1 tsp vanilla extract
1 large egg

1 ½ cups almond flour
½ tsp baking powder
½ tsp xanthan gum
¼ tsp salt

Directions and Total Time: approx. 25 minutes

Preheat oven to 350 F. Line a baking sheet with parchment paper. In a bowl, using an electric mixer, cream butter and sugar until light and fluffy. Add vanilla and egg, and beat until smooth. Add almond flour, baking powder, xanthan gum, salt, and whisk the mixture until smooth dough forms. Fold in chocolate chips. Roll the dough into 1 ½-inch balls and arrange on the sheet at 2-inch intervals. Bake for 12 minutes until lightly golden. Let cool completely.

Storage: Place in airtight containers in the refrigerator for up to 5 days (or in the freezer for up to 3 months).

Per serving: Cal 233; Carbs 15g; Fat 16g; Protein 6g

Walnut & Chocolate Bars

Ingredients for 8 servings

8 oz cream cheese, softened
½ cup butter, softened
2 cups brown sugar
2 eggs
2 tsp vanilla extract
1 cup almond flour

1/3 cup coconut flour
¼ tsp salt
1 ½ tsp baking powder
½ tsp xanthan gum
1 cup dark chocolate chips
1 cup chopped walnuts

Directions and Total Time: approx. 45 minutes

Preheat oven to 350 F. Line a baking sheet with parchment paper. In a food processor, blitz cream cheese, butter, and sugar. Add in eggs and vanilla and mix until smooth. Pour in the flour, salt, baking powder, and xanthan gum; process until smooth. Fold in the chocolate chips and walnuts. Spread the mixture onto the sheet and bake for 30 to 35 minutes or until set and light golden brown. Remove from the oven, let cool completely, and cut into bars.

Storage: Place in airtight containers in the refrigerator for up to 5 days (or in the freezer for up to 3 months).

Per serving: Cal 227; Carbs 14g; Fat 17g; Protein 5g

Glazed Lemon Cookies

Ingredients for 8 servings

For the lemon cookies

¼ cup cream cheese	1 egg
¼ cup unsalted butter	2 cups almond flour
5 tbsp brown sugar	1 lemon, zested and juiced

For the lemon glaze

¼ cup brown sugar	1 ½ tbsp lemon juice

Directions and Total Time: approx. 40 minutes

Preheat oven to 375 F. Line a baking sheet with parchment paper. In a food processor, beat cream cheese, butter, brown sugar, and egg until smooth. Pour in almond flour, lemon zest, and lemon juice. Mix well until soft batter forms. With a scoop, arrange 1 ½ tbsp of the batter onto the sheets at 2-inch intervals. Bake for 30 minutes or until set and lightly golden. Transfer them to a wire rack to cool. In a bowl, whisk brown sugar and lemon juice until well combined. Drizzle over the cooled cookies.

Storage: Place in airtight containers in the refrigerator for up to 5 days (or in the freezer for up to 3 months).

Per serving: Cal 285; Carbs 21g; Fat 18g; Protein 3g

Mixed Berry Muffins

Ingredients for 12 servings

1/3 cup melted butter	½ tsp baking soda
1 cup mixed berries	1/3 cup almond milk
2 ½ cups almond flour	3 large eggs
1/3 cup brown sugar	1 tsp vanilla extract
1 ½ tsp baking powder	½ lemon, zested

Directions and Total Time: approx. 35 minutes

Preheat oven to 350 F. Line a 12-cup muffin pan with wax paper liners. In a bowl, mix almond flour, sugar, baking powder, and soda. In another bowl, whisk butter, almond milk, eggs, and vanilla. Combine the mixtures until smooth. Fold in berries and lemon zest and fill the muffin cups two-thirds of the way up. Bake for 25 minutes. Cool.

Storage: Place in airtight containers in the refrigerator for up to 5 days (or in the freezer for up to 3 months).

Per serving: Cal 197; Carbs 11g; Fat 15g; Protein 4g

Lemon Shortbread Bars

Ingredients for 12 servings

For the shortbread crust:

¼ cup melted butter	¼ tsp salt
2 ½ cups almond flour	1 large egg
¼ cup sugar-free maple syrup	½ tsp vanilla extract

For the lemon filling:

1/3 cup sugar-free maple syrup	
¼ cup blanched almond flour	¾ cup lemon juice
4 large eggs	

Directions and Total Time: approx. 40 minutes

Preheat oven to 325 F. Line a baking sheet with parchment paper. In a bowl, whisk almond flour, maple syrup, salt, butter, egg, and vanilla until smooth. Spread the mixture onto the sheet and bake for 13 minutes. Let cool.

For the filling, in a bowl, whisk maple syrup, flour, eggs, and lemon juice until smooth. Spread the mixture over the crust and bake further for 18 minutes or until the filling sets. Remove, let chill, and slice.

Storage: Place in airtight containers in the refrigerator for up to 5 days (or in the freezer for up to 3 months).

Per serving: Cal 169; Carbs 13g; Fat 13g; Protein 2g

Amazing Chocolate Cookies

Ingredients for 12 servings

12 tbsp butter, softened	¾ cup brown sugar
1 ½ cups almond flour	2 eggs
½ cup cocoa powder	1 tsp vanilla extract
1 tsp baking soda	1 cup dark chocolate chips

Directions and Total Time: approx. 35 minutes

Preheat oven to 350 F. Line a baking sheet with parchment paper. In a bowl, mix almond flour, cocoa powder, and baking soda. In a separate bowl, cream the butter and brown sugar until light and fluffy. Mix in the eggs and vanilla extract and then combine both mixtures. Fold in the chocolate chips until well distributed. Roll the dough into 1 ½-inch balls and arrange on the sheet at 2-inch intervals. Bake for 22 minutes until lightly golden. Cool.

Storage: Place in airtight containers in the refrigerator for up to 5 days (or in the freezer for up to 3 months).

Per serving: Cal 242; Carbs 15g; Fat 21g; Protein 6g

Halloween Cookies

Ingredients for 12 servings

1 oz cream cheese softened	9 tbsp sugar-free maple syrup
3 tbsp butter softened	1 tsp vanilla extract
3 eggs	¼ tsp salt
½ cup pumpkin puree	¾ tsp baking powder
2 tsp pumpkin pie spice	8 tbsp coconut flour

Directions and Total Time: approx. 60 minutes

Preheat oven to 370 F. Line a baking sheet with parchment paper. In a food processor, add eggs and butter and blend until smooth. Top with cream cheese, pumpkin puree, pie spice, maple syrup, and vanilla. Process until smooth. Pour in salt, baking powder, and coconut flour and combine it until soft thick batter forms. Using a cookie scoop, arrange 1 ½ tbsp of the batter onto the sheet at 2-inch intervals. Refrigerate the dough for 30 minutes and then bake for 25 minutes, until set and lightly golden. Let cool completely.

Storage: Place in airtight containers in the refrigerator for up to 5 days (or in the freezer for up to 3 months).

Per serving: Cal 217; Carbs 12g; Fat 17g; Protein 5g

Lime-Avocado Custard

Ingredients for 4 servings

½ cup heavy cream
¼ cup water
2 tsp agar agar powder
3 soft avocados
½ lime, juiced
Salt and black pepper to taste

Directions and Total Time: approx. 10 minutes

Pour ¼ cup of water into a bowl and sprinkle agar agar powder on top; set aside to dissolve. Core, peel avocados and add the flesh to a food processor. Top with heavy cream, lime juice, salt, and pepper. Process until smooth and pour in agar agar liquid. Blend further until smooth. Divide the mixture between 4 ramekins and chill.

Storage: Keep in the refrigerator for up to 3 days.

Per serving: Cal 299; Carbs 17g; Fat 23g; Protein 3g

To-Go Pancake Muffins

Ingredients for 12 servings

2 tbsp butter, melted
½ cup coconut flour
½ cup brown sugar
1 ½ tsp baking powder
1 ½ tsp vanilla extract
6 eggs

Directions and Total Time: approx. 35 minutes

Preheat oven to 350 F. Line a 12-cup muffin pan with paper liners. In a food processor, blend coconut flour, sugar, baking powder, butter, vanilla, and eggs until smooth. Pour the batter into the muffin cups two-thirds way up and bake for 25 minutes or until a toothpick inserted into the muffins comes out clean. Let cool completely.

Storage: Place in airtight containers in the refrigerator for up to 5 days (or in the freezer for up to 3 months).

Per serving: Cal 156; Carbs 1.8g; Fat 12g; Protein 8.6g

Mascarpone-Chocolate Mousse

Ingredients for 6 servings

For the mascarpone chocolate mousse:

8 oz mascarpone cheese
8 oz heavy cream
4 tbsp cocoa powder
4 tbsp brown sugar

For the vanilla mousse:

3.5 oz cream cheese
3.5 oz heavy cream
1 tsp vanilla extract
2 tbsp brown sugar

Directions and Total Time: approx. 15 minutes

In a bowl, using an electric mixer, beat mascarpone cheese, heavy cream, cocoa powder, and sugar until creamy.

Do not over-mix, however. In another bowl, whisk all the mousse ingredients until smooth and creamy. Gradually fold the vanilla mousse mixture into the mascarpone one until well incorporated. Spoon into dessert cups and chill.

Storage: Keep in the refrigerator for up to 5 days.

Per serving: Cal 412; Carbs 15g; Fat 32g; Protein 8g

Caramel Nuts & Lemon Curd Mousse

Ingredients for 4 servings

For the mousse

8 oz cream cheese
1 cup cold heavy cream
1 tsp vanilla extract
¼ cup brown sugar
½ lemon, juiced

For the caramel nuts

2/3 cup brown sugar
A pinch salt
1 cup mixed nuts, chopped

Directions and Total Time: approx. 15 minutes

In a stand mixer, beat cream cheese and heavy cream until creamy. Add vanilla, brown sugar, and lemon juice until smooth. Divide the mixture between 4 dessert cups, chill.

For the caramel nuts:

Add the brown sugar to a large skillet and cook over medium heat with frequent stirring until melted and golden brown. Mix in 2 tbsp of water and salt and cook further until syrupy and slightly thickened. Turn the heat off and quickly mix in the nuts until well coated in the caramel; let sit for 5 minutes. Top the mousse with caramel nuts.

Storage: Keep in the refrigerator for up to 5 days.

Per serving: Cal 485; Carbs 15g; Fat 44g; Protein 6g

Avocado Chocolate Mousse

Ingredients for 4 servings

1 cup coconut cream
1 avocado, pitted and peeled
1 heaped tbsp cocoa powder
2 tbsp cream of tartar
1 cup Greek yogurt

Directions and Total Time: approx. 10 minutes

In a food processor, add coconut cream, avocado, cocoa powder, tartar, and Greek yogurt. Blend until smooth. Divide the mixture between 4 dessert cups and chill.

Storage: Keep in the refrigerator for up to 5 days.

Per serving: Cal 333; Carbs 12g; Fat 29g; Protein 5g

Speedy White Chocolate Mousse

Ingredients for 4 servings

1 ½ cups cold heavy cream
6 oz unsweetened white chocolate, chopped

Directions and Total Time: approx. 10 minutes

Add white chocolate and ½ cup of heavy cream to a microwave-safe bowl. Microwave until melted, frequently stirring, about 60 seconds. Let cool at room temperature. Pour the mixture into a stand mixer and whisk with the remaining heavy cream until soft peaks form. Divide the mousse between 4 dessert cups. Chill.

Storage: Keep in the refrigerator for up to 5 days.

Per serving: Cal 425; Carbs 19g; Fat 27g; Protein 3g

Seedy Tahini Twists

Ingredients for 8 servings

For the puff pastry:

4 tbsp cream cheese, softened | ½ tsp salt
¼ teaspoon cream of tartar | 3 whole eggs
¼ cup butter, cold | 3 tbsp brown sugar
¼ cup almond flour | 1 ½ tsp vanilla extract
3 tbsp coconut flour | 1 whole egg, beaten
½ tsp xanthan gum

For the filling:

2 tbsp sugar-free maple syrup | 1 egg, beaten
3 tbsp tahini | 2 tbsp poppy seeds
2 tbsp sesame seeds

Directions and Total Time: approx. 1 hour 30 minutes

Preheat oven to 350 F.

Line a baking tray with parchment paper. In a bowl, mix almond and coconut flour, xanthan gum, and salt. Add in cream cheese, cream of tartar, and butter; mix with an electric mixer until crumbly. Add brown sugar and vanilla extract until mixed. Then, pour in 3 eggs one after another while mixing until formed into a ball. Flatten the dough on a clean flat surface, cover with plastic wrap, and refrigerate for 1 hour.

Dust a clean flat surface with almond flour, unwrap the dough, and roll out the dough into a large rectangle. In a bowl, mix maple syrup and tahini and spread the mixture over the pastry. Sprinkle with half of the sesame seeds and cut the dough into 8 strips. Fold each strip in half. Brush the top with the beaten egg, and sprinkle with the remaining seeds and poppy seeds. Twist the pastry three to four times into straws and place on the baking sheet. Bake until golden brown, 15 minutes. Let cool.

Storage: Place in airtight containers in the refrigerator for up to 5 days (or in the freezer for up to 3 months).

Per serving: Cal 238; Carbs 11g, Fat 17g, Protein 7g

Macadamia Bars

Ingredients for 8 servings

1 cup macadamia nuts, chopped
¼ cup coconut oil, solidified | 1 cup coconut flakes
½ cup smooth peanut butter | 1 tsp cinnamon powder
½ cup pepitas | 2 tsp vanilla bean paste

Directions and Total Time: approx. 10 minutes

Line a baking sheet with parchment paper. In a bowl, mix macadamia nuts, pepitas, coconut flakes, cinnamon powder, peanut butter, coconut oil, and vanilla bean paste. Spread the mixture onto the sheet and refrigerate until firm. Cut into bars.

Storage: Place in airtight containers in the refrigerator for up to 5 days (or in the freezer for up to 2 months).

Per serving: Cal 353; Carbs 18g; Fat 29g; Protein 10g

Printed in Great Britain
by Amazon

37550942R10071